Greetings from Saudi Arabia

Visit www.booksurge.com to order additional copies.

JUDITH C. CARROLL

GREETINGS FROM SAUDI ARABIA

2007

Greetings from Saudi Arabia

CONTENTS

To Sister Deb, My Muse And Painter Of Soul,
To Uncle Otto, Who Led A Seriously Adventurous Life, And...
To My Husband Wayne, A Lover Of Life, Who Fought The Good
Fight.

FOREWORD

After the Gulf War, there was a sense of hope about Middle East relations. The events in this story occurred during that time—before the devastations of 9-11 and Hurricane Katrina.

Names and some of the circumstances were changed for protection, but the cultural climate remains accurately depicted.

So, why are there humor and cartoons in a book regarding the cultural and sexual clashes in a carefully concealed society? First, to attempt to provide a more balanced perspective, and second, because the author, who draws for children, can only produce cartoons.

I hope you enjoy *Greetings from Saudi Arabia.*

Judith Carroll, Ph.D.

CHAPTER 1
Two's Company

The Mississippi Gulf waters were calm, as usual. The barrier islands sheltered this stretch of the coast from the pounding ocean waves. Sometimes the water was so placid and lazy, it looked like smooth glass stretching for miles on the horizon.

Spanish moss draped through the live oaks like soft, dark lace. Flowers lined the medians between roads, and when the brilliant pink azaleas were in bloom, the view was captivating.

The addition of a dozen major Las Vegas-style casinos had somewhat diminished the laid-back ambiance, but, as usual, the coast people graciously accepted the newcomers. They'd seen people and businesses come and go for three hundred years. Between a large international shipping port, Keesler Air Force Base, and New Orleans, the coast natives accommodated most of the people and their behaviors with amused leniency.

Given the nature of the calm waters, it was not surprising to find this was the birthplace of yachting. The nature of the people was also reflected in the water. Its native sons and daughters were genteel by birthright. A laborer in a pickup truck, if born here, could innately show a sense of refinement and impeccable manners. The titles, "Miss Sally" and "Mister Jim" rolled comfortably off the native's lips. Confrontation was not their way.

Even during the Civil War, there had been no real confrontation. Unlike neighboring New Orleans, there were no major battles. The Union troops had positioned themselves offshore when they spied the heavy cannons and guns stationed near the Biloxi lighthouse. For several weeks the Union troops waited on their ships, determining their next move. While they waited, the calming water of the Mississippi Sound worked its subtle tempering effect.

Finally, the troops left their ships and with some trepidation came ashore. Surprisingly, no guns were fired. No cannons volleyed. On closer inspection, the invading troops were relieved and somewhat amused to discover that the imposing cannons were just wooden carvings placed to appear as if the shores were protected.

Nestled on the Gulf waters was the picturesque town called Biloxi. For all its small-town beauty, it was unpretentious about its area attractions. The community was home to a university campus overlooking the Gulf. One could walk up the steps of a deck built in the magnificent 600-year-old live "Friendship Oak" tree.

Local historians were proud that this tree was thriving before Columbus stepped foot in America, and survived every hurricane ever recorded. There was an idyllic small craft harbor and seafood restaurants. New technology firms had recently settled here, too.

There were, of course, exceptions. City Council meetings were usually better than prime time TV. A new mayor was trying to straighten out the budget debacle left by the previous administration. With a CPA and impressive corporate track record, he had the qualifications for the job. A native himself, he had been away at college when Hurricane Camille devastated the Mississippi Coast. As he watched his neighbors suffering, he vowed some day he would return and help his home town.

Now Mayor Bob was wondering about his decision. His blue eyes glazed over as he sat at his desk, head in his hands. In front of him was a petition from one of his constituents, Camille Ladnier-Kohl. Camille had been aptly named for the Category Five hurricane that had destroyed much of their little town, along with the rest of the coast. Camille was a natural blonde with large, dark, fiery eyes and good bone structure. It was always assumed, or hoped, that Camille would marry well and settle down.

Camille had married a young Air Force doctor from Sheboygan, Wisconsin, stationed at Keesler Air Force Base in Biloxi. Hans Kohl was the son of German immigrants, and had a stiff, strange accent. Locals said, "He talks like a hockey player." At a robust six foot five, people also assumed he was well-equipped to handle Camille. Most times they were right.

Camille's father, A.J., was a dignified-looking Southern gentleman with light green eyes, graying hair and beard. His wife had died in childhood during the birth of their second daughter, Ashley. A.J. had continuing opportunities to remarry, but never did. Camille sometimes wondered if there was someone in his life, but never was quite sure.

Ashley was as different in temperament from Camille as she was in looks. Ashley's cream-colored skin was framed with dark auburn hair, and she had the same light green eyes as her father. Camille was too proud, unemotional, and demanding. Ashley was too demure and sentimental.

On the day of Camille and Hans' wedding, Ashley had sniffed and delicately wiped her eyes.

"Oh, Camille, it was such a beautiful wedding."

Camille had turned back toward her younger sister with a look of disapproval. "Let's not go on so, Ashley. Let's just get this reception over with!"

When their son, Beau, was born, Camille was pleased. Beau was a handsome, healthy little boy with Camille's natural towhead hair and Hans' blue eyes.

Now Beau was a tall, gawky twelve-year-old with an adventurous spirit, quick wit, and easy, infectious laugh.

Camille was also pleased with her chosen career, but Hans liked to have her available—too available to her liking. Hans' Yankee relatives, some of whom liked to stay for months, sporadically interrupted this idyllic arrangement. To placate Camille, Hans had built an addition on the house for his visiting family. The relatives were actually very friendly people. Yet, to Camille, they always seemed to be underfoot and wanting her to accompany them to some local casino or Mardi Gras parade.

Uncle Otto

On the two flagpoles out on the patio, the German flag and the French flag flapped wildly in the breeze. When Hans had launched his German flag, Camille had insisted that her heritage not be ignored. Today, the flags seemed to fight each other even more, as if it were an indication of the mood inside the house. It had been a hot, humid day when Uncle Otto and "Mabel Baby" had announced their arrival with a loud honk of the car horn.

"Well, Camille, baby! Come here! Let me give you a 'buss'!" The feisty old man grabbed Camille and planted a sloppy, wet kiss on her cheek. He started to instinctively administer a pat on the rear, but Camille gave him a stern warning look and backed away in time.

Hans had prepared his wife in advance, but she still groaned inwardly as Uncle Otto carried in a box of groceries and his own coffee pot. Hans and she had fought that morning about the unknown planned length of stay for this visit. Hans figured that Uncle Otto had earned the right to stay as long as he wanted, and Camille would just have to understand.

Uncle Otto was a frisky seventy-five-year-old widower and a retired electrical engineer. Seven years after his wife's death, he'd found love again with "Mabel Baby", a young chick of sixty-eight. They'd met on a polka bus tour from Sheboygan, Wisconsin. Camille plastered on the most pleasant smile she could muster.

"Well, Uncle Otto, how are you? Miss Mabel, how was your trip?" She helped the elderly couple lug in several large, heavy suitcases. Since the car appeared to be loaded, it seemed all the more ominous that this would be a very long stay.

Uncle Otto and Mabel Baby were quite a handful by themselves. However, Hans' older brother, Gordy, his wife, Linda, younger brother, David, and his wife, Dianne, were also flying down to spend two weeks. Hans had orchestrated the visits to coincide with Oktoberfest. With imported German bands and German beer served in large, open-air tents, Hans liked to make the once-a-year event an extended family occasion.

Camille liked Gordy and Linda. They were lively, funny, and picked up after themselves. David was the most mellow of the group. He blended easily with the coast people. Dianne, his wife, had a wonderfully infectious laugh and upbeat attitude. Camille even grudgingly admitted to herself that she like the old codger, Uncle Otto. It was just that they disrupted her routine, a fact that her husband didn't seem to appreciate.

Camille had helped settle Uncle Otto and Mabel Baby into their bedroom and fixed them a light lunch. Uncle Otto wolfed down his sandwich.

"Is the hot tub ready? Mabel Baby, bring us some beer, then put on that sexy new swimsuit of yours!"

Camille turned away as she rolled her eyes. She snuck back to her computer. Her son Beau threw open the screen door.

"Hey, Mom…did you hear that a hurricane is heading this way? Man, we may get some days off school!"

"Yes, I heard. Go and say 'hi' to your Uncle Otto."

"Alright."

Camille typed furiously as she heard the muted conversation on the back porch. The back door opened, and Beau returned to Camille's office.

"Oh, Mom!" he exclaimed in hushed tones. "I went out there to say 'hi' to Uncle Otto, and Mabel Baby was sitting on his lap in the hot tub. She was kissing him. Yuk! I mean, wrinkles on wrinkles!" Beau made a twisted, joking face. "Man, I may be warped for life!"

"Yeah, yeah. Listen, we're all going to the Quarter tomorrow afternoon. Do you want to come along?"

Beau's ears seemed to visibly perk up. "The French Quarter? Sure, what time?"

"About one o'clock."

"Can I bring a friend?"

"May I?" she corrected him. "No, you may not. Uncle Gordy, David, and their wives are also going, so it's going to be packed as it is."

"Aw, OK."

Beau foraged through the refrigerator, then disappeared into his bedroom.

Camille saved her work, then logged onto the National Weather Service website. It had been a busy hurricane season, and she had hoped that this last hurricane would stall out until they made it to October. After all, it was the last week in September. She frowned as she looked at the hurricane track. The pressure readings were dropping, meaning it was gaining strength.

Uncle Otto came dripping into her office, holding his beer bottle precariously over her keyboard.

"What's that on the screen?" he asked, apparently fascinated.

"That's our latest hurricane."

"Huh…" he replied. He took another sip of beer, then let out a loud, unapologetic belch. Camille visibly cringed.

"Listen, you don't have to worry about dinner. Mabel and I stopped at the grocery store on the way over here. I'm going to make my special pork loin and sauerkraut steamed in beer!" Uncle Otto glanced at the clock. "In fact, I'd better get started. The pork loin has to be roasted slowly."

"But, Uncle Otto," Camille protested to the back of the retreating elderly man. "Miss Kay-Dee is coming over here to make Creole food—" She realized Uncle Otto wasn't wearing his hearing aid and she didn't feel like shouting. She heard the pans rattling in the kitchen.

Camille sighed and logged onto the website of her professional organization. It was a form of escapism. She had been born and raised on the Mississippi Coast. Everybody knew her business, and she knew everybody else's business. Camille had hoped to travel the world and have adventures. Meeting and marrying Hans had been good—her son was good. But, she felt she had missed out on her one big world adventure. She scanned the "Help Wanted" classified ads on the national website. Fascinated, an overseas ad caught her attention.

"Clinical Director needed to help start the first clinic of its kind in the Kingdom of Saudi Arabia. Ph.D. required. Western housing and travel reimbursed. Western schooling for up to two children paid."

Another person entering the front door interrupted her reading.

"What in God's name is dat awful smell?" Camille looked up to see Miss Kay-Dee, their Creole cook, standing by her side. She sniffed the smells of the kitchen with obvious disgust. Miss Kay-Dee was an exceptionally striking woman in her early fifties who had practically been Camille and Ashley's mother after their own mother had passed away in childbirth. Camille still was slightly in awe every time she saw Miss Kay-Dee. The woman looked more thirty-ish than her true age. The Creole woman had flawless bronze skin, high cheekbones, full lips, light golden eyes, and a slim figure.

Camille's father, A.J., had chosen well for his daughters' caretaker. Miss Kay-Dee now had a thriving catering business and drove a big white Cadillac. She'd never married, but seemed content, somehow. With her busy schedule, Miss Kay-Dee was now only occasionally available to cook her famous dishes.

Kay-Dee looked at Camille for an answer. "What goes on in my kitchen?" she demanded again in her unique accent.

Camille gave a huff and cast her eyes up in disgust. "Uncle Otto is baaaack. And he's making his special pork loin and sauerkraut steamed in beer."

"He's making what? Not in my kitchen he's not! I have fresh shrimp and spices here!" Camille started to grab for Miss Kay-Dee's hand before she could get to the kitchen. At that moment, Hans walked in.

"Hi, Kay-Dee." He sniffed the air with a pleased expression. "Uncle Otto, you're making pork roast and sauerkraut? Alright!"

Camille and Miss Kay-Dee looked at each other with resigned disgust. "Miss Kay-Dee, just put the shrimp in the freezer. We'll make it tomorrow."

"Alright. Den I go. Dees smells do not agree with my nose."

Miss Kay-Dee quickly crossed over to the second refrigerator in the large bar room and stuffed the bag of shrimp into the freezer. She gave a perfunctory, silent nod to the intruders. But Uncle Otto was not to be ignored.

"Oh, Kay-Dee. They can have your Cajun food tomorrow. Today I make my special pork roast."

Miss Kay-Dee's back arched and her eyes blazed. She raised her finger to punctuate her words. "I tell you this one time only. I am Creole, not Cajun!" She gave an indignant huff as she trounced out the door and peeled away in her big white Cadillac.

Uncle Otto gave a sideways belch as he poured beer on the pork roast. "Yah, yah…Cajun, Creole, so what's the difference?"

Hans was already in the bar room socializing.

"Hey, Hans, I brought you down that special micro beer from the brewery in Madison. And—look what other special treat I brought you—" Uncle Otto pulled out a package wrapped in thick brown paper.

Hans sniffed appreciatively. "Alright! You brought me some head cheese!"

Camille slapped her hand onto her forehead. Headcheese stank. And it would stink up her refrigerator for the next month. She looked back at the computer screen, and the Clinical Director job in Saudi Arabia seemed to beckon her with the lure of exotic destinations and job challenge. Her fingers lovingly paused over the keys, ready to respond. Naw, she could even handle the stinky cheese. Garbage pickup was in two days, when the stinky cheese would mysteriously disappear.

"And—oh, ho, ho," Uncle Otto chuckled mischievously, "look at this!"

There was a pause as Hans examined his new present. Then Camille heard him laugh.

"Wow! Is this great! Hey Camille, come and look at the terrific bar sign Uncle Otto made out of stained glass."

Knocker's Bar

Camille steeled herself. Hans' "bar room" was already filled with neon beer signs and other tasteful decorations. It was as bad as she thought. Hans had built an eighteen-foot bar as competition with his brothers. Gordy had held the record for the longest bar until two years ago, at an ample seventeen feet. But Hans had always wanted a bar that was high enough for him to stand and lean his elbows on the top. Since Hans was six foot five, this meant the top of the bar was at the height of Camille's breasts. Henceforth, Hans' family had affectionately named it the "Knocker's Bar." To commemorate the special bar, Uncle Otto had obviously spent many hours making a stained glass sign with a picture of a woman sporting a large pair of knockers. Uncle Otto had painstakingly welded on the letters "Knocker's Bar."

"Uh—um, that's great, Uncle Otto. Looks like this took a lot of work," Camille responded with as much enthusiasm as she could.

"Oh, you know it took a lot of work—almost two whole months."

"Uh, let me just shut down the computer now," Camille promised as she exited the room.

Maybe it was the low pressure from the impending hurricane affecting her judgment. Maybe it was too many well-meaning family intrusions. Maybe it was anger at Hans for his insistence on allowing Uncle Otto free reign in the kitchen. Whatever it was, Camille pulled out her resume, copies of degrees, and licenses. She prepared to upload them to the requested website address in Saudi Arabia. Ready to transmit, her fingers paused on the keyboard. What was she doing? This was silly.

At that moment, Uncle Otto felt a familiar gaseous cloud ready to be relieved from his rear. Uncle Otto wasn't as insensitive as Camille thought. He just felt that he'd lived long enough to do pretty much as he pleased. But he knew his limits. After Hans had alphabetized all the canned goods in the kitchen cabinets, he had posted written kitchen rules on the wall. Camille had only one inviolate rule, which she had written in large emphatic letters at the end of Hands' multiple listing—"NO Farting in the Kitchen!"

Uncle Otto quickly appraised the situation. He wouldn't have time to make it very far from the kitchen, and he didn't want to upset Camille so soon after his arrival. Frantically, he looked around. Next to the kitchen door, just inside Camille's home office, was a swinging laundry chute door. Uncle Otto quickly backed his rear end up to the laundry chute door and blasted the small hinged door open with a massive fart, apparently the culmination of three days of confinement in a car.

It was too much for Camille. "Oh, Uncle Otto! How could you?"

Uncle Otto looked confused at her reaction. After all, he thought he was using the utmost in manners and German efficiency in relieving his gaseous load.

Beau walked in on the scene and doubled over in laughter. "Uncle Otto, when I get to be your age, you're my role model!" Beau laughed appreciatively.

Camille clamped her teeth together in desperation. This was just the start of a prolonged visit? "Hans," she called, "would you come here a minute?"

Hans grudgingly walked into the office, ready for a fight.

"How long?" Camille whispered. "Did you ask them for, like a rough estimate of how long this visit is going to be?"

Hans narrowed his eyes in defiance and turned away in an angry huff.

"Hey, Uncle Otto! I just wanted you to know we're really glad you're here." Hans turned back to Camille for emphasis, "And—you may stay as long as you want!"

Camille took a deep, angry breath. She'd had it. Hans had been all over the world. She had never been farther than Sheboygan, Wisconsin. Camille remembered the first time Hans had taken her to meet the folks in Sheboygan. They were engaged, and the trip, for her, was quite an adventure. It was Christmas, and Camille couldn't believe all the snow.

She wasn't quite prepared for "the Bros," as they were called. One by one, each entered the kitchen with a stocking cap on his head and a bottle of beer in his hands. Hans' brothers were not the world travelers that he was. Their accents were even much more pronounced. Each talked rapidly in a dialect she could barely understand.

Camille was brought back from her reverie by a loud belch. This time it emanated from her husband. Her fingers hesitated briefly over the "send" button. Maybe she shouldn't.

"Hey, Uncle Otto. This is great beer, 'en so. Do you want to play a game of cribbage?"

"Yah, yah. I just have to put my new polka tape from Germany in..."

The loud blare of polka music resounded through the house with a dominant insistence. The word "blitzkrieg" came to Camille's mind. There was no doubt left now.

Camille raised her right index finger, made a frustrated circle, and hit the "send" button. All her documents were on their way to this mysterious clinic in Jeddah, Saudi Arabia. Her attention was diverted to something red on her son's head.

"Beau, is that a Confederate flag wrapped around your head?"

"Yup, Me and Shiyou are going mudriding on his land." Beau hurried toward the door and accidentally knocked his bag against the wall. A small round tin can rolled out and landed at his mother's feet.

Camille picked up the can. "Chewing tobacco?"

"Well, Mom, I just wanted to get the complete experience, you know?"

"What experience is that, son—the total 'Bubba' experience?"

"Yes, ma'am, that's the one!"

"Do you know what your dad would do if he saw this?"

"Oh, Mom, please don't tell Dad. Please…"

Camille picked up the can and tossed it in the garbage. "This time I won't. Aren't you going to stay and have supper with your 'role model'?"

"Are you kidding? Everything around here is cooked in friggin' beer—steaks steamed in beer, chicken steamed in beer, spaghetti steamed in beer, peanut butter and jelly sandwiches steamed in beer…" he exaggerated. "Shiyou's dad picked us up some crawfish, and tonight we're gonna have a crawfish boil outside. OK, Mom?"

"Well, alright. You may spend the night, but just be home in time to do your chores before we leave for New Orleans."

"Thanks." As Beau ran past Camille, she grabbed the Confederate flag from his head and laid it on the shelf. Beau was out the door and jumped into the back of the big dented pickup truck the boys used to drive around in the back woods.

"Hey, Hon, shut the computer down and join us," Hans said with a trace of disapproval at her isolation.

"Yah, yah, come and get some real culture," Uncle Otto added.

"I'll have you know," Camille stood up, "D'Iberville founded Biloxi in 1699, 150 years before Wisconsin even became a state."

"Yah, that may be so, en hey, but Nicolet landed his boat in Green Bay in 1634," Uncle Otto proudly countered.

"True," Camille's dark eyes flashed, "but when he got off the boat, he was wearing a Chinese robe."

Uncle Otto appeared confused at this information. "A Chinese robe? Why?"

"Because he thought he'd discovered China!" Camille laughed victoriously.

Uncle Otto appeared thoughtful. "Well," he finally recovered, "I'll have a beer on that!"

"Cammy, shut that computer down now!" Hans ordered.

"Jawohl, *mein Führer*! I'm just logging off now," Camille answered through gritted teeth. She knew she wouldn't be getting much work done for the next several weeks.

In the morning, Hans drove out to the Gulfport airport to pick up his brothers and their wives. By midmorning, the new guests had settled into their rooms. Gordy liked to razz Camille with "dumb blonde" jokes. After watching her on the computer for a few moments, he started in.

"Hey, Camille, did you hear about how the blonde corrected typing mistakes on her computer?"

"Yeah, yeah, she painted 'White Out' on her screen."

"Oh, well...what's this?" Gordy flapped his hands around his ears.

"I don't know, Gordo, what is that?"

"That's a blonde recharging her head."

"What?"

"You know," he flapped his hands by his ears again. "She's getting more air into her head." Gordy laughed maniacally.

"Hey, Camille, I got one for you..." his wife, Linda, joined in. "Do you know how to kill a blonde?"

"No," Camille shook her head.

"Easy. You just put a 'scratch and sniff' sticker at the bottom of the pool!"

Gordy and Linda laughed again. Camille managed a polite little chuckle.

Brother David sauntered up to Hans.

"Hans, Dianne and I have been watching Chef Emeril Lagasse on his cooking show. We want to take you all to his restaurant in the French Quarter for lunch."

"You mean NOLA's?" Camille asked. "That would be a pretty expensive lunch."

"What's NOLA's?" Uncle Otto asked.

"That's the name—it stands for New Orleans, Louisiana. They serve mostly gourmet French food," Camille explained.

Uncle Otto threw his hand forward in a German gesture of dismissal. "Aw, I'm not into that crap. While you're having lunch there, Mabel Baby and I will be down the street at the Crescent City Brew Pub having a sandwich."

"Yeah, Crescent City sounds good to me," Gordy agreed.

"That's fine," Hans agreed. "In fact, I'll go with you. Uncle Otto, Beau would probably want to have a sandwich with us. Camille, you can go with David and Dianne to that fancy place."

"How much could it be, I mean just for lunch?" David wondered.

"Let's see—with the three of us? And a few drinks? I'd say around a hundred bucks."

Now it was time for David to make the same dismissive gesture. "Aw, come on…well, even if it is, we still want to go."

The group loaded into the large van and Hans skillfully negotiated the sixty miles to the French Quarter. Locking the van in the parking lot, the group split into two and headed toward their respective restaurants. Camille guided David and Dianne to the street where NOLA's Restaurant was located.

The young couple seemed happy with the upscale décor. A handsome young waiter dressed in professional black attire immediately seated them.

"Do you want flat water or bubbly?" the waiter asked.

David appeared confused. He looked at Camille for help, but she just shrugged.

"Uh, flat water," he guessed.

"Very good, sir." The young man disappeared and quickly came back with bottles of water. He skillfully poured water into each stemmed glass garnished with fresh lemon. The diners paused a few moments over the lunch selections, then ordered. The meal was enjoyable.

"And it's so nice of them to keep filling up our water glasses without even being asked," David commented. He rose from the table. "I'm going to the bathroom."

The young waiter appeared with the bill.

"Just a second, Hon," Dianne said as she picked up the bill. "Guess what? They actually charged us for that 'flat' water! Can you believe it?"

David threw three $20 bills on the table.

"More..." Dianne advised.

David threw another $20 bill on the table.

"More..."

Dianne checked the bill again. "One more. That'll cover the tip, too, then."

David's eyes opened wide as he threw down the fifth $20 bill.

"Geesh! Now can I go to the bathroom?"

Camille covered her smile with her hand. "Gee, thanks, bro, for the nice meal."

David had seemed to recover from the $100 lunch after he returned from the bathroom.

"I saw Chef Lagasse make a blue martini on one of his shows. Let's go sit at the bar and have one."

The three sat down at the small bar.

"Give me a blue martini and a good cigar," David ordered.

Beau opened the door to the restaurant and approached his mother. He'd run the seven blocks between the restaurants.

"Hey, Mom—Dad went over to Fritzel's. He said to ask you."

Fritzel's was a German bar in the Quarter. There had even been an episode from a cancelled TV show, The Big Easy, where the TV cameras had filmed the walk-up bar, and the large, muscular backside of Hans in his green Pumas were caught on film forever.

"Ask me what, Beau?"

"If I could walk around the Quarter by myself for twenty minutes."

"Beau, you're twelve years old. What do you need to be walking around the French Quarter by yourself for?"

"Please, Mom? I've been sitting with those guys all this time, and I just want to walk."

"Alright, Beau," she sighed. "But, you've got exactly twenty minutes. Be back here precisely at 2:20. If you get lost or mugged, I'll finish the job. Do you understand me?"

"Yeah!" Beau raced out the door. Something wasn't quite right here; Camille just couldn't put her finger on it. For the next twenty minutes, she waited anxiously.

Exactly on time, Beau came bursting back into the door. "Hey, Mom, guess what?"

"What son?"

"You know that topless bar down on Bourbon Street? Well, I decided to take my allowance and try to get in. The bouncer looked at me and said, 'Boy, not only no, but HELL, no!'" Beau threw his head back and laughed heartily.

Camille sighed loudly. "You know what, son? There are probably some things you shouldn't tell your mother."

"Are there a lot of strip clubs in the French Quarter?" Dianne asked innocently.

"Dianne, if you want the ultimate astral experience, New Orleans is the place," Camille commented as she finished her wine.

Dianne gave Camille a puzzled look. She didn't understand, but thought better about pursuing the topic.

The Kiln

David looked at his watch. "Uh, it's time to get back to the car. Camille, do you think we can stop and see that bar Brett Favre goes to in his hometown—you know, the Kiln?"

"You mean the 'Broke Spoke?' I'm sure Hans won't mind."

"Yeah, that's it. Uncle Otto said he made a big sign and put it in the bar last time he was down here."

Everyone piled into the large van, and within thirty minutes they were turning down a country road. There were dozens of motorcycles parked around the area. In the middle of the street, a fight had broken out and the crowd was cheering. A huge black man was fighting a drunk, skinny white man with stringy hair and a tattooed body. The crowd seemed good natured, not angry. They were encouraging the black man.

"Come on, Ham, don't take crap off Rooster—give him hell!"

Hans continued to drive the van toward the fight.

"Hans, don't! Don't get in the middle of it!" Camille pleaded.

"Alright, Dad, go for it!" Beau encouraged.

Hans slowly drove the van between the two fighters. "There now, time to break it up!" he commanded in his German accent. Apparently, Hans knew what he was doing. The two fighters looked confused and walked off in separate directions. The crowd seemed to lose interest and also dissipated.

"Hey, David—you and Dianne come and write your name on the building, too," Hans stepped out of the van with a black magic marker.

Linda and Gordy walked around the dilapidated wooden bar in reverence, snapping pictures. This was, after all, the birthplace of the Green Bay Packers' famous quarterback. The owner, Steve, grinned and shook his head. He couldn't understand why his bar in Brett Favre's hometown was such a big attraction to these Wisconsin visitors. It was as if it were a pilgrimage. After the 1996 Superbowl game in New Orleans, there was a continuous crowd to the Broke Spoke bar in out-of-the-way Kiln, Mississippi. The state police had been called to direct the heavy onslaught of traffic for two days, and the beer truck had to make four extra deliveries.

Satisfied with visiting the football bar-shrine, Gordy looked at his watch. "You think Jerry Fisher is at the 'Dock of the Bay' this afternoon?"

"What time is it?" Hans asked. He never wore a watch, which was rather curious given his compulsive temperament.

"About three-thirty."

"Yeah, he should be there by now."

Jerry Fisher was the former lead singer with the rock band Blood Sweat and Tears. Years ago, while on a plane going to his next concert, he'd met a pretty dark-haired woman named Melva from the Mississippi Coast. They'd married, and now he had a restaurant on the water in Bay St. Louis called Dock of the Bay. Jerry had always been inspired by Otis Redding.

The group was able to park in front of the restaurant.

"How ya doin', Hans? See your relatives came down from Wisconsin again. Well, Camille…"

Camille walked over to Jerry and lightly rubbed the side of his beard. "You have the softest beard of anyone I know," she laughed.

Hans nodded, and everyone sat at the bar. Jerry was rehearsing. He finished the arrangements with the band, and started singing, "Georgia, Georgia, the whole night through. Just the sweet, sweet song of Georgia on my mind…"

Jerry finished the set, having a little difficulty remembering the words to a new song. Laughing, he approached the bar. "Guess I've got that thing called 'Old Singer's Disease'." He stopped to look at one of the men at the bar. "Gordy," Jerry shook his hand. "Got another gig for me at the Horse and Plow? I liked that place."

The Horse and Plow was part of a five-star complex owned by the Kohler company near Sheboygan.

Gordy grinned. "No, I haven't checked that out, but I did bring you something from there…" He handed the singer a hat with "Horse and Plow" embossed on the front.

Jerry grinned as he put on the hat. "Thanks."

Gordy pulled out one of Jerry Fisher's CDs. "Would you mind signing this for one of the guys at work?"

"Sure, no problem."

Camille looked at her watch. "Oh, boy. We'd better leave if we're going to meet Ashley."

"Ashley? Where are we meeting her?" Uncle Otto asked.

"Uncle Otto, remember we were going to the Grand for steamed oysters? They're the only place around where the oysters are pasteurized, so you don't have to worry so much about getting sick," Hans explained. "Ashley's meeting us there."

Miss Ashley

Ashley was seven years younger than Camille. In college, she'd majored in Deaf Education. Camille had always hoped Ashley would marry her high school sweetheart, Remmy. Remmy was a true Southern gentleman, with a quiet, easy sense of humor. He wasn't bad on the eyes, either. His family owned a lot of commercial property, and Remmy had easily taken to the business.

But to Camille's disappointment, in her senior year, Ashley, the shy, younger sister overshadowed by her flamboyant, older sister, had married a large, robust blonde college student named Jimmy. Jimmy was vacillating between a career in theater or religion at that time.

Ashley encouraged Jimmy to go into the ministry. Ashley had always been religious. During her childhood, she had sat in the church pew on Sundays, listening reverently to the pastor, while her older sister fidgeted and whispered to her friends. Little Ashley would put her finger to her mouth to hush Camille. This scenario went on until Camille was in high school and quit going to church altogether.

Ashley, however, was involved in every committee the church offered. She was thrilled when Jimmy took her advice and went into the ministry.

However, Jimmy had his problems. He couldn't seem to get enough of other women, although Ashley was constantly covering up this fact. After all, he was a local pastor in the area. Camille didn't even know, Ashley did such a good job of covering his tracks. This arrangement probably would have gone on for the rest of their marriage, until the fateful theater production. Jimmy had seemed unusually restless.

"Jimmy, I think you've been working too hard lately. Why don't you try out for the lead in 'The Music Man'? It'll be good for you to do something you like. I'll even help make the costumes," Ashley volunteered.

With Jimmy's blonde good looks and booming voice, he was a natural for the part of Professor Harold Hill. The female lead in the play, Suzie, was a recently divorced bleached blonde with a child, and a less than savory reputation. Jimmy started coming home later and later. In a desperate attempt to get some control of the situation, Ashley had volunteered to watch Suzie's young son for the night while Suzie was supposedly going to Jackson to "take care of some business." That night, Jimmy didn't come home at all.

Even with Ashley's ongoing attempts to cover Jimmy's tracks, the word finally got out into the community. Jimmy was less and less careful. One night, he and Suzie even fogged up the car windows in downtown Gulfport.

The word spread quickly to Camille. Camille called Ashley. "What were you thinking, girl, actually offering to baby-sit for Suzie when you knew she was seeing your husband?" she asked her sister angrily.

"But I didn't know then...not for sure."

"You—you didn't know? What—do they have to do it in the middle of your living room before you know for sure?"

Jimmy had come home and asked Ashley for a divorce. Ashley cried and went into shock for a month. Then Jimmy went before the elders of the church board to try to talk his way out of his latest escapades. Jimmy had been able to talk his way out of a lot of things in his life. This time, it didn't work. Jimmy was asked to resign as the pastor of the church. With his master's degree in counseling, he hung out his shingle. His specialty, the sign said, was "marriage counseling."

Hans and Camille dropped Beau off at a friend's house.

"We'll pick you up at nine-thirty sharp. Be waiting," Camille instructed.

"But, Mom..."

"Nine-thirty, Beau," Hans reminded him.

Hans, Camille, and the Wisconsin visitors met Ashley at the Bistro in the Grand Casino.

"Ashley, baby! How are ya?" Uncle Otto had a live one. He gave Ashley a wet, sloppy kiss on the cheek, then slapped her on the rear.

"Uncle Otto, please don't..."

"Oh, ho-ho-ho, you're looking good," said Uncle Otto, ignoring her protests.

"Thanks." Ashley wiped the wet kiss off her cheek, and Camille slid in next to her sister.

"When are you going to tell the old fart to keep his hands off your ass?"

"Well, hello to you, too, Cammy. I guess I just don't know how to be rude."

"Rude? It's called covering your ass. You should learn to do that a little more, Ashley." Camille studied her younger sister for a moment, then let out a disapproving sound. "Didn't you get that non-smudge mascara yet? Look, you've got some smudged underneath your lower lashes. My God, girl, you look more like a lounge singer than a teacher."

Camille took a tissue and dabbed at Ashley's face. "And...sweetie, you always wear your pretty hair in that tight little bun. You're not a minister's wife anymore."

"Alright, Cammy." Ashley was exasperated. "Decide which one I look like—a lounge singer or a minister's wife."

Camille studied her for a moment. "I don't know, Ashley. You are sending out mixed signals, you know."

"Just quit picking on me. I actually plan on having a good time tonight."

"And how are you going to do that?"

"I'm going to sit at the video poker bar and have a glass of wine."

Camille choked on her drink. Ashley had never taken a drink of alcohol in her life and disapproved of all forms of gambling. Suddenly, the big sister in Camille felt torn between Ashley's need to have a little fun and the naiveté that summarized Ashley's whole outlook on life.

"Uh, Hans? Ashley wants to try her hand at video poker."

"She does?" Hans was just as incredulous.

"I'll just go over there with her," Camille decided. "Would you mind sending my oysters over?"

"Sure. No problem."

Ashley and Camille sat at the video poker bar. A huge Cajun named Tony grinned at them. He'd gone to the same school as the two sisters.

"Hi, Camille. Want your white wine and club soda in a tall glass?"

"Sure, Tony."

"Ashley, I'm surprised to see you at a casino. You want a Coke or something?"

Ashley lifted her head in defiance. "No! I think I'll have a glass of wine."

Camille and Tony exchanged helpless glances. Tony also knew about the rough times Ashley had been through with Jimmy. He didn't want to offend her, but still felt protective.

"Um, Ashley, why don't you try what I'm having? It's light, and I'm sure Tony will put a fresh slice of lime in it."

Tony hoped Ashley would go for this suggestion.

Ashley hesitated.

"Heck, Ashley, I'll even put some fresh cherries in your drink, if you want," Tony offered.

Ashley cocked her head, apparently satisfied. "Yes, I think I'll have my drink with some fresh cherries, Tony."

Camille pulled out a roll of quarters. Ashley didn't make much money as a teacher, and although she'd kept the beach house her father A.J. had bought her as a wedding present, Jimmy had stripped the furniture and bank accounts.

"Here, sweetie, start with these."

Tony sat the drinks down on the bar. "Here, let me explain this game to you..." he offered.

Camille smiled at the sight of this huge Cajun man being so patient with her petite, younger sister.

Hans approached the bar. "Hey, Ashley, you're playing poker!"

"And she's even winning," Tony bragged.

"Yah, yah, I see. Listen, Cammy, I'm getting tired. If we don't get everybody out of here now, we'll be waiting all night. I've got them talked into stopping to see Mack Taylor for a few songs. Then we can get them home."

"Sounds good," Camille responded. "Besides, it looks like Ashley just ran out of quarters."

The group drove the three blocks to where Mack was singing. As they entered the lounge, Gordy's wife, Linda, scrutinized the singer's face.

"Looks like he's been rode hard and put away wet."

Camille chuckled. Mack had led quite the life.

Mack sang with a gravelly voice and played the piano. Hans' ears perked up at a conversation in German at the next table. He stood up and walked toward the tourists.

"Welcome. I hope you're enjoying your vacation," he said in German.

The German tourists were surprised to hear their native tongue in this unexpected place. They invited Hans' group to sit with them. Uncle Otto immediately regaled the tourists of his latest European adventures in fluent German.

Mack stopped singing for a moment. "This one's for Camille and Ashley. In fact, why don't you girls come up here and sing it with me?"

Camille looked at her sister. "I will if you will."

Ashley hung her head in embarrassment. "Camille, I can't sing."

"You can't sing? Why do you think Daddy paid all those years for your piano and voice lessons?"

"No!" Ashley was adamant.

"Sorry, Mack," Camille answered.

Mack shrugged and continued with the song.

Hans turned to address the tourists. "Have you ever heard the song 'Red Neck Mother' in German?"

Hans turned to Camille.

"Don't do this to me," she warned through clenched teeth.

Hans stood up. "Hey, Mack. Would you mind playing 'Red Neck Mother' for our new friends? Camille's going to sing it in German."

Camille gave Hans a searing look, and then focused on Ashley. "I'll do it if Ashley accompanies me with her sign language. It's the least you can do if you're not going to sing."

Ashley sighed and stood next to Camille, signing the words to the song—"Up against the wall, red neck mother. Mother who has raised her son so well—so well, so well! He's thirty-four and drinking in a honky-tonk café. Kicking hippie's ass and raising hell..."

As Camille sang and Ashley signed the words, the German tourists shrieked their enjoyment. Song finished, the women walked back to their seat.

"I feel like a trained seal." Camille looked at her sister. "What happened to you? You used to love singing."

Camille saw tears drop from her sister's eyes. "Jimmy wanted to be the one in the spotlight. He made fun of my singing. He said he was just being honest about my voice because he loved me, and I need to know."

"Needed to know what?"

"He said I had no singing range."

"My God, girl. You can do three octaves easily. Don't you know he just didn't want you competing with him?"

There was a commotion at the table as the Germans pulled something out of a travel bag. "This," the elder German announced, "is our last bottle of Bitters. We present it to you for giving us such good times!" Many Germans traveled with a bottle of Bitters for medicinal purposes, to settle their stomachs from strange water and foods. It was indeed an honor to be given their last bottle.

The weekend passed, and Hans went back to his medical practice. Beau went back to school. "I just know we're gonna have some hurricane days," the twelve-year-old hoped as he headed out the door.

Camille set her morning coffee on the desk and booted up her computer. She would have closed the office door, but that would have been too obvious. She logged on and checked her email. One of her friends, Sheila, was currently living in San Juan, Puerto Rico, with her engineer husband and their three small boys.

'Camille', the email message began, 'Hurricane Georges is due to hit tonight. I'm shutting down the computer after sending this message. Pray for us.'

Camille put her hand to her lips and tears welled in her eyes. The building codes in San Juan were nowhere as strict as the States. And their electrical service had never been dependable. Thoughts of Sheila's plight were interrupted by a now-familiar voice.

"Camille, come here a minute!" Uncle Otto commanded.

Camille groaned quietly to herself and headed toward the kitchen.

"I just finished sharpening all your knives. Now, I also made you some knife covers. You just can't set these steak knives in the drawer, or they'll get dull," he lectured.

"Well, that was nice of you, Uncle Otto, but you didn't need to..."

Uncle Otto grunted his reply. "Just see that you use the knife covers."

Camille turned to leave.

"Now, wait. I have to show you what I did in the main bathroom—"

Camille cast her eyes upward for some kind of divine intervention, but none was forthcoming.

"See—see this?" Uncle Otto pointed to the shower head. There was a new one installed, and the old one was lying in a black puddle in the sink. "You didn't have a water saver on this shower. Watch this—if you turn the lever on the shower head, then you can control the water better."

"Thanks again, Uncle Otto." Camille couldn't recall asking for a new shower head, but, if it kept him busy...She headed back to her computer. She only had one more lesson to complete.

"Hey, Camille," Mabel Baby called. "Why don't you come and play a game of cribbage with us?"

"I'd love to, Miss Mabel, but I'm kind of working under a deadline here..."

Uncle Otto crossed the room and stood over the computer screen to see what was so important. "Aw, you work too hard. Why don't you go with us to the prize drawing at the Copa Casino this morning?"

At that moment, Camille's hospital pager mercifully started beeping loudly.

"What's that?" Uncle Otto wanted to know.

"Oh, no!" Camille feigned regret. "It's the hospital! And I was so looking forward to going with you!" Camille grabbed her briefcase and lab coat as she headed out the door.

The staff at the nurses' station was in a giddy mood.

"I've just never seen y'all act so silly," Camille laughed.

"Maybe it's the pressure drop from the hurricane," Miss Sandy, the head nurse, speculated.

Camille cocked her head in thought. "You know, Miss Sandy, you may just be right."

Camille was charting when her beeper went off again. It was a number she'd never seen before. She dialed the number.

"Casino Magic," the voice answered.

"What?" Camille asked, confused.

"Casino Magic," the voice repeated. "May I help you?"

"Uh, this is Dr. Kohl. I received a page to this number, but it must be a mistake..."

"You said your name was Kohl?"

"Yes, but—"

"It's no mistake, ma'am. Your brother-in-law, Gordy Kohl, is here. He's won the daily jackpot, and he wants you to come over and help him."

"Help him? I don't understand."

"That's what he said, ma'am. He's on the first floor Golden Pharaoh machine at the west end."

"Uh, thanks..."

Camille shook her head and hung up. She made the twenty-minute drive to Casino Magic and parked. As she walked toward the west end, she could see the smoke from Gordy's celebratory cigar curling into the air.

"Oh, there you are, Cammy. Linda went shopping. I'm just so hot on this machine, it's unbelievable. Could you take these buckets up to the cashier and cash them in for me?"

"Gordy—I'm working here!" Camille tried to contain some of the exasperation in her voice.

"Yah, yah..." Gordy piled six buckets of dollars into his sister-in-law's arms. Camille sighed and turned toward the cashier. She dutifully cashed in the buckets and collected the money. Her eyes alerted to a drift of smoke from another cigar. Looking across the gaming tables, she spotted the former Chicago Bears coach, Mike Ditka.

"Hi, Mr. Mike!" she waved.

"Iron" Mike looked up and grinned. "Hi, Camille, how you doing?"

"Fine. I'm just on my way back to work," she emphasized for her brother-in-law's sake.

Gordy had been watching with interest. "That's Mike Ditka."

"Yes, I know, Gordo. He does his radio show here."

"How do you know Mike Ditka?"

"Oh, I met him during a charity drive. I don't know why everybody says he's so mean. I mean really, he's just so sweet..." she drawled.

"Geez..." Gordy took one last reverent look. Then the lure of another machine called. "I think I'll go beat that old lady for the nickel machine..."

Hans was catching up on some paperwork in his office when an Air Force Reserve pilot walked in. "Hans, the hurricane hunters just sent their new report back to Keesler. This hurricane is a strong one."

Hans put down his papers and looked at his friend. With his family visiting the coast, the hurricane would definitely cause some logistical problems. Still, he wasn't going to worry his relatives until the hurricane track was certain.

By the time Hans returned from work, Camille was in an irritable mood. Hans, however, was happy to see his uncle. "Gordo called me about his winning the jackpot. That son of a gun is always lucky. Where's David?" he asked.

"Oh, he and Dianne have been gone all day. I think they said he went to Ship Island."

"What's for supper?" Uncle Otto called from the barroom.

Hans turned to his wife. "Camille, haven't you started dinner yet?"

"The chicken is in the oven," Camille yelled back, determined not to be disrupted again from her work. "It'll be ready in about thirty minutes."

This time, Mabel Baby got up and walked into Camille's office. She had a serious, questioning look on her face.

"What is it, Miss Mabel?"

"I was just wondering..."

"Yes?"

"Where did you buy the chicken?"

Camille frowned. "At the grocery store. Why?"

"Do you know where the chicken came from?"

"Came from? I don't understand."

"Did the package say what state the chicken came from?"

"I'm sorry, I'm not following this. I assume it was from around the area."

Mabel hesitated for a moment. "You think it's Southern chicken, then?"

"Southern chicken? Why, I guess so..."

"Oh. I'd rather not eat it."

Camille let down her guard enough to show her exasperation. "Miss Mabel, I made chicken especially for you, since you won't eat seafood. Would you mind telling me what the difference is between Northern chicken and Southern chicken?"

Mabel could see her hostess was irritated, but felt rather strongly on this point. "Well, Northern chickens are fed a better quality of grain. It makes a difference in the meat."

Camille rocked back and forth for a moment in her office chair.

"Really!" she answered sarcastically. She leaned forward, ready to defend Southern chicken, when Hans intercepted.

"That's OK, Mabel. We've got some ham in the refrigerator. Camille, why don't you make her a ham sandwich instead?"

"That would be good," Mabel answered, appeased.

"Mabel Baby, why don't you put on some polka music?" Uncle Otto called from the barroom.

Mabel dutifully picked through the next selection of polka torture.

Camille looked at her husband through angry, narrow eyes. "Did you hear that? Cam you believe that crap—better grain?"

"Well," Hans replied, "it could be true."

"What? Incredible!"

Camille huffed into the kitchen and slammed the cutting board onto the counter. Just then, the polka music blared through the house. Camille could actually see the dishes on the wall vibrating.

"Uncle Otto! Turn it down!" Hans shouted above the racket.

"What?"

"Turn the music down. Put your hearing aid in."

"Oh, OK."

As the week progressed, Uncle Otto and Mabel Baby continued blithely along in their routine. They might disappear somewhere for a few blessed hours of silence during the day, then return home to "keep Camille company."

Camille struggled to finish the last lesson in the online course, which had been promised for delivery on Thursday. Despite the constant interruptions, the completed course was ready Thursday afternoon. Camille breathed a sigh of relief as she made back-up copies of her work. Even Uncle Otto's projects couldn't ruffle her feathers today. She'd met her deadline.

"Camille, I just realized what you're missing around here," Uncle Otto started.

"What, Uncle Otto?" she replied pleasantly enough.

"Well, when we're outside, we have to keep the doors open to hear the polka music, but that isn't so good with the air conditioning running."

"This is true," Camille responded.

"So, I went to Home Depot. I'm going to rewire the barroom and put loudspeakers out on the patio, so we can hear the polka music outside better."

Camille felt a laugh welling up inside her. What a way to get even with Hans, and she didn't even have to plan this one.

"Sure, why not?" She tried to keep the sarcasm from coming through.

"Right, then. Where's your toolbox?"

"Just let me get that for you, Uncle Otto," Camille gushed sweetly.

Hans returned home from work thirty minutes later. As he walked into the barroom, he saw the wiring on the switch plate pulled out. He walked back out and gave his wife a questioning look.

"Uh, where's Uncle Otto?"

"Oh, I think he's back by the fuse box."

"What's he doing?"

"Well, Hans..." she drew this out for a moment—this was just too much fun—"he's decided to rewire the barroom and put loudspeakers out on the patio for his polka music."

"He—he's what? And you let him?"

Camille looked up at her massive husband innocently. "Well now, Hans, he does have a college degree in electrical engineering."

"Yeah, in 1939."

Camille shrugged. "He's your uncle," she said with some relish.

Hans shook his head. "Well, I'd better go stop him now before he goes any further. I don't want a neighborhood riot on my hands."

Camille could hear the muffled sound of Hans and Uncle Otto's voices in the back room. She hummed happily, her work finished. She logged onto the internet and pulled up the National Weather Service's website. Her triumphant mood melted away. The hurricane's course was tracking straight for the Mississippi Gulf coast. The phone rang.

"Hello?"

"Hi, honey."

"Well—hi, Daddy. Where've you been?"

"I've been moving my boat to the Back Bay. They're getting ready to close the bridge. It looks like the hurricane is going to hit us after all."

"Oh—you think?"

A.J. chucked softly. "Sweetie, you know I've never missed predicting one in thirty years."

The realization hit Camille suddenly. "I know."

"Listen, I'm leaving the coast tomorrow morning. Going up to that spread of land I bought north of Hattiesburg. There's a big house up there, though I'm not sure what shape it's in. Do you want to bring everybody up there?"

"Well, I'll ask. But, tonight is Oktoberfest, and I doubt if you could blast them away."

"Cammy, why don't you meet me at the Waffle House at eight-thirty tomorrow morning on my way out of town?"

"Sure, Daddy, I'll be there."

Robert, the mayor, had come back to town to try to fill his father's shoes. It was a big task. His serious blue eyes now evaluated the latest weather reports. It was his first term, and it looked like a big storm was going to directly hit his cherished hometown. He sighed. All he could do was prepare the city as best he could. He switched on the intercom.

"Miss Maria?"

"Yes, Mr. Robert?"

"Please call the Public Works Department immediately. Have them dredge out all the drainage ditches. We want to have the water drain as fast as possible. And start the emergency callbacks."

"Yes, sir."

CHAPTER 2
Hurricane

Camille drove down the street the next morning and saw work crews from the city busily dredging the drainage ditches. Uh oh, she thought to herself. The mayor must think the hurricane was coming their way, too. She'd have to thank him for his preparations at the next Rotary meeting. She drove up to the Waffle House and parked.

"Hey, Miss Camille!" Miss Trudy called. "Do you want the usual?"

"Sure, Miss Trudy. Just make sure to get it light."

Miss Trudy had been a waitress at the Waffle House longer than anybody on the coast. She did alright—stock options, pension plan, and on the side dabbled in community theater. In her early fifties, she was a diminutive spitfire.

"Pecan waffle, extra light," Miss Trudy called out.

"Isn't that a contradiction in terms—light waffle?"

"Morning, Daddy." Camille smiled and gave her distinguished-looking father a light kiss on his bearded cheek. "Your boat all secure?"

"All secured."

"Hey, Mr. A.J., you want your usual?"

"Sure, Miss Trudy."

Camille studied her father. "You look a little tired."

"Well, I was up most of the night helping friends get prepared for the hurricane." His daughter, he noticed, missed the obvious emphasis on the word "friends." It continued to amuse him that his daughter was so clueless about his love life.

"Nash Roberts said that the hurricane is going to New Orleans. They're already evacuating people, and using the Super Dome as a shelter," Camille reported.

"Nash has to play it safe. There are thousands of people to evacuate, and the floodgates might not hold. I, however, don't have to consider the politics," he answered.

"That's true."

"What about Hans' family? Are they going to evacuate?"

Camille threw her head back and laughed. "Are you kidding? Tonight is Oktoberfest. They don't see how a hurricane would dare interrupt that! Besides, Hans has volunteered to help out in the E.R. at the hospital. Kind of 'shape 'em up', you know. He's good at that."

"Well, if the hurricane does change course, they're welcome to come up north to the property. It'll be harder than hell trying to get a hotel room within three hundred miles of the coast. Here—" A.J. passed a sheet of paper to his daughter. "Directions and phone number to the property if they change their minds."

"Thanks." Camille studied the paper. "Daddy, do you think our house will be safe?"

"Well it's twenty-seven feet above sea level and survived your namesake, Camille. This storm will only be a Category Three or Four. I'm more worried about your sister right now."

"You mean, Ashley's beach house?"

"Yes. It's newer construction. It's got hurricane straps and shutters, like yours, but being right on the beach, I don't know. Camille, will you ask Ashley to stay with you? She's all alone now, and I'd feel better."

Camille felt somewhat ashamed that she hadn't thought about her sister's safety. Hans' family had kept her constantly busy.

"Uh, sure. I'll call her when I get home."

"Good. Now—did you back up your computer programs?"

"Yes, I did." Camille looked serious. "Daddy, speaking of being all alone, don't you think it's time you found someone?"

A.J.'s green eyes twinkled. "Someone?"

"Don't be coy, Daddy. You've been alone forever. I've been looking around, and there's a really nice lady in the Biloxi Historical Society..."

A.J. chuckled. "You know something, darlin'? I think I'd rather pick out my own women." After all these years, he thought, she kept missing the signs...

Camille made a little sound of disapproval. She pulled herself up in the booth. "Well, I was just trying to help."

"I know you were." A.J. looked at his watch. "I've got one more stop to make on the way out of town. I'd better be going."

Camille suddenly looked frightened. A.J. gave her a gentle hug. "It'll be alright, sweetie. Hans has good sense; he won't let anything happen to you."

Camille watched as her father left in his large truck. She stood there for a moment, and then realized her father's last words. "Hans won't let anything happen to you?" Geesh!

As soon as Camille was back at her house, she turned on her computer and pulled up the National Weather Service website. It looked like the hurricane was on a direct track for Gulfport. She reached for the phone.

"Ashley, we're going to get something from this hurricane. I want you to come and stay with us."

"Why, hon, that's nice of you to think of me. Do you need some of my extra batteries? The stores are already out."

"Extra batteries? Being married to a prepared German? No, keep them for later."

Uncle Otto finally realized that Camille was home. "Hey, what's up?"

"I was just looking at the hurricane tracking chart..."

"Oh?" Uncle Otto seemed surprised. "I thought it was going to hit New Orleans."

Gordy and Linda walked into the room.

"Gordy—you and Linda are actually home during the day?"

"Yeah, this hurricane's got me worried." Gordy studied the screen closely.

"My father says it's going to hit the coast. He just went up north this morning. You can still drive up there if you want," Camille offered.

"And miss Oktoberfest?" Uncle Otto was somewhat incredulous. "Oh, no—no—no," he chuckled.

Mabel seemed curious about something. She walked out the front door, stood in the middle of the road, and looked down at the beach two blocks away. Camille watched as she just stood in the middle of the road, staring at the Gulf waters. Finally, Camille's curiosity got the better of her. She walked out to the middle of the road.

"Miss Mabel, what are you looking for?"

"The hurricane."

"The hurricane?"

"Yes. I thought I'd be able to see it by now."

"No, Miss Mabel," Camille chuckled, "the hurricane is still one hundred miles out."

"Oh…do you think we can see it later?"

Camille realized Mabel had seen many snowstorms, but never a hurricane. "Well, for our sakes, I hope we don't. I'm going to get Ashley. If Beau comes home early from school, will you tell him to start putting the lawn furniture in the shed?"

"Alright."

Camille grabbed her keys and backed out of the driveway. When she returned with Ashley, Camille found Beau and Miss Mabel moving the last chaise lounge into the storage shed.

"Beau, check all around the house, and make sure there isn't anything loose that could fly around in the wind."

"Yes, ma'am." Beau went seriously about his task.

Hans pulled up in the driveway.

"Well, you're home from the office early," Camille remarked.

"It was a slow afternoon," Hans lied. He didn't want to upset his wife, who could get a little emotional about these storms.

Camille shrugged and went to the sink to fill empty soda bottles with water.

"What are you doing?" Miss Mabel asked.

"In case we have a 'boil water' alert—that happens sometimes during a hurricane."

"Look, Camille," Hans' voice seemed testy. "We're not going to have a hurricane!" He didn't want his brothers to get any more worried. "Let's play a game of cribbage, and then it'll be time to go to Oktoberfest."

Beau came in the back door. "All finished, Mom."

"Good, son. Are you going with us to Oktoberfest?"

Beau shook his head in disbelief as he laughed. "I don't think so! I'm not about to do the Chicken Dance, and I don't like bratwurst."

"Ho—ho—ho! Beau, you don't know what you're missing!" Uncle Otto chided the boy.

"Oh, yes I do." Beau turned to his father. "David, me, and Jason rented a whole bunch of movies. They were having a 'hurricane special' at Super Video. Can I stay there overnight?"

"Do we have Jason's phone number?

"Dad—it's been on the bulletin board for the last five years!"

"Well, alright then. Just be home by ten tomorrow morning."

"Dad, that's pretty early."

"Ten o'clock."

Beau sensed that his Dad was more firm than usual on this point. "Yes, sir."

"OK!" Hans slapped his hands together. "Who's ready for a game of cribbage?"

Most of the group was busy playing cards when Ashley walked in. "I don't want to go to this Oktoberfest," she announced.

Linda had gotten bored with watching the cribbage game, and came over to talk with the sisters. "Why not?" she asked.

Camille looked at her sister knowingly. "Because Jimmy, her skirt-chasing ex-husband will probably be there. He always goes."

Ashley nodded. "And he'll probably bring his new wife, Suzie."

Camille sneered and stuck her nose up in the air. "Just imagine—he cheated on you with that sleazy thing. And her bleached blonde hair needs a serious toner—"

"I don't want to go!" Ashley reiterated.

"You have to, babes. I kind of got you—a date."

"What? You did what? Cammy, I don't know if I'll ever be ready for another man in my life, let alone tonight."

"Look, Ashley, you just have to sit next to him at the picnic table. It's just for show, you know."

"Well, who is it?" Ashley wondered.

Camille hesitated. She didn't quite know how her sister would react to this meddling. "Uh...it's Remmy."

"Remmy?" Ashley seemed to brighten. "I thought he was engaged to be married."

Camille tilted her head and grinned. "Not anymore."

"Cammy, are you sure?"

"Yes, darlin', I'm sure." Camille put her arm around her younger sister. "You have to go and show Jimmy you just don't care about him anymore."

"Yeah, girl," Linda agreed in her husky voice. "You gotta show that son of a bitch a thing or two."

Oktoberfest

The sun was setting as the group loaded in the van and headed to Oktoberfest. As they approached the intersection leading to the Gulfport International Harbor, a policeman put his hand out to signal traffic to stop. Dozens of huge semi-trucks followed one another out of the port and headed north on Highway 49.

"My God, they're completely evacuating the harbor," Hans quietly realized aloud.

The night was warm and humid, but now that the sun had set, it was finally cooling off. Hans had reserved two large tables for family and friends. He was in an exceptionally good mood this evening. "Well, Father Ryan! It's good of you to come!"

Father Ryan, the hospital priest, raised his mug in welcome.

Camille saw her younger sister, Ashley, freeze in her tracks. She looked toward the table across the room. It was Jimmy, her ex-husband, with his new floozy wife, Suzie. Suzie had her arms wrapped around Jimmy's ample belly as a further proclamation of her ownership.

Camille gave Ashley's hand a reassuring pat. "Don't worry, my dear, I'll take care of this." Camille narrowed her eyes. Her face and body language took on the characteristics of a Cheshire cat.

"Cammy, please don't..." Ashley pleaded weakly to her sister's retreating back.

Jimmy glanced up and saw his former sister-in-law headed toward him. He puffed out his chest in a show of bravado and waved at her. "Well, Camille! So nice to see you!" Jimmy rose from his chair. "You've met my wife, Suzie.."

"Oh, yes-s-s," Camille hissed.

"And this is the pastor of the new church Suzie and I have joined," Jimmy said in a booming, sanctimonious voice.

"Well now, Reverend Bob," Camille purred, "it's just been ages!"

"Camille, it's so nice to see you again. I see your beautiful sister is here..."

Camille paused for effect. "Oh, that's right. You and Ashley used to date each other," she emphasized, glancing meaningfully at Jimmy.

"Just how is Ashley?" Reverend Bob inquired.

"Oh—she had a big problem..." Apparently, this was another piece of information Jimmy had withheld. "...but she was able to get rid of him."

Camille watched with some satisfaction as Jimmy's face turned white. Then, she made a point of staring into Jimmy's famous "coffee" mug. Jimmy had steadfastly denied that he ever drank.

"Well, Jimmy, still drinking your whiskey out of a coffee cup, I see." She smiled sweetly to make sure her words had their intended effect. They had.

Camille turned her attention to Jimmy's new wife, Suzie. Suzie had been sitting quietly, hoping that Camille would just go away. Not quite yet, however. Camille scrutinized the top of Suzie's hair.

"Oh, my dear," she said in a mock voice of concern. "I'm just sure you had no idea how long your black roots were. Really, sweetie, I know Jimmy can't afford much, but you just have to go to a professional if you want to pretend to be blonde!"

Satisfied, Camille started to walk away. The band hadn't started playing yet, but there was a CD playing over the loudspeakers. Camille stopped and listened to the words, then laughed. She turned back toward Jimmy.

"Hey, Jim-bo, they're playing your song!" Camille broke out in a strut and circled once around Jimmy's table. "Da-da-da-da, I'm just a love machine..." Smugly, she walked back to her table.

Ashley had a look of trepidation on her face. "Camille, what were you saying over there? I hope nothing bad."

Camille took a sip of beer and savored it. Oktoberfest was one of the few occasions she drank it, and she felt philosophical now. "You know, Ashley, what's the point in living if you can't show your ass every now and then?"

The band from Germany was getting ready to start. "Oh, ve have an announcement—someone left de car lights on, a white Ford. Vould you please go make out de lights? Und now, ve have a new polka song for you!"

"Father Ryan, would you like to dance?" Camille asked.

"Sure, let's go!"

Uncle Otto had his tape recorder up and running, doing his commentary along with the recording of the band. "Here we are in Biloxi, Missi-iss-iss-iss-ippi," he slushed. "We're having a great time at Oktoberfest, and the band is from Weisbaden, Germany."

Ashley watched silently as Remmy's truck pulled into the parking lot. Remmy approached the table.

"Well, Miss Ashley, it's been a long time. Would you care to dance?"

Ashley gave a quick, frightened glance toward her older sister, then shyly took Remmy's hand.

"You know," Remmy started, "I was really quite peeved with you when you married Jimmy."

"I—" Ashley started to defend herself, but Remmy interrupted.

"Hush, girl, that's alright. You're well out of it now."

"But, Remmy, I thought you were getting married this fall—"

"Oh, I was, darlin', I was. But...I don't know, it just didn't seem right, somehow." He looked down at Ashley and showed the slightest trace of a smile. "Would you mind, Miss Ashley, if I give you a call next week?"

Ashley looked shyly away. Somehow, she felt she'd let Remmy down. After all, she was a divorced woman now. "I—I suppose that would be alright, Remmy."

"Good." Remmy looked at his watch. "Darlin', I have to leave now— got some properties to get secured for the storm. I'll talk to you later, hear?" He gave Ashley a soft kiss on the cheek and walked away. Confused about her feelings, Ashley watched as he disappeared into the dark.

Gordy and Linda look bored. "Hey, Hans? We've been to enough Oktoberfests. Do you mind if we disappear for a while in the Beau Rivage Casino?"

"Sure—you'll be back in a couple of hours?"

"Yah, yah. It won't take us that long to spend our money." They got up and left the tent.

Mike Reader, the Biloxi TV station meteorologist, had just announced the beer drinking contest. During her study of anatomy, Camille was fascinated by the obscure fact that the Germans had developed the ability to keep their throats open and pour beer down in one continuous gulp, rather than having to swallow repeatedly. Everyone laughed as the Americans gulped and slobbered beer down their T-shirts.

"And here's our winner!" Mike Reader announced over the microphone. Everyone clapped and cheered. Florence, the wife and owner of the sponsoring restaurant, hurriedly walked toward the meteorologist. She looked fearful as she whispered a message to him. Camille watched curiously as the meteorologist disappeared from the tent.

Florence picked up the microphone. "OK, everybody! It's time for the Chicken Dance contest!"

Camille looked at her sister, sitting sullenly at the table.

"Want to try this?" a clean-cut young officer asked Ashley.

"No, thanks," Ashley brushed a fly away. She was still confused about her feelings for Remmy and needed time to think.

Casinos are Closing

Camille and Hans saw an agitated Gordy enter the beer tent.

"What's up?" Hans asked. "You've only been gone thirty minutes."

"They closed all the casinos due to the hurricane. They're evacuating all the guests from the hotels."

"What? You're joking, right? The casino would lose too much money, and they're all built to withstand 160 mile per hour winds," Hans responded, trying to process this new information.

Florence appeared nervous as the word spread around the tables. She quickly took up the microphone again. "Hey, everybody! It's time to line up for the rumba! Let's go!"

The band members' wives, dressed in German costumes, got behind Florence. Hans wanted his family to end Oktoberfest with a happy memory. He stood up. "OK, gang, let's go!" He turned to his wife, "You, too, *mein Schatzi!*"

The family sat there, stunned at the news.

"Look," Hans bargained. "If you do this last dance, then we'll go. Now—c'mon!"

One by one, the family rose and hooked onto the back of the line. They laughed in spite of themselves.

Back at home, there was quiet conversation around the bar.

"What should we do?" Uncle Otto asked.

"Look," Hans said, "it's too late to get hotel rooms away from the coast, and it's too late to drive anywhere tonight. The roads are still congested with the New Orleans people evacuating. Let's just get a good night's rest, and make our decisions when we're fresh tomorrow morning."

Everyone nodded. It seemed like a logical plan.

In the morning, everyone was up early, gathered around the TV, transfixed. The Weather Channel showed the hurricane only fifty-five miles away. It had veered slightly more to the west, homing in on New Orleans.

"That's good, isn't it?" Gordy asked hopefully. "I mean, it looks like the hurricane is going toward New Orleans instead of us."

Hans and Camille looked at each other.

"We'll be on the east side of the hurricane," said Hans with a sickening realization.

"So? What difference does that make?" Uncle Otto wanted to know.

"The east side is the worst side of a hurricane. It drives the flood waters in," Hans explained.

Gordy had a worried, serious look for a change. He turned to his wife. "You know, David and I have to be back at work on Tuesday. If the flights get jammed up, we might not make it."

"You're right, Gordo," Linda agreed. "We'd better call the airport, and see if we can change our tickets to today instead." Linda picked up the phone, dialed, and then frowned. "The number's busy," she reported.

Linda redialed. Still busy.

Gordy looked thoughtful. "Maybe," he said softly, "we'd better pack and go out to the ticket counter in person. At least we'd have a better chance that way."

The couple quickly packed their belongings, got in their rental car, and backed out of the driveway. Uncle Otto and Mabel Baby silently watched them drive down the road. Uncle Otto was not his usual feisty self this morning.

Camille realized she had to take their minds off the storm, at least for awhile. "Homemade coffeecake!" she announced, pulling the warm pastry from the oven. "And, there's a fresh pot of coffee ready. Come and get it!"

Everyone was eating coffeecake and watching the Weather Channel when the phone rang.

"Hello, Hans?"

"Yeah, Gordo, what's up?"

"We got the tickets changed for all of us. Tell David and Dianne to get out to the airport as fast as they can. The last flight is overbooked, and then they're closing down the airport."

David and Dianne gave each other a frantic look, then started throwing their belongings into suitcases. Five minutes later, they were heading toward the door.

Hans walked to the door and waved goodbye to his brother's quickly disappearing back. "Bye, Bro! See you next trip!"

Brother David turned around. "Yeah—after hurricane season is over."

At the airport, David and Dianne just made last call before the gantry pulled away. Back in the airport, an announcement came over the loudspeaker. "Folks, we're sorry, but that's our last plane out. The airport is now officially closed."

The fear and frustration in the crowd was palpable as the announcements continued. "We have busses to take passengers without transportation to the shelters. For people with cars, we have printed directions to get to the shelters."

Relieved that the brothers had made it out on the last flight, Camille relaxed for a moment. Then she realized, "Where's Beau?"

"Didn't he call?" asked Hans.

"No...oh, my God..." Camille was starting to worry. She knew how her son liked to take risks.

The Hurricane Walk

At that moment, Miss Kay-Dee was driving down Highway 90 in Gulfport. She was on her way out of town. The Gulf winds were coming in so strong off the beach that her big, heavy Cadillac had trouble staying on the road. Sand particles blasted the side of her car, as the swirling sand blew across the road with fierce intensity. Miss Kay-Dee glanced out into the Gulf waters and saw two boys one hundred feet out, challenging the pounding wind and surf.

"Crazy tourists!" she muttered. Then she saw Jason's pickup truck and screeched to a halt. Miss Kay-Dee honked her car horn loudly to get the boys' attention. She flung open her car door and marched angrily toward the two boys on the beach.

"Beau! Jason!" she screamed.

The two boys had heard the car horn and now were looking at the figure of the approaching woman, her large beach hat and long dress flapping wildly in the wind.

"Is that your mom?" Jason asked, trying to peer through the blowing sand.

"It's worse. It's Miss Kay-Dee," Beau said with some justifiable fear.

"Not Miss Kay-Dee—" Jason didn't relish an encounter with her anymore than Beau did.

"You two boys get your skinny white asses out of the water now! You hear me?"

It had taken Beau and Jason twenty minutes to fight the wind and waves out to the channel markers, which was what the challenge was all about. Now, with the motivation of Miss Kay-Dee and the wind at their backs, they were back onshore in less than four minutes.

Miss Kay-Dee was waiting, arms crossed. "Jason, the wind is too strong for you to get back to the Pass. Doesn't your Uncle Robert live just up Courthouse Road in Bayou Estates?"

"Yes, ma'am."

"Is your uncle staying or leaving?"

"He's staying. We were just there an hour ago."

"Well then, you get in your truck and go up there right now. I'll call your mama."

Jason knew better than to argue. "See ya, Beau."

Miss Kay-Dee turned with purpose to her young charge. "And you, Beau…"

Beau hung his head.

"What are you using for brains? I know you mama must be worried sick about you right now." She stopped for a moment to think. Well, she reasoned, they all had to learn the truth sometime.

"Beau, you're coming with me."

Beau got into the Cadillac. Miss Kay-Dee picked up her cell phone and dialed Camille's number.

"Hello?" The voice was anxious.

"Cammy, it's me. I found Beau and Jason on the beach. They were doing the hurricane walk."

"The hurricane walk? No matter how many times he's been warned—"

"Cammy," Miss Kay-Dee interrupted, "I've got to get out of here. I'm taking him up north with me. I'll call you when I get there."

Miss Kay-Dee turned to the chastised young boy next to her. "And Beau," she stated flatly, "you're gonna pay for this stunt."

The Cadillac spun its tires in the sand as Miss Kay-Dee put the hammer down.

Camille hung up the phone, mentally exploring Beau's punishment options when the hurricane was over.

"Camille! Come here!" Hans ordered. She had rarely heard Hans that excited. She ran into the living room.

"What is it?"

There was a newsman with a very serious expression saying something while a message ran across the bottom of the screen.

"Hurricane Georges is starting to slowly move to the east, and is expected to hit Slidell, Louisiana, by midnight. A no-driving order is being posted from Slidell, Louisiana, to Pascagoula, Mississippi, starting at six p.m. I repeat, there is a driving ban starting at six p.m. tonight. Drivers without official business will be arrested."

Now Camille was caught between a rock and a hard place. If she urged Uncle Otto to leave, it might look as if she'd finally found her excuse to get rid of him. If she didn't urge him to leave, she'd be stuck with him in a house which, at the very least, would have no electricity or running water for an indeterminate amount of time.

Uncle Otto looked toward Hans for guidance.

"Well, we can all go to A.J.'s place up north," Hans offered.

This was an even worse scenario than Camille could have imagined— stuck in an enclosed car in a traffic jam with Uncle Otto blaring loud polka music. She had to think quickly.

"Uh, Uncle Otto...we're only two blocks from the beach, and there's no room for your car in our garage. I don't want your new car to be damaged..."

Uncle Otto thought about it for a moment. "Yah, yah, you're right. This is the first trip in my new car..."

At that moment, Hans' beeper went off. "It's the hospital," he announced. He crossed the room to the phone. "Hello? Extension 240 please...Yes, this is Dr. Kohl. You need me now? Alright, I'm on my way."

Hans and Camille exchanged looks. Hans turned toward his elderly uncle.

"Uncle Otto, I think it's better if you get up north before the driving ban goes into effect at six. Here's the map to A.J.'s house. It's just north of Hattiesburg, so even with the traffic, you should make it in two hours."

Uncle Otto filtered this information through his brain. "Right! We'll get packed."

Hans looked pointedly at his wife, who was trying to look both concerned and innocent at the same time. "Camille will help you pack," he volunteered.

Camille stuck her tongue out at her husband's retreating back.

Hans stopped and turned back toward his wife. "Cammy." His voice had softened. "If it looks like the weather is going to be really rough, get your hospital badge and bring Ashley with you to the hospital. You promise?"

"I promise."

Hans gave his wife a light kiss. He turned to his uncle. "Bye, Uncle Otto. We'll be up to see you soon." He gave Mabel Baby a hug. "Take care now. Drive safe." Hans jumped into his SUV and drove off.

"Ashley!" Camille realized. She went to the phone. "Hey, Ashley, did you hear about the driving ban? You didn't? Look, girl, pack up what you need and get over here right away!"

"Camille!" Uncle Otto called. "Could you put our food in my cooler?"

"Sure. I'll even make you some sandwiches for the road."

With Uncle Otto's usual precision, he and Mabel Baby were packed and loaded within twenty minutes.

"Now, here's an extra copy of Daddy's directions and phone numbers, just in case."

"Got it! Well, we'd better be going!"

Camille gave Uncle Otto and Mabel Baby a quick hug. Then the couple opened the screen door and started toward their car.

"Bye!" Camille waved. Still smiling sweetly, she muttered under her breath, "and don't let the screen door hit you in the ass."

She watched them walk away. Triumphantly, she returned to her empty house. For just one brief moment, Camille missed them already. She shook her head, as if to get rid of that silly thought. She had a lot of work to do in the next few hours.

Hurricane on Shore

Camille was busy putting all her important files in a large, waterproof case when she saw Ashley drive up.

"It's about time!" she greeted her sister. "It's quarter after five already."

"You should see the traffic out there; it's just crazy," Ashley explained.

"Here, let me help you. I iced down a mess of boiled shrimp we bought for the Bros. We'll at least have one good meal before the storm hits."

The two sisters ate a leisurely meal while they watched the developing path of the hurricane on TV. There were continuous news bulletins with safety instructions. Pictures of ten-mile long traffic jams from New Orleans to Interstate 55 North flashed across the screen. Ashley and Camille were too worried to sleep. Another bulletin came on.

"The hurricane is slowly moving east. It now looks like it will make landfall at midnight in the Bay St. Louis-Waveland area," Mike Reader, their meteorologist, announced gravely. He knew better than anyone that this position put the major portion of the Mississippi Coast in the worst possible path.

Frightened, Ashley turned to her big sister. "Do you think we should leave? We can still make it to the hospital."

Camille looked outside. The winds were even stronger now, and she could see smaller trees bending with the force. A bright flash of lightning illuminated the living room as it hit a large tree in the neighbor's front yard. The lights flickered a few times, then the house went dark.

"This house withstood Hurricane Camille, which was a Category Five, and this storm won't even be a Category Three when it makes landfall," she answered. Camille was glad Ashley couldn't see her worried expression in the dark. "Besides," she continued brightly "Hans has everything we need here."

Camille switched on one of the battery-powered lamps, and then switched on the battery-operated television. The room glowed with a soft, reassuring light.

"Folks," Mike Reader reported with some irritation, "we've just lost our feed from the National Weather Service. Our last coordinates showed probable landfall in the Bay St. Louis-Waveland area. If you're in this general area, would you call the station and let us know which direction the wind is coming from? With your help, we can continue to track its movement."

"Ashley?"

"Yes?"

"We've got to try and get some sleep. There's nothing we can do right now by worrying, and we'll have to be rested for tomorrow's cleanup."

"You're right, I guess. I'll try..."

"Goodnight, babes."

Ashley took her lamp and went into the guest bedroom.

Camille gently pulled back the covers on her bed and settled into fitful dreams. She dreamt of a war-like background of planes and guns. A missile came from the night sky and arched toward her. As she ran toward a large white palace for protection, she looked down to see herself covered in black robes. The loud boom of the missile exploding jolted her awake and upright in bed, disoriented. Outside, the intense, roaring sound of the wind brought her back to the present threat. She looked at the time—four a.m.

"Camille?" a small, frightened voice asked.

"Ashley?"

Ashley padded into her big sister's bedroom. "I'm scared. I think we're in the middle of it now."

A large object crashed against the hurricane shutters in the bedroom. Both women jumped.

"I'm afraid!" Ashley cried.

Camille thought quickly. "Listen, hon. Let's take our pillows and blankets to the middle hall. And bring your guitar—it'll help keep our minds off the storm."

Ashley thought it wasn't much of a plan, but at least it was something. The two women closed the doors and settled into the hall. Ashley strummed softly on her guitar. Then, Camille tried to accompany her with her flute. Ashley laughed to herself. Her big sister could do a lot, but nobody wanted to tell her how bad her flute playing was.

"Cammy, can we talk for awhile?"

"Sure, hon."

"I'm sorry it didn't work out with Jimmy and me. I tried—really hard."

Camille reached over and gently patted her sister's hand. "There, there," she reassured. "Jimmy was just the wrong person for you. I mean, girl, he couldn't even buy you a decent diamond ring. Remember that little bitty chip he gave you?"

Ashley let out a huff. "Camille, why do you think true love is based on the size of a diamond ring?"

Her sister thought about this for a moment. "Well, Ashley, in Jimmy's case, it was a good predictor, now wasn't it?" Then she became serious. "Ashley, you know Remmy still cares about you."

"I don't know that for sure."

"Well, he does."

Ashley looked up at her sister. Camille could just make out the tears streaming down Ashley's face. "I'm not good enough for him."

"What do you mean, not good enough for him?" Camille asked angrily. "You're pretty, talented, educated—"

"I'm damaged goods," Ashley interrupted, "I was married, cheated on, and divorced."

"So? My friend Brittney has been married three times already. She oughta just marry her divorce lawyer, and get some of that money back... Besides, now you've got some real world experience."

Ashley brightened. "No, not yet. But I may have soon."

Camille frowned. "May have? What do you mean?"

Ashley backed away a little. She didn't know how Camille would respond to her news. "Uh, you know that clinic job you applied for in Saudi Arabia? Well, I applied, too—as a deaf education teacher. They say there's a lot of need over there..."

"You did what?"

Ashley was defiant now. "Hey! It's my turn now. I want to have some real adventures and some new experiences!"

Camille put her head down on her knees and was quiet for several minutes.

"Cammy?" Ashley questioned softly. She heard her older sister sigh.

"Alright, Ashley, I can see that. You're young, and you have no ties—yet."

Ashley laughed delightedly. "Oh, thanks, Cammy, for understanding."

The roar of the wind suddenly became so loud and ominous; the two sisters held each other and shook.

"Cammy—why did you quit going to church?"

"Oh, I don't know. I just wasn't getting anything out of it anymore."

"Do you believe in God?"

"Sure, honey, of course I do. I've done a lot of thinking about what rules I should have in life. There's a man who studied all the laws in the world and wrote a book about it. His name is Richard Maybury, I think. He found that all the different laws could be condensed down into two basic rules."

"Two rules? What are they?"

"The first is, 'do everything you have agreed to do.' The second is, 'don't get into other people's space'."

Ashley gave her busybody sister a sideways glance.

"I know, I know...I'm still working on rule number two."

The power had also gone out at the hospital four hours earlier. The backup generators were working, but electricity had to be rationed. Hans, known for his efficiency, had supervised the move of all the patients to the second floor in case of flooding. The water pressure was down, so toilets wouldn't flush. Hans instructed the nurses to restrict the patients from using the toilets.

"What are we going to use, then?" one nurse peevishly asked.

"We have a stock of heavy-duty plastic bags for contaminated waste disposal." Hans walked to the storage room. "Yes, here they are. We'll use these."

"That's fine and dandy, Dr. Kohl." The tired nurse put her hands on her hips. She'd already pulled two shifts, and this certainly wasn't a pleasant development. "But now that the exhaust systems aren't working, we've got a real problem."

"And what problem is that?" Hans asked, tired of all the complaining.

"Do you know what Joey stocked for emergency food rations?" Joey was the director of Food Services.

"No, what does he have for rations?"

"Beans. Cases and cases of pork and beans."

Hans looked incredulous. "You're kidding, right?"

"Go and look for yourself, doctor."

"I will." Hans threw open the door to the stairs and walked down to the kitchen.

"Joey, what kind of emergency provisions do you have?"

Joey pointed proudly to dozens of cases stacked against the wall. Hans saw the large black and white print on the side of each box—"Pork and Beans." He looked at Joey, still proudly beaming in the pale light.

"Good, Joey," he said as he turned to the door. "Very good."

Hans walked back upstairs to the second floor.

"Well?" the same nurse greeted him. "We've got a new problem with the plastic bags. Perhaps you want to suggest a solution?"

Hans sighed. He was tired. He followed the nurse into a patient's room, then bolted backward. The smell of gaseous beans hung like a heavy cloud. The nurse held up the red plastic bag, which now looked like a big, inflated balloon.

"So doctor—whaddaya think? Here's Mr. Jackson's B.M. The question is—do we let the gas out of the bag, or leave it in? The conference room is almost full up with red bags."

Hans' beeper sounded for the sixteenth time that night.

"Do what you want. I have to go to the E.R." Hans threw open the door to the stairway. "What's this?" he muttered under his breath in his thick staccato accent, "I have to do 'Stupid Patrol' along with everything else?"

A few miles down the road on Biloxi Beach, the huge casino boat, Treasure Bay, lay moored near the docks. It had been anchored securely since its arrival in Biloxi, but the City Council had also insisted on a large chain cemented to the docks. With the casino closed due to the impending hurricane, only a lone security guard was on duty. Alerted by the changing movement of the deck beneath his feet, he suddenly realized that the huge ship had broken away from its moorings and was slowly drifting out to sea. In desperation, he watched as the few lights still burning on the shoreline began to slowly fade from view.

"God help me," he prayed aloud, "I'm all alone here."

Just as suddenly, the ship lurched to a halt. Then the security guard remembered the extra chain cemented to the dock. He clasped his hands in prayer. "Please, let that chain hold!"

A mile east on the beach, the intense wind filled the newly renovated lobby of Casino Magic with fish from the Gulf.

On Highway 49 North a hotel filled with local residents who had left their homes in low-lying areas and sought shelter away from the rivers and back bays was also facing the onslaught of the storm. Most of the refugees were asleep in their rooms when the howling wind lifted the roof off the hotel, drenching them in hard-pounding wind and rain.

In Ocean Springs, Judith, a friend of Camille's, felt her whole house suddenly pitch forward into the angry river currents. Judith screamed as she and her husband raced out the back door and clung to a tree.

Back at the hospital, Hans slumped into an office chair in the E.R. "I can't remember being this tired since my residency," he remarked to no one in particular. Dr. Dan appeared in the doorway. Dr. Dan was a wiry, wise-cracking young doctor who'd grown up tough in the Bronx and had to work his way through medical school. Hans liked him. Dr. Dan's patients loved him.

"Yo, Hans! I'm relieving you. Go on home now."

"I won't argue with you on that, Dan."

Dan looked serious for a moment. "Any casualties?"

Hans turned and suddenly realized, "Amazingly, no. We've had no reports on anyone being killed." Hans suddenly felt tired and drifted off to sleep in his office chair. He awoke several hours later, and realized he'd better drive home and check on his family.

Hans walked out into the morning sun and looked at the devastation around him. It reminded him of war zones he'd lived in during his early military years. He drove carefully around downed power lines. A massive palm tree had fallen across Highway 90. He drove his SUV around it over the medians.

Hans took a deep breath as he drove down the street to his house. He knew Camille and Ashley were safe, but how much damage would there be? He breathed a sigh of relief as he pulled into his driveway. There didn't seem to be any damage at all. Those years of removing trees, against Camille's protests, had seemed to pay off.

He quietly unlocked the door and tiptoed back toward the bedrooms. As he opened the hall door, he found his sleeping wife and her sister in the middle of the hall, blankets and pillows piled all around them.

Camille woke up and looked at her husband. She carefully eased herself up and quietly pulled the hallway door closed behind her.

"Everything OK at the hospital?"

"Yeah. All reports indicate that nobody was killed." Hans leaned against the wall for a moment, and a worried look crossed his face. "No one was killed—this time. We were lucky to dodge the bullet..."

Camille could hear the fear in his voice, and for a moment, felt it, too. She pushed the fear back down. "Well, we all were lucky."

Hans looked at the blankets spread everywhere. "Why were you sleeping in the hallway?"

"Oh...Something heavy hit the bedroom window around four in the morning. We may have a window out."

"Oh, well, we'll deal with it later." Hans suddenly was hungry. "We still have the steak and eggs iced down in the cooler, don't we?"

"Yes, but, hon, the power is out."

Hans shook his head. "That's why I have a gas grill. You get the plates ready, and I'll grill up the steak and eggs."

Ashley had smelled the grilled food. She padded out to the kitchen, still sleepy but amazed. "Food? You cooked food?"

After breakfast, Hans walked over to the beer refrigerator. "I think I'll have one beer before I go to bed, 'en so." Then he realized. The power was out. "My beer!" Before his brothers and Uncle Otto had come for their extended visit, Hans had carefully stocked the beer refrigerator with all their favorites—Heineken, Red Stripe, Pilsner Urquell, Foster's Lager...Now all his beer was going to get warm!

Hans quickly pulled out two large insulated coolers and threw bags of ice in each of them. He carefully packed the still-cool beers in the coolers and lovingly wrapped the top with towels. He stepped back to look at his salvaged stock.

What in the world would he do with all this beer before it got warm? He thought for a moment, and then a smile crossed his lips. Hans crossed over to the kitchen phone and leafed through the phone book until he found the radio station call-in number. Other people were calling the radio station to offer help, and so would he. He felt somewhat altruistic as he dialed the phone number.

"Hello? I want to offer some refreshments. OK, I'll hold…Oh, you want to put me on the air? That's fine." Hans waited. The radio station host came back on.

"Sir, you're on the air."

"Yes, I'm at the 'Back Door Pub', and our power went off last night. We still have a lot of good imported beer on ice that we want to give away before it gets warm."

"Well, that's an unusual offer," the radio announcer laughed. "Sir, what is the address of this 'Back Door Pub'?"

Camille had been in the living room listening to K99 Live when she heard the start of the announcement. She knew where this one was going, and she would not be known around the coast as the "free beer lady."

"Hans! What do you think you're doing?" she interrupted. "Put that phone down right now!" As she said the word "now," she stamped one well-pedicured foot on the floor.

Hans realized his wife felt very strongly about her reputation, and it wasn't worth the month of retribution it would take. He turned back to the phone.

"Oh, it looks like we have to close down now," and hung up the phone.

Camille glared at him. "I think it's time you got some sleep. You're not thinking as sharp as usual."

Hans walked into the bedroom, pulled off his clothes, and collapsed into bed. Camille closed the blinds and gave her husband a kiss on the forehead.

"Goodnight."

The next three days, Hans stayed home with his wife. They were still without power and watched in amazement as power company trucks from five neighboring states came to help. Without the usual distractions, it gave husband and wife a chance to talk. As the couple sat in rocking chairs on the front porch, Camille felt philosophical.

"You know, Hans, if something happened to you, I don't think I'd ever get married again."

"I feel the same way," Hans replied.

"You do? How sweet." Camille fanned herself with some satisfaction.

"Yeah," Hans continued, his eyes focused far off into the distance. "I would never want to go through all of this again."

Camille's head jerked toward him in surprise. "Well," she huffed, standing up, "I guess I'll just leave you alone in your thoughts. I'm going to get a waffle at the Waffle House."

It was oppressively humid, and her hair had fallen from its prim ponytail to hot, sticky blonde strands against her neck. Camille struggled to gather her hair up off her neck.

"And why don't you just get your hair cut, so you won't have to keep doing that?" Hans asked with some irritation. "You look like a librarian with that long hair."

Camille grabbed her keys and drove to the Waffle House. Most of the restaurants were still closed, but gratefully, the Waffle House had massive generators running.

"Hey, Miss Trudy...Light pecan waffle, please."

Miss Trudy sighed. "I'd like to help you, dear, but we're only using the gas grills to make sandwiches."

"Oh, no!" Camille protested. "Now this is real trauma! Oh, alright. Give me a BLT."

The tired, sweaty woman listened to the noise of the huge generators. Her eyes were drawn to the name on the side—Kohler generators, from Hans' Wisconsin hometown. There was just no getting away...

Camille finished her sandwich and drove home. Hans was still sitting on the porch and now some of the neighbors had gathered there. Suddenly, a convoy of power company trucks came rolling down their street. The neighbors waved and cheered them on.

"It won't be long now," Hans predicted. As usual, he was right. Within an hour, power was restored.

Camille quickly plugged in her computer and logged on. She pulled up her email, anxious to see how Sheila had survived the hurricane in Puerto Rico.

'Hello from the survivors of Hurricane Georges—' the email started. 'It's been three weeks now, and we're still without power. I'm contacting you from Mike's office, where they have a backup power source. We were lucky that our home wasn't significantly damaged, but many others weren't so lucky. The damage to property and the loss of lives still hasn't been totaled yet. I hope so very much that you and your family are safe. Love, Sheila, Mike and the boys.'

Cruisin' the Coast

On the coast, the estimated damage from Hurricane Georges was over $50 million. But officials decided not to call off the scheduled "Cruisin' the Coast," an annual meeting of vintage cars and their owners.

As the sun set on Friday night, one of the most brilliant rainbows ever seen on the Mississippi covered half the sky. It was almost as if it was a gift from above—you survived, you've earned this.

Shortly afterwards, Hurricane Hugo devastated Honduras. Coast doctors, knowing what living through a hurricane meant, volunteered their services and supplies.

As Hans leaned back in his recliner to watch the ten o'clock news, he suddenly frowned.

"Honey," he called to Camille, "has anyone heard from Uncle Otto since he left?"

CHAPTER 3
The Offer

Camille breathed a sigh of relief as she sat down at her computer. Now, maybe, things could get back to normal around here. She opened her email program. There were 112 messages to clear out. She quickly deleted about thirty, and scanned through others. Then her eyes stopped. "Greetings from Saudi Arabia..." the message began. Camille quickly read the long message.

'Camille, do you remember me? We took a workshop together. You have the qualifications we're looking for. If you're serious, it will take about five weeks to complete the paperwork and get the visas. Could you be ready to come by then? Naomi Ryals.'

Camille typed a quick reply. 'Greetings from Biloxi. Yes, I remember you, Naomi. Glad to know I'd be working with you. I'm going to talk to my husband, and will get an answer back to you in 24 hours.'

Camille printed out Naomi's email message, then picked up the phone. "Hans, I'm coming over to your office. I need to talk to you about something."

Camille nervously entered her husband's office. She had mixed emotions about Saudi Arabia.

"Hans," she began, "you know how I've told you that I would like chance, just once, to go overseas?" She handed him the Saudi message.

Hans took the message and scrutinized it for what seemed to Camille like ages. She feared his response.

Her husband slowly looked up.

"Do you want to go?"

"Well, it would be a chance to help set up the first clinic of its kind," she offered.

"That's not what I asked you. Do you want to go?"

Camille lowered her head and her voice. "Yes, Hans, I do."

"Then you should go."

Camille's expression was one of astonishment. "You can come, too, Hans. I'm sure there are plenty of jobs for doctors in Jeddah."

"I'm sure there are, but I can't leave my practice right now—maybe later." Hans suddenly frowned. "What about Beau?"

"He can come. He said before he wanted to…" Camille flipped to the second page, "Look, they'll pay for his schooling."

Hans carefully read over the material. "Yes, this looks reasonable." He took a long look at his anxious wife. "You know, Camille, maybe we do need a break from each other for a few months. It's been kind of tense for all of us lately. And…" he added, "maybe you'll get this wanderlust out of your system and be satisfied."

Camille bristled inside at his answer, yet she knew it was true.

"Maybe," she answered. "I think I'll go pick Beau up from school, and talk to him about this."

Camille pulled her car up to the curb of the middle school. She waited. Beau's blonde head eventually appeared. He saw her immediately, and glanced nervously around to make sure no one of importance had also seen his mother picking him up.

"Next time, darlin', I'll wear some hair rollers and a fuzzy bathrobe," she greeted him.

"Why are you picking me up?" Beau returned.

"I have something to talk to you about. Want to go get some pizza?"

Beau brightened. That might be worth the potential embarrassment. "Yeah."

Beau ordered his special pizza and grabbed the French dressing off the counter. He happily dipped his pizza in the sweet, orange-colored dressing. "So, Mom, what's up?"

Camille grinned mischievously. "Remember, son, how you've always wanting to have a big adventure?"

"Yeah…"

"Yes, ma'am," she corrected him. "Well, how would you like to go to Saudi Arabia with me for awhile?"

Beau pulled himself up and looked at his mother with rapt attention. "Really? Saudi Arabia? When?"

"Well, I have to go over by myself first and get things settled. Then, you'll come over a few weeks later."

"Aw…can't I go sooner?"

"No, there's a lot of preparation. And—you can start studying Arabic."

"Do I have to?"

"You want to be prepared, don't you?"

"I suppose…but, what about Dad?"

Camille sighed softly to herself. She really didn't know exactly where she really stood with her husband about this, but she was willing to take the chance. "Dad can't come right away, but he said he might come over after a few months."

"Well, that's alright. Hey, Mom, can I order another pizza—we can take some home for Dad."

"Sure, why not?"

Within a week, a large batch of papers arrived for Camille. After a flurry of activity, the papers and medical exams were completed. Camille emailed Naomi for further instructions.

'Don't pack any books that have 'God' in the title', Naomi cautioned. 'Being American, you won't have to wear an *abaya*, but your arms and legs will have to be covered.'

Camille had a trusted seamstress sew long, light cotton skirts and blouses. As she walked around the house, she repeated Arabic phrases from her headphones.

"*Titkallam arabi?* (Do you speak Arabic?) *Allah yisallimik* (May Allah make you safe). *Laazim tistajil* (You must hurry). *Al-arkaan al-xamsa humma; as-sihaada, as-salaa, as-Hansaa, as-soom, wal-Hajj* (The five pillars are: the declaration of faith, prayer, almsgiving, fasting, and the pilgrimage)."

She passed by her son, sprawled on the living room floor playing video games. "Boy, you'd better start your Arabic lessons."

"Yeah, yeah, I'll get to it…Hey, Mom, are you gonna answer the phone?"

Camille pulled off the headphones. "Hello? Oh, hi, Georgene. You're planning a what? That's awfully nice of you. Yes, the Blow Fly Inn would be fine," she laughed.

Goodbye Party

Later that week, the family walked into a roomful of friends. Everyone seemed to be in a light-hearted mood.

"Oh, Camille, look at the cake!" one of her friends pointed out proudly.

"A camel cake?" Camille laughed. She didn't have the heart to tell them that she was going to a port city on the Red Sea, not the desert.

Camille looked around the room. "I'm gonna miss y'all!" She glanced over at the bar. Her husband was sitting alone, ordering a beer.

"Well, here's the food!" someone announced. Waitresses carted in buckets of crawfish and shrimp.

Hans had ordered a steak instead, which he seemed to be enjoying immensely. Camille watched as he slowly savored every morsel of meat, with accompanying sounds of pleasure. With every sound of enjoyment, she became more irritated.

"Hans, that's almost obscene," she complained. She turned and walked away, muttering, "I'm actually jealous of a steak."

After the party, Camille packed the last of her belongings. She would be leaving the next morning. She peered at Hans watching the 10:00 news. "I'm going to bed now," she announced somewhat expectantly.

Hans seemed intent on the TV remote control, clicking through channels. "Good night," he uttered.

The next morning, Hans seemed cheerful as they loaded the car with Camille's luggage. After all the luggage had been checked, Hans and Beau accompanied Camille to the gate. Camille pulled out her tickets, ready to board, when Hans suddenly broke out in sobs.

"Oh, Dad!" Beau groaned. He turned toward his mother. "Bye, Mom!"

"Bye, Beau. I'll let you know as soon as we have your travel dates. Be good, and don't do too much 'mud riding' and—"

Camille looked at Hans, tears streaming down his face. "Uh, and take care of Dad, OK?"

Beau looked up at the massive figure of his father, sobbing and blowing his nose.

"Gheeze—c'mon, Dad. You're making a scene here..."

"Ma'am, you have to board." The gate attendant's voice was insistent. Camille turned and walked down the ramp.

Camille met Naomi and her family at LaGuardia. After a brief layover in London, they all boarded the final jet to Jeddah.

As the passengers settled down for the night on the jumbo jet, Camille looked around. Each passenger had their own dreams, their own aspirations. What kind of events would unfold for each of them? What lessons would they learn? What lessons would she learn?

"Come up front and meet Safiya's husband, Sami," Naomi interrupted Camille's reverie. Safiya was the exceptionally wealthy Saudi woman who was funding the new clinic from her own money. Camille walked the aisles to first class. A nice-looking, clean-cut man in his late thirties grinned at Camille and shook her hand.

"Nice to meet you, Doctor Camille." He sounded as if he were from California rather than Saudi Arabia. She liked him instantly, and relaxed somewhat. If he was this nice, she reasoned, could Safiya, her employer, be that bad?

Camille walked back to her seat and made herself as comfortable as she could for her night's sleep.

The next morning, the sound of food carts wheeling down the aisles and the smell of fresh coffee was a pleasant wake-up call. By the time the passengers had eaten breakfast, the pilot announced, "Folks, we've been cleared for landing at Jeddah International Airport. Thank you for flying Swiss Air."

A large entourage with signs was waiting as the clinic group deplaned. The group was hustled to a different part of the airport. Camille watched her baggage come down the conveyer belt.

"This is the part I'm dreading. I heard they go through all your suitcases with a fine-tooth comb," Camille whispered to Naomi's husband, Gerald.

The suitcases were taken off the conveyer belt without being opened.

"Perhaps they need my keys," Camille naively remarked, searching frantically through her briefcase for her suitcase keys.

Naomi put her hand over Camille's arm. "Stop! We're not going to have to go through that procedure," she whispered.

The Saudi expediters, special employees trained to deal with the conflicting myriad of rules and customs, motioned with a flourish to a line of limousines. The cavalcade wound its way through the maze of seemingly haphazardly planned streets.

Jeddah

"Look ! Look at the garbage men!" Camille laughed like a delighted school child. Hanging onto the back of speeding garbage trucks, men in *thobes*, which were the standard white robes of the mean, flapped merrily in the breeze. She pointed to another sign and chuckled, "Look! Pizza Sheik!"

The limousine procession halted in front of huge gates.

"This is American compound," the chauffeur informed the passengers in broken English. The chauffeur showed a pass, and the limousines slowly continued, stopping occasionally for groups of women and children.

"It's a disgrace women would dress such!" The chauffeur appeared genuinely upset. "This is allowed here!" He made a disgruntled noise.

Camille glanced out the window at the young mothers in jeans pushing baby carriages. One young woman jogged past in a T-shirt and exercise shorts.

The chauffeur made an even louder disapproving noise. "Such an insult!" he clucked.

The limos stopped in front of a group of town homes. Car doors opened. Camille gathered up her purse and briefcase.

"You—uh, won't need to take those," Naomi instructed.

"What? Why not?" Camille took out the sheet of written instructions Naomi had sent to her in their final correspondence. "It says here we're all to stay in the American compound. Am I in a different section?"

Naomi glanced uncomfortably at her husband, Gerald. "Well, we had to make some last-minute changes. We've put you in a different compound."

"Different? Now I'm confused. I thought there was only one American compound."

Naomi didn't want to explain this in front of the Arab staff. "Come into our place. We'll talk inside."

Camille entered the bright, freshly painted two-story villa. "Wow! This is nice!"

Naomi and Gerald exchanged more uncomfortable glances.

"We put all the new furniture in here for you, Doctora Naomi," an Arab worker explained with great pride.

Naomi glanced hesitantly toward Camille, quietly confiding, "Uh— it's not exactly the style I would have picked out."

"They gave us new furniture, too?" Camille commented appreciatively.

Naomi grimaced, "Well, I don't know if you have—"

"Doctora Naomi, where do you want these boxes?" an Arab woman interrupted.

"Oh, Camille, the chauffeur will now take you to your villa," Naomi announced, glad at the diversion.

"Well, good, I guess I can pick up a few groceries at their store," Camille assumed. Another uneasy look passed over Naomi's face for a moment, and then she returned to her unpacking.

"Come, Doctora," the chauffeur said softly.

The lone limousine left the huge compound and drove through more disjointed, haphazard streets.

"Suleiman—your name means Solomon in English, doesn't it?" Camille asked the chauffeur.

He grinned at the recognition. "*Aiwa* (yes)."

"Suleiman, how do you keep from getting lost with these unmarked roads?"

"Many years I practice. Sometimes the holy men take down English signs. That makes it harder. Then, they put English signs back up."

The Compound

Camille was pondering the politics of road signs as the limo pulled up to a small gated complex. The chauffeur showed the guard a pass, and the gates opened.

"This—" he gestured around him, "is where your villa is. Most British here. Maybe two American families."

Camille stepped out into the brilliant sunlight and looked around. "Where are the stores?"

"The stores?" Suleiman was busily supervising smaller Arabs, who were carrying the American woman's luggage into an open villa door.

"Yes. Naomi said there'd be a grocery store, a beauty parlor, and a gymnasium..."

Suleiman looked perplexed. "No, Doctora. No such things here."

"But—how do I get milk?" she asked to no one in particular as she followed the workers into her villa. The workers bowed, and the head worker ceremoniously handed her a large key ring with at least twenty keys attached.

"Some of these keys work for your doors!" the worker proudly explained. "You figure out which. You may keep others. They open some things." Satisfied that they had taken care of business efficiently, the Arab workers exited.

Camille stood in the hallway of her new home, looking with amazement at the large key ring with assorted shapes and sizes of keys.

"And some of these may even work!" she repeated incredulously.

The tired woman paused to look around her new home. Bare light bulbs hung from electrical wires. Although the villa was the same size as Naomi and Gerald's, it obviously hadn't seen a paint job in years.

"Is that actual mold growing on the living room wall?" Camille wondered aloud. She eyed the couch. It at one time had apparently been white, but now had a grungy, grayish cast. There were suspicious yellow stains near the legs of the sofa, as if an unattended animal had taken comfort in relieving itself on a regular basis. Against her better judgment, Camille sat down and took a whiff.

"Oh, just as I thought!" she exclaimed as she reeled from the smell. "Cat pee!" Disgusted, she made her way to the kitchen. The dining room table had a black veneer that had been peeled back in sporadic spots to reveal yellowed pine.

"Well, at least the floors appear clean." She opened a cupboard.

"Oh, yuk, there's mold growing in the back of the shelves!" She slammed the cupboard door, angrier now. She tentatively opened the refrigerator door. "Well, at least that's clean," she continued her commentary.

A voice from behind startled her.

"You'll notice that the manager has provided you with some different foods to get you started," a proper English voice explained. "We call it our 'care package'."

Camille spun around to face a tall, distinguished man in his fifties.

"Hello, Camille. I'm Jack Daniels."

Camille grinned. "As in the whiskey? Sorry, I guess you hear that a lot. Oh...you're the personnel director. We talked on the phone."

Jack smiled. "Yes, I remember. How do you like your new living quarters?"

Camille frowned. She knew Jack had heard her comments. How could he ask such a question?

"In your letter, Mr. Daniels, you said my living quarters were already prepared."

"Why, yes. I supervised the preparations myself."

Camille scrutinized the man's face for a moment. She realized there was most likely some passive-aggressive behavior going on here—possibly because she was American.

"Well, Mr. Daniels, do you think we might be able to get this villa cleaned and painted? I'd like that." She delivered these last words with sickening sweetness, and hated herself for the way they came out.

"Oh, I think we might manage that," Jack answered magnanimously.

"Great—I'd appreciate that. Oh…one other thing, Jack. How did you ever happen to come by such an interesting set of furniture?"

Camille thought she saw a slight amount of embarrassment come across his face, though it quickly passed.

"Oh, that…well, I'm afraid it's a bit of a game the tenants play in the compounds. When someone moves away, the other tenants pick over their furniture, then leave their old furniture in its place."

"Oh, I understand. I'm just sure we could do something about that later, now, couldn't we?" Camille drawled with some exaggeration.

"Quite sure," Jack reassured. "However, the reason I am here is that, in my capacity as personnel director, I like to welcome all the new employees with dinner out the first night. I though we might go to the downtown Hilton. They have the most marvelous seafood there."

"That sounds good. I am hungry."

"Very good. Let's get you settled in, and I'll pick you up about seven-ish?"

"Fine." Camille closed the door behind him, glad at last to have some privacy.

"What a dump!" she pronounced as her final assessment of her new living quarters. She thought she heard the crackle of static somewhere, but dismissed it. She was tired and probably hearing things.

Camille headed up the stairs for a shower. She was talking to herself again. "Hopefully, the shower works."

The bathroom was bare. "Oh—no towels." Tired, she pulled a sheet off the bed. She stepped into the shower, and was relieved when the warm water poured over her body. As she rinsed the last traces of soap from her back, she heard the phone ringing downstairs.

Frantically, Camille grabbed the sheet and threw it around her as she skipped down the stairs. Lunging toward the ringing phone, Camille stepped on the corner of the sheet. It crumpled to the floor. Camille stood clutching the phone receiver, horrified to realize she was standing totally naked in front of a large picture window. The curtains were fully opened. She saw people walking in the bright sunlight several villas away, who apparently hadn't noticed.

"Thank God," she muttered, reflexively crouching down on the floor.

"Hallo? Hallo? Are you there?" a British voice was asking.

"Uh, yeah—hello?"

"Oh, there you are. Is this Camille?"

"Yes."

"Oh, forgive me. My name is Sam. I'm the manager for the Western compounds. My wife, Katie, and I wanted to invite you over for a spot of lunch. Are you available?"

"Lunch...what time is it?"

"It's just one p.m."

"Why, yes, I'm available."

"Well, then anytime you're ready, dear. We'll be waiting. Just go to Apartment 2B across from the pool."

Camille replaced the phone receiver, then labored to wrap the wet sheet around her. "I'm here for less than an hour, and I'm already flashing the entire compound," she whined to herself. She quickly bolted back up the stairs.

Dressed casually in a loose pullover top and denim jumper, Camille followed the signs to the manager's apartment. She noticed that this section of the compound had only small flats. Camille realized that she'd been somewhat honored with a spacious, two-story villa, even if the inside needed work. Perhaps she should be more grateful. She knocked on the manager's door.

Her gratefulness abated somewhat as the door opened. The apartment's interior sparkled with fresh paint and luxurious furniture. A Siamese cat meowed and brushed against her leg.

"Rubbles! Come back here!" a chubby woman with sparse, stringy gray hair commanded. "You must be Camille. Come in," the woman ordered in a curt Irish brogue.

"Well, welcome, Camille!" a pleasant-looking man greeted with more warmth. He paused to look her over. "My, you're much prettier and younger than I would expect for a doctor."

His wife 'harrumphed' from the kitchen. "Would you like tea or beer?" she called out.

"Beer? I thought liquor wasn't allowed in the Kingdom."

"Of course not," Sam agreed, "frightfully archaic law."

"Well, then," Camille countered, "maybe you shouldn't have gotten your ambassador shot, and mucked it up for everybody."

"What's that?"

Camille was proud of her research in preparation for this trip.

"You know. The Brits brought the liquor to the party. The Arab prince got drunk and shot the British ambassador. The Arabs needed the Brits to work. So, thinking he was appeasing the British, the king outlawed liquor."

"Oh, I'm quite sure you're right, dear. But, the liquor law goes back a few centuries, you know."

"Yes, of course…that's just one incident," Camille acknowledged. "But, how do you have beer?"

"It's homemade. The shopkeepers are ever so thoughtful. They put all the ingredients—malt, yeast, sugar—in one aisle so it's much easier to find. I'm sure the *matawain* (religious police) will figure it out one day."

"Huh. Imagine that. Well, maybe I will try a beer."

Sam grinned and proudly handed her over a chilled mug with the foamy liquid. Camille took a tentative swallow.

"Sam, this is actually very good."

"Yes, it is, isn't it? It's actually one of Katie's culinary efforts."

"Thanks, Katie." Camille hoisted her mug to the woman. Katie let a small smile escape, appeased somewhat that she'd been recognized.

"Of course," Sam started nonchalantly, "it's nothing as good as what's at the American embassy…" He paused expectantly.

"The American embassy? I haven't had time to even think about that yet. What kind of beer is at the American embassy?"

"Oh!" Sam was happy to fill her in. "I heard they had Schlitz beer!"

Camille choked on a sip of beer. "Schlitz?" she asked, and broke out into guffaws of laughter. "SCHLITZ?"

Sam seemed confused and somewhat dismayed by her reaction.

"Ahem, I just thought—if you ever got the chance," he continued sheepishly, "that you might remember us sometime when you go?"

Camille wiped the tears of laughter from her eyes. She hoped she hadn't hurt his feelings too much. "Oh, I'm sorry, Sam. If you and Katie would like to go drink Schlitz beer at the American embassy, I'm sure we can do that. Forgive me. It's just that a lot of Americans prefer other beers."

Sam relaxed and appreciatively poured Camille another round.

"Well, my dear," Katie smoothed her apron as she headed back toward the kitchen, "are you ready for your food now?"

Camille was about to answer when Sam interrupted. "I can't think of why Charles is late. He's usually very punctual. Perhaps we should wait a few more minutes, darling."

The Greek Statue

Camille was ravenous by now, and not excited about waiting for an unknown dinner guest. Just as she was crossing to the kitchen to forage for a snack, the doorbell rang. Katie dropped a pan on the floor and raced excitedly to the door.

"There's Charles now," she said, smoothing her stringy gray locks before pulling open the door.

Camille glanced casually toward the door, then studied the man standing there. Sam had been waiting to see her reaction and smiled contentedly. In the doorway stood possibly one of the most classically handsome men Camille could ever remember seeing. He reminded her of a Greek statue. His finely chiseled face extended to a strong, sleek, perfectly proportioned body. His close-cropped silver hair was complemented by the most startlingly vivid aquamarine eyes, the color of which reminded her of the Gulf waves in Destin, Florida. Fascinated, she watched as, just like the waves, their color changed ever so slightly with his change in emotions.

Yes, he truly was something to look at. But even at that, he wasn't her type. Now her sister, Ashley...he was definitely Ashley's type, Camille mused idly. Camille wistfully thought of her big, muscular husband back home. Her face saddened for a moment as she realized how much she already missed him.

The living Greed statue handed Katie some fresh flowers, then flashed a pair of even white teeth at her. Katie accepted the flowers as if she'd received the crown jewels.

"Charles, I'd like you to meet Camille," Sam introduced.

"So sorry I'm late. I got held up at the office, you see."

Camille heard a slight trace of a melodic accent—it wasn't quite standard British. Where was he from?

Katie proudly turned to her female guest. "Camille, Charles is the executive director of the whole plant!"

"Camille," the aquamarine eyes fixed on her, "I heard you were coming. I hope you like it here." Charles openly studied her for a moment.

The two couples sat down for lunch.

"Katie, this food is really good," Camille remarked honestly.

Katie grinned in spite of herself, and then settled back into her habitual scowl.

Not Really Southern

After lunch, Charles reclined casually on the sofa. Katie meekly sat next to him, as if receiving some special favor. She obviously doted on Charles. Sam didn't seem at all threatened or concerned. Charles seemed to take little notice of Katie's obvious adoration. The two men joked easily back and forth.

"What part of the States did you come from?" Charles asked.

"Very Southern—Biloxi, Mississippi."

"Mississippi?" Charles leaned forward, intrigued. "You don't seem to have much of a Southern accent."

"Well, we're on the coast, with a large international port. And, we're between Florida and New Orleans."

"Sounds nice," Charles commented, a far-away look in his eyes.

"New Orleans, New Orleans...let me see," thought Sam. "Charles, what song do we know about New Orleans?"

"I know—" Charles broke out into a baritone voice. "New Orleans ladies—"

Sam laughed and joined in the singing. Camille laughed delightedly at the entertainment. Although she was enjoying herself, she suddenly felt tired. "This is great, but I have to unpack. Thanks for the lunch. It was nice meeting y'all." Camille rose and headed toward the door.

"That's it, then? Your one Southern word?" Sam chuckled.

"What?"

"What he means is," Katie broke in, "you don't seem to be really Southern."

"Really Southern? As different from 'General American' dialect?"

"Well, now," Katie smoothed out her apron, confident she held the upper hand, "you really don't act very Southern, my dear."

Camille was growing more tired from her long journey. However, these were her hosts, and she didn't want to disappoint them. Camille turned and looked at Katie. Katie had her head cocked and mouth slightly twisted in the knowledge that this American woman hadn't somehow lived up to the group's expectations.

"Oh, Southern. Like—Scarlett O'Hara in 'Gone with the Wind'? Katie, are you really sure that's what you want?"

"Yes, that's what I want."

Camille sighed. "Well, you are the hostess. If that's what you want..."

Camille opened her eyes wide and aimed them at Katie.

"Well, Miz' Katie," she drawled as she touched her arm, "thank you ever so much for the just scrumptious meal. I'm sure you do your momma proud." Then Camille turned her attention on Sam. She lowered her eyes, and gave his beard one light stroke. "As for you, Mister Sam—you're just the finest host that anyone could ever want."

Camille grinned toward Charles' direction. "Bye, now." She turned back briefly, then closed the door. Walking down the steps, she quietly commented to herself, "be careful what you wish for..."

Sam felt a slight, inexplicable stirring. Katie saw the look of intrigue on her husband's face and rage welled up inside her. She threw a pan of food across the kitchen, where the contents slid down the newly painted wall. Charles threw his head back and laughed heartily.

After Camille was out of the building, Sam turned expectantly to Charles. "Well, what did you think of her?"

"I could see why men would find her attractive," Charles answered, taking a reflective sip of beer. "However, I prefer brunettes with blue eyes...not that I've found someone like that here..." Tears welled up in his eyes, but he fought them back. His wife had been killed in a car accident in Jeddah two years ago, and he was just now able to think about her memory without searing emotional pain. Charles took another sip of homemade brew to clear this throat. "Besides," he continued, "with that huge diamond, she's quite married, you know."

Camille set her alarm for a few hours of rest. As she lay down on her bed, she smiled. So far, she enjoyed it here. Jeddah was a beautiful port city, and the people seemed colorful, yet genuine.

Promptly at seven p.m., there was a knock on her villa door.

"Well, Doctor Camille, look at you."

"Hello, Mr. Daniels. Are we ready to go?"

Camille bent down to pick up her purse. "Oh, Mr. Daniels, even though I'm completely covered, should I wear an *abaya*?"

"Oh, no, my dear. That won't be necessary. You're with me, you see."

Jack drove skillfully through the streets toward downtown Jeddah.

"Look at that huge fountain!" Camille exclaimed. The remarkable fountain was illuminated in the night sky with lights, and the spray of water seemed to go hundreds of feet into the air.

"Oh, yes," Jack answered knowingly, "they pump the water for that fountain from the Red Sea. It's probably the largest fountain of its kind in the world. If you look close enough, you'll see fish flying through the spray."

Another mile passed, and a large statue came into view.

"Look!" Camille pointed with child-like awe. "It's made totally out of car parts! And the car lights are even blinking! Oh, Jack, may we stop and take a picture?"

"Oh, no, my dear," he chuckled. "Unfortunately, pictures are not allowed to be taken in the Kingdom."

Camille turned to him, dismayed. "No? Why not?"

"The Saudis are a very private people."

Jack drove into the circular drive of the downtown Hilton. Two small Arab men respectfully opened the doors of the Volvo as the couple alighted into the glare of the bright neon lights of this monolithic American franchise.

Seated between palm trees and surrounded by four eager waiters, Camille decided she'd try to get as much information out of the personnel director as possible. "Jack, tell me about yourself. How did you get into this business?"

"Well, my first position was in Africa. I was a petroleum engineer at the time. One day, while I was out in the bush, I was suddenly surrounded by natives."

"What happened?"

"Of course, I worried I was a goner. The head bushman came up to me with a spear and pointed it at my stomach. He looked at me again, and in perfect English asked, 'Mr. Jack, is that you?' I looked at him more closely and realized it was one of my engineering students from Oxford. I relaxed, and we all went to camp for a good meal—which was not me, by the way."

Apparently, Jack liked to tell that story. His pleasant facial expression suddenly changed to one of anger. He looked at his American companion through narrowed eyes.

"What I can't understand about you Yanks is that way you treat your Indians. When the British Empire ruled the world, if we had trouble with the natives, we just shot one of them as an example. Then the rest fell back into line. You, however," Jack snarled viciously, "just killed the whole bloody lot of them!"

Stunned at this unexpected outburst, Camille was pensive for a moment. Then she shrugged her shoulders. What could she say? Thankfully, the four waiters arrived with their dinners, and Jack lapsed back into his pleasant mood.

After dinner, the couple walked leisurely back to Jack's Volvo.

"The bloody asshole!" Jack spit out. Camille was startled as she watched the rage overcome his face again. A Mercedes sedan was parked in front of Jack's Volvo, effectively cutting him off from the hotel exit. He muttered curses as he bent down over one of the Mercedes tires and unscrewed the valve stem.

Camille could hear tire air escaping. "Jack! What are you doing?"

"The son of a bitch is going to pay—"

"Jack, wait, please. Let's go in and ask the concierge to find the owner. Please? We'll probably get out sooner that way."

Jack relented. He screwed the valve stem back on. They walked back to the hotel lobby. Using fluent Arabic, Jack explained the situation to the concierge. The concierge nodded, wrote something on a small blackboard, and walked quickly through the lobby striking a small xylophone for attention. Within minutes, an Arab in the characteristic white *thobe* got up from his seat and quickly moved the offending Mercedes.

Jack seemed to brighten again, another angry storm forgotten. "Dessert!" he snapped his fingers. "Camille, I know a market that has the most fantastic desserts! And you'll get to see a little local color."

Jack drove as if on a racetrack now, defiantly cutting off cars and passing within a split second before contact with an oncoming car. Camille could see the gleam in his eyes. It was better not to even try to intervene in this man's manic pace. She was thankful when the car halted in front of a small market, gaily lit with hanging lamps.

Jack opened the car door for his guest with some excitement. "Here we are!"

Camille quickly noticed there were no other females except her. Approximately forty white-*thobed* Arab males watched the Western couple with great interest. As the two stood in line for their dessert, an Arab approached Jack with a knowing smile. He looked at Camille—blonde, fair, and many years younger than Jack, then asked a question in Arabic. From the context and a few key words, Camille knew the question: "She's not your wife, is she?"

"*La* (no)," Jack answered pleasantly.

Camille realized Jack enjoyed putting himself and others in situations just at the edge of culturally acceptable behavior—pushing the envelope, so to speak. She pretended she didn't understand the question. "Jack," she asked innocently, "what did the man say?"

"Oh, he just wanted to know if we were married," Jack answered with unexpected truthfulness.

Completing their desserts under watchful eyes and whispers, Jack finally stood up. "Come, Doctora."

Having had his fix of subtly thumbing his nose at the local mores, he appeared smug and at his most pleasant demeanor. As Camille entered the Volvo, she decided the personnel director's methods of coping were erratic, but certainly inventive.

CHAPTER 4
Working At The Palace

The dawn prayer call woke Camille. She didn't mind, finding the voice on the loudspeaker hauntingly compelling. After breakfast, Naomi and Gerald picked Camille up at her villa.

Gerald complained bitterly as he drove through the streets of Jeddah. "I've been to Safiya's place several times already, but not from this direction. Naomi, is this where we turn? Naomi, tell me!"

Naomi tried to calm Gerald, and appeared somewhat embarrassed that Camille should see her husband's temper so soon.

"Ah! Here we are!" Gerald seemed relieved as they pulled up to the gates of the palace. The large, white stone mansion with classic pillars looked surprisingly like a Greek temple. A small Arab man ran out to the gate, recognized Gerald, and let him in. Camille followed the couple around to the back of the building.

"Camille, this is Safiya."

Camille grinned at the woman and shook her hand. "It's nice to finally meet you, Madame Safiya. I appreciate you inviting me to be a part of this project."

Jack Daniels entered the room in a business-like manner. "Ah, good. I see you're all here. We're going down to the bank to open your accounts now. If you'll just follow me..."

Jack escorted them to a van, and sat in front with the driver. They drove through the architectural potpourri of the city streets now illuminated in bright morning sunshine. The van pulled up in front of the Saudi bank. Jack went ahead, spoke a few sentences of Arabic to the manager, and handed him some documents. The manager nodded and approached the three Americans.

"Welcome." He bowed with characteristic Arab flair. "Our clerk, Rashad, will take care of your needs."

"Let's get this over with." Gerald pushed ahead impatiently. While Camille sat waiting, two more American men walked in.

"Bob," the one man addressed the other, "so it looks like you might take that Air Force contract at Keesler?"

Camille looked up reflexively at the mention of the large Air Force base in Biloxi.

"Bob? Bob Hoffman?"

"Camille? What a surprise! Where's Hans?"

Camille flushed slightly. "Oh, he'll be along..."

"Well, I never thought I'd see you in Saudi. Here—here's my business card. Call me and we'll all get together for dinner, OK?'

Camille took his business card. "Sure. That sounds good."

Jack, the ever-watchful personnel director, drifted over to her side. "Camille," he asked in a conspiratorial tone with a touch of amusement, "do you know how many laws you just broke then?"

"What? By saying 'hi' to an old friend?"

"Well, my dear...over here, it's called soliciting."

Camille shook her head in amazement. "Huh. Imagine that."

Naomi, Gerald, and Camille completed their banking and returned to the van. Within twenty minutes, they were back at Safiya's pool house, which was their temporary office until the new clinic construction was completed.

Naomi appeared ready to do business. "Alright, we've got our banking finished. Now we need to get these books catalogued. Camille, bring those boxes of books in."

Naomi waved her hands in the direction of about sixty mildewed boxes of books. "And figure out some classification system as you put them on the shelves."

Naomi sat in a lounge chair, leisurely chatting with Safiya. Gerald seemed engrossed in moving pictures of office furniture around on his computer. Camille began dragging boxes of dank, musty books across the brick floor. The task was made more difficult by the long, loose skirt she wore, which always seemed to be underfoot.

"What am I, a friggin' slave?" Camille thought to herself. Naomi continued her unhurried chat with Safiya while the servants respectfully brought Safiya, Naomi, and Gerald beverages.

"I'd like something to drink, too," Camille thought to herself as she finished the seventeenth box. The servants seemed to ignore her when Safiya was present. At twelve-thirty, the servants brought in trays of sandwiches and fresh vegetables.

"You may come and eat now," Naomi informed Camille. Camille wiped the sweat from her brow and sat down.

After the short lunch break, Naomi addressed Camille curtly, "Try to get those books finished up today."

Camille was muttering silently over the piles of moldy books when the clinic door opened. A pleasant-looking man entered.

"Is Dr. Gerald here, please?"

Camille nodded and pointed to Gerald, still sitting intently in front of his computer.

"Ah, there you are, Dr. Gerald. I'm Arthur from the company. I'm a computer scientist specializing in mainframe applications. Madame Safiya asked me to help you pick out a computer system for the new clinic."

Gerald looked up, less than enthusiastic.

"Uh—may I sit?" the Brit asked uncomfortably.

"Go ahead."

"Well, now," Arthur began, opening a notebook. "Tell me about the kind of applications you need."

Gerald frowned. "We already know what kind of computers we want."

"But—" Arthur insisted, "Madame Safiya asked me to help decide whether the clinic would be better served by IBMs or Macintoshes. If you will just tell me what kinds of application needs you have, I'll be able to help pick out the most compatible system."

Gerald spun around in his swivel chair, visibly angry. "That's none of your business!"

The dismayed Brit stood up, fumbling for words. "Very well, I'll check with Madame Safiya and see if I misunderstood."

"You do that."

Arthur's look was one of stunned confusion as he left the clinic.

Camille paused for a moment. She knew she should stay out of it. "But, Gerald," she asked softly, "how is he going to help us if he doesn't know what applications we need?"

Gerald continued to peer into his computer screen. "If he ever asks me again," he spun around to face her and delivered the words in a hard staccato, "I will put —him —in —his —place!"

Camille shrugged her shoulders and went back to dragging around smelly boxes of books, realizing they must have been sitting in a humid warehouse for some time now.

She continued through the afternoon as Naomi rearranged her office space to achieve maximum privacy.

Camille stopped to notice the sun setting, and heard the prayer call in the distance. She glanced at her watch, six-fifteen p.m.

The glass doors slid open, and Camille recognized Sami, Safiya's husband. "Hey, Camille. Nice to see you again."

Camille was happy for a friendly face. Naomi glanced over at her.

"Oh, you didn't get all the books put away. Well, I suppose you may as well come and sit down. We're having a meeting now, and you may take the minutes."

Out of the Way

Camille sat with the group, organizing the clinic's first minutes as the meeting proceeded for another hour. It was after seven p.m. now, and she was hungry.

Gerald finally glanced at his watch. "I guess we'd better get going. We have to drop Camille off at her place, and it's so far out of the way," he grudgingly explained.

Camille tried to contemplate on how she had regressed from an equal colleague to a low-caste inconvenience in the span of one day.

Safiya stood up and tossed on her tailored, obviously expensive *abaya*. "Gerald, I'll go with you to help, until you get a little more used to Jeddah," she offered.

Camille was grateful. She was hungry, tired, and rather exasperated about her day's treatment. She wasn't ready to endure Gerald's theatrics as he tried to find his way back to her apparently out-of-the-way villa.

With Safiya riding in the front seat with Gerald, he was on his best behavior. After ten minutes of driving down dark streets, Safiya remarked in a dismayed tone, "Oh, Gerald, I think I got you lost. Stop here. I'll ask that man for directions."

Safiya rolled down the car window and hailed the passing man. In Arabic she asked, "Could you tell me if we're close to the Hijaz District?"

The man poked his head in the car window and looked curiously at the three attractive women—white, black, and Arab. Without a word, he circled around the car and addressed his question in Arabic to Gerald.

"How much for your women? Are they different prices?"

"What are you jibbering to me about?" Gerald asked in irritated English.

Camille put her hand over her mouth to stifle a laugh. She was amazed that after living in the Kingdom for five years, Gerald still didn't know much of the language.

The man continued, gesturing toward the women.

"Hey, man, do you speak English?" Gerald asked, becoming more annoyed.

"How much for your women?" The man became louder and insistent.

Safiya seemed horrified when she realized what the man was asking.

"Gerald! Close the window! Drive on immediately!"

Gerald put the car in gear and drove off. He turned to Safiya. "What was that all about?"

"Nothing, Gerald. Oh, wait a minute. I recognize this building. We're alright after all. Camille," Safiya looked back to explain. "There are no strict building codes in Saudi Arabia. You can build a factory next to a house. The roads developed in the same fashion. Even natives in Jeddah sometimes get lost, especially in the less-traveled districts."

Camille appreciated Safiya's explanation, yet was dismayed to find she'd been dropped in the "less-traveled district" of Jeddah. She wondered about the safety of her new, out-of-the-way home, and was relieved when the car finally pulled up to her compound.

"Thanks, everybody!" she said, jumping out of the Volvo. The tired woman took out her huge chain of keys. She tried four of them before finally finding one that unlocked the front door. She wearily dropped her briefcase in the dining room. Ravenous, she opened the refrigerator door.

"Wow! Let's see—I could boil an egg, or make a peanut butter sandwich...without jelly, of course. Milk, I need milk." Camille picked up the phone and called the guardhouse.

"Milk," she asked, "where can I buy some milk?"

"We can order a limo for you, but it will take forty-five minutes or more. You should have ordered a limo earlier," the guard scolded.

"I just want some milk," she persisted. "Didn't I see a small grocery store about six blocks from the compound?"

"Yes, there is such a store. But you can't walk by yourself. Very risky. You must go by limo."

"Forget it." Camille hung up the phone, frustrated. She went to the back door and peered toward the far-off lights of the small shopping district.

"Very risky," she repeated sarcastically. She realized, tired and unhappy, that she was not up for the challenge this night. There seemed to be a knocking sound coming from the front end of the villa. Camille slid the patio doors closed and crossed to the front door. A heavy-set blonde man and a heavy but attractive blonde woman stood on the doorstep.

"Hi, Camille!" The couple walked right in. "I'm Janice, and this is my husband, Henry." The voices were twangy, Midwestern American. "We volunteered to be your newcomer hosts." Janice wandered around the room, inspecting the furniture. "Oh, my God. I can't believe they pulled this on you...this stuff is just awful!"

Henry was already sprawled on the sofa, arms behind his head. "Yeah," he agreed, "this place looks like crap, alright. You really shouldn't let them do this to you. As an American, you're expected to ask for more."

Camille was still holding the front door open. "Make yourselves at home," she said with some sarcasm. "It's nice to meet y'all, but I've had a long day. And I still haven't had dinner yet."

"We can fix that. Henry grilled some steaks and we've got a couple of extras. C'mon over."

"You're on. I'm starved."

Camille followed the couple down the sidewalk. Their villa was one of the largest she'd seen in the compound.

"Yep, except for Charles, we've got the biggest villa in the compound. See? An extra family room. They let us go to Ikea to pick out our furniture. Get them to take you there."

Henry flopped a sizzling steak on Camille's plate. "Thanks. This beats the peanut butter sandwich I was going to have."

After dinner, Janice brought Camille some coffee.

"Well," Janice asked expectantly, "tell us all about yourself."

A warning bell went off in Camille's head. They were just a little too friendly, a little too eager for information.

"Oh," she waved her hand in dismissal, "there's nothing much to tell. I have a husband and a son. They'll be joining me soon."

Janice realized she wasn't getting anything juicy from this new woman. Maybe if she primed the pump a little...Janice lowered her voice in a confidential manner. "So," she asked, "have you heard about the Arab women yet?"

"What about them?"

"They shave, you know."

"Well, Janice, so do we."

"No, I don't mean their legs or underarms. I mean their—you knows..."

"Their—'you knows'?"

"Yes...down there—"

Henry lumbered in from the kitchen with more coffee and poured some in Camille's cup. "The Arab men wouldn't touch 'em if they didn't!" he declared.

Camille suddenly felt very tired. "You know, Henry. I grew up sixty miles from New Orleans. If you want real titillation, that's the place you should go." She stood up. "I really don't care who shaves what. I'm more concerned about how I can buy a gallon of milk without paying twelve bucks for a limo."

Henry sneered as he held up his glass of Coke. "It won't be your only concern, believe me," he said ominously. He raised his glass in a toast, "Welcome, my dear, to the Magic Kingdom!"

Chased by the Matawain

Within a few more days, Safiya, apparently satisfied with the clinic progress, left on a ski trip. Camille received a special treat. Safiya had ordered her personal chauffeur, Suleiman, to drive Camille back and forth from work in her Jaguar. No more having to endure Gerald's impatient honks, or his angry looks he shot from his rearview mirror. Camille felt like a princess.

Suleiman parked the Jaguar in front of the neighborhood grocery store he personally owned. "Take your time shopping, Doctora," he offered graciously.

This seemed to be a more traditional part of the city. Two black-robed women with matching black face masks stared at the blonde American woman before passing down the street. Camille looked at her clothes. She was completely covered in a long cotton blouse and skirt.

"Uh, Suleiman? Do you think it's OK that I don't have on an *abaya?*"

Camille knew that Naomi steadfastly refused to own an *abaya*, and had advised Camille that the black robes weren't necessary for Americans. The chauffeur looked uneasily around. Camille could see he was caught in a political dilemma.

"This is my store!" he decided aloud. "You are welcome in my store without an *abaya.*"

Camille followed Suleiman into the store. She grabbed a basket and meandered off down the aisle, happily exploring the exotic goods. Her thoughts were interrupted by the now-familiar sound of prayer call.

"Come to prayer, come to prayer," the singer admonished over the loudspeakers. Dutifully, shoppers put down their groceries and filed outside the store.

Suleiman walked quickly downstairs to lock the front door.

"Suleiman, should I go outside, too?"

Suleiman looked at Camille, then at the crowd outside. These were people not used to foreigners in their midst. Even though it was risky keeping her inside, he knew it would not be safe for her outside.

"No, Doctora. You stay and shop. Prayer call will be over soon."

Suleiman disappeared back upstairs, hoping he'd be lucky enough not to have any matawain passing by his shop.

Camille wandered through the freezers of various wrapped meats. It was interesting to see the lack of pork, but an ample stock of veal. A loud, demanding rapping on the store window disrupted her musings. Camille looked up to see a scraggly-looking man in an ankle-length robe. He was brandishing a stick. She'd never seen a matawain, one of the religious police, up close yet, but had heard many stories. She looked at him curiously. His eyes seemed strangely dilated, and he was furiously shouting something at her. By his angry gestures, Camille assumed he wanted her to come outside.

The door was locked, and Camille felt safer in the store. The matawain continued screaming and waving his stick menacingly. Frightened, Camille froze. She couldn't believe this man's zealous tenaciousness.

Prayer call was ending. The matawain lined up at the door to be first in the building. Camille glanced around, determining her escape strategy. The men's bathroom—with luck, he might not expect her to enter there. As Suleiman unlocked the door, five other Arabs pushed the matawain out of the way and crowded in first. Camille had made it to the other side of the store, bolted into the men's bathroom, and slid the lock securely on the door. She waited several minutes, then cautiously opened the door a few inches. No stick-waving matawain to be seen…

"Doctora Camille," her chauffeur's anxious voice called, "where are you?"

Later that afternoon, Camille happily unpacked her groceries. Milk. She hadn't bought milk. She decided defiantly that she was going to walk the six blocks and get herself a gallon of milk. After all, she'd been taking karate classes for several years now, and got around New Orleans alright. And, she was packing mace.

Camille grabbed her keys and mace, then started walking briskly down the street. Cars honked. Men shouted at her from passing cars. One of the men pulled up and jabbered something which Camille recognized as less than gentlemanly.

"Go away, you perverts! Go harass someone else!" She walked even faster.

She entered the small store and paid for her milk. Having accomplished her mission, she steadied herself for six blocks of more harassment. The sun was almost below the horizon now, and Camille was getting concerned. She suddenly recalled about the young Arab girl who had been raped on this same street a week before.

Camille made it one more block before a car slowly pulled to the curb across the street. Two Arab men got out and approached her. Another car suddenly appeared, stopping between the Arab men and her. With relief, she recognized the two men. They were Australians from her compound.

"Camille, get in. We'll drive you back. What are you doing out here by yourself?"

"Just wanted some milk, that's all."

"Well, just tell us next time you need some groceries. We'll be glad to take you."

Camille made a mental note. Maybe she should get one of those *abayas* after all. At least she would be a little less conspicuous.

The Welsh Love to Sing

The phone was ringing as Camille opened her front door.

"Where have you been?" She recognized Charles' voice and smiled.

"Buying milk."

"Buying milk? At this time of night? Listen, we're having a little celebration party at my villa. Do come over, will you?"

"Sure. May I bring something?"

"Just yourself. Do hurry."

Camille walked past the pool to the other side of the compound. Music and laughter emanated from Charles' villa. She knocked on the door.

Sam, the compound manager, answered. "Well, my dear—come in, come in."

Camille glanced around Charles' villa. It was as large as Janice and Henry's villa. The furnishings were more traditional, but elegant.

Charles approached with a glass of wine. "There you are, Camille. Please, have a seat."

More relaxed than she felt in a long time, Camille happily swapped stories with the lively group. "I can't get over this country," she blithely related. "Safiya, Naomi, Gerald, and I were lost, and just stopped to ask for directions. This man thought we were some kind of international smorgasbord. Boy," she chuckled, "was Safiya upset!"

Arthur, the computer specialist Gerald had curtly dismissed, was sitting next to her.

"Speaking of Safiya, I checked with her again. She told me she wants me to thoroughly study the needs of the new clinic and determine the best computer system. I've spent hours going over the data I have. I want to make the right decision—IBMs or Macs."

Camille laughed. "Arthur, that's simple. Just order Macs."

"Macs? Why?"

"Because that's what Safiya has all her cookbooks on."

Arthur looked crestfallen. "Oh," he said dejectedly.

Camille patted him on the back. "Arthur, cheer up. Your work is finished. Now you can relax and have fun."

The others laughed. However, the two Americans, Henry and Janice, seemed to be mentally filing this information about Safiya's private life away for future use.

The distant warning bells went off in Camille's head again, and she decided not to relay anymore stories about what went on in the palace.

"Well, Camille, what are you going to do with all that money you're making? It's quite a bit," Henry announced knowingly.

Camille put down her glass of wine. "Henry, just how would you know what I make?"

Henry squirmed in his chair. "Umm...uh—until you get your own personnel department, all your records are going through Sami's company."

"And do you work in the personnel department, Henry?"

"Well, no..."

"Henry, just to clear this matter up...my salary is no more than what I make in the States. That's not why I'm here. What about you?"

Janice looked nervously at her watch. "Henry, we've got to go pick up our son. His karate class will be out soon."

The couple made some perfunctory good-byes and exited quickly. Camille felt irritated, but this quickly passed as Charles, Sam, and another man burst into song.

"Isn't Charles a good singer? You know the Welsh—they love to sing." Katie smiled adoringly at Charles.

"Welsh? So that's the accent."

The singing was interrupted for a moment by a heavy pounding at the front door. Nobody seemed much interested in the commotion.

"Uh, you want me to get the door?" Camille asked.

A playful smile crossed Charles' lips. "Oh, would you?"

Camille opened the front door and looked up into the face of a huge man. He had a shaggy beard and an even shaggier mane of wild red hair. The giant hulk's eyes appeared to be glazed over, as he visibly swayed back and forth in the doorway. Camille caught the strong scent of alcohol wafting toward her as he started to speak.

"Cedric!" someone called from across the room. "Get your bloody drunken ass in here!" With some effort, Cedric focused his eyes on Camille. A heavy Scottish brogue poured forth.

"Good God, darlin', look at the nice, big pair of knockers on ye!"

Two big paws extended out toward Camille. She instinctively put her arms up and stepped back, which was enough to throw the swaying Cedric off balance. Cedric wore a look of amazement as he reeled backwards out the door, landing with a heavy thud.

"Oh, no!" Camille cried out. "What did I do? Oh, I'm so sorry, Cedric."

Two of the men grabbed Cedric's feet and dragged him into the study. They stepped over the large Scot to rejoin the others.

"One of these days, he'll learn," Charles pronounced. "However, with Cedric, that will be many, many more days from now."

Within the hour, most of the partygoers had left. Charles had even poured some coffee into Cedric and walked the massive, unsteady Scot back to his villa.

Sam smiled wickedly at Camille. "Well, Katie, it's time we took our leave."

Katie was hesitant, but Sam pulled her up from the sofa. "Come, darling."

Katie shot the American woman a begrudging glance. It was obvious what the couple expected. Camille decided to have some fun with it. As Charles said goodbye, Camille shook his hand.

"Bye, Charles. Great party. See y'all around sometime."

A look of disappointment crossed his eyes, but he said nothing. Camille walked out the door with a surprised Sam and Katie, and then walked toward her villa. She stopped and watched the couple go into their apartment, then circled around and skipped over the low wall to Charles' patio.

"There you are!" Charles greeted her almost expectantly. "Want some coffee?"

"No thanks. Charles, would you mind doing me a favor?"

"Name it."

"Would you mind taking me shopping for an *abaya* tomorrow? I think I'd better buy one."

A slow grin spread across Charles' classic features. "That's probably a wise precaution. Of course I'll take you shopping. How about after mid-afternoon prayer call?" Charles made a quick check in the green newspaper. "That's around five-thirty."

"Great. I'll be ready." Camille walked to the door. Charles suddenly looked lonely. She gave him a gentle hug. "Goodnight, Charles."

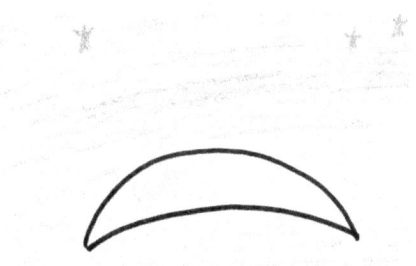

Camille walked out into the warm night air. She looked up at the large, luminous moon. Apparently, due to the longitude, the moon's phases were at a different angle here. The pull of the moon seemed stronger here. Maybe that's why, she reasoned, the Saudis were such a passionate people. Camille couldn't go back to her villa of mildewed walls and pet-stained furniture just yet. She pulled up a deck chair by the pool and sat quietly, feeling the gentle warm breezes on her skin as the crickets chirped in the background. She hadn't heard from Hans this week. Most likely the phone lines were messed up in this technology-challenged country.

Back at her villa, the phone was ringing. After the twelfth ring, the man at the guardhouse interrupted.

"I'm sorry, sir. Doctora is not at her villa."

Hans sighed unhappily and hung up. Where could she be at this time of night? Was she safe?

JUDITH C. CARROLL

First Abaya

The following article appeared in the day's newspaper:

ARAB NEWS: Religion

About dress regulations:
Q: I would be grateful if you would advise me on how a Christian woman should dress while she is shopping in this country. Recently, a friend of mine was approached by a group claiming to be policemen who told her that to conform to Islamic law, she must wear an abaya and a headscarf. At the time she was wearing a long-sleeved, high-necked blouse and a skirt which was almost ankle length. What those people told my friend is at variance with the directive given by different consulates to the nationals living in the country. Please provide some clarification.
H.C., Dhahran

A: What the law of the country says is that foreign nationals should respect the laws, traditions, and cultural values which prevail in the Kingdom. As you realize, this is a general statement, which is liable to be strictly or liberally interpreted. Hence, you can easily find variations in its implementation...

Camille didn't mind the hard work at the palace. In fact, it kept her mind off the tension she felt from Naomi and Gerald.

"There's a fax for you," Gerald announced. "It's from your book publisher. I can't see why they're using our fax machine to get messages to you!" He tossed the faxed pages onto the table. "And I don't know what the big deal is anyway." Gerald returned to his computer, turning his back to Camille. "Anyone can write a book."

Camille was tired of taking Gerald's snide comments for the sake of a peaceful work environment. "Right. Anyone can write a book." She strolled by him, leisurely pouring herself a cup of coffee. "I guess that's why, Gerald, you've written so many of them."

Naomi looked out from behind her private screen and stared at Camille. Then Safiya poked her head out from the screen, looking curiously at her. Safiya's head disappeared back behind the screen.

"What was that all about?" she heard Safiya ask Naomi. Naomi whispered something to Safiya, and the Arab woman's head popped out again.

"Oh, Camille, you're not writing a book, are you?"

Camille chuckled. "Relax, Safiya. I'm writing a therapy book."

Safiya got up from behind the screen, walked across the room, and sat at Camille's worktable. "Oh, I'm so relieved. My brother was married to an American woman. After a while, the woman wanted to go home, but my brother wouldn't let her. She ended up leaving anyway, and she wrote a book all about our family. Perhaps you've heard of it—*Behind the Veil?*"

"No, I haven't."

Safiya continued, enjoying the diversion to chat about her family history. "Have you heard about my grandfather? The story of how he saved Jidda (Jeddah)?"

Camille brightened. "No..."

"Well, the Sauds were taking over the country. The opposing armies had retreated to Jidda, where my grandfather was governor of the city. No food could get through the barriers the Sauds had put around the city, and the people of Jidda were starving. My grandfather went out to meet the enemy. He explained how they would have a much easier time with the majority of the people in Jidda if they appeared generous and fed them. Then, the last small faction of resistance would not have the people's support. Well, the Sauds saw the logic and agreed. There was no more bloodshed, and everyone was happy. My grandfather gained a great deal of respect for his diplomacy. He was given much land and treasures in gratitude."

Camille smiled appreciatively. These were the kind of stories and experiences she had hoped to find in Jeddah. "That's quite a proud heritage, Safiya."

"Safiya, I need you to check these budget figures," Naomi interrupted from behind the screen. Naomi's head popped out again. "Camille, have you finished writing the clinic manual?"

"I'm on Chapter Twelve, Naomi. Have you proofread any of the other eleven chapters I've given you?"

"I'll get to them when I'm finished with more important matters," she sniffed.

The tension would have been more tolerable for Camille if she could have gone out for lunch somewhere, anywhere. But she was bound to that one room in the palace. She dreaded lunchtime, when she had to sit at the same table with Naomi and Gerald.

Camille was relieved when another twelve-hour marathon day was completed. Tired, she was glad to reach her villa that night, even with the moldy walls.

Her front door was wide open. Camille walked around several Filipinos scurrying up and down ladders.

"American?" one of the Filipinos asked.

"Yes."

"Good. Americans treat us nice."

"Hallo? Well, my dear, what do you think of the paint job?"

Camille spun around to see Sam, the compound manager.

"Sam, you got this going? I should have guessed. Come in."

Sam's wife, Katie, was hovering ten feet away.

"Well, come along, Katie. It's alright."

Camille glanced up at the ceiling lights. Where once hung barren light bulbs, there were now new lampshades. "Oh, look!" she squealed delightedly. She bounded up the steps, quickly checking the upstairs rooms. All were fitted with new lampshades.

"Sam!" she called as she descended the stairs. She'd guessed correctly that he'd done this thoughtful deed. Camille didn't see the frozen smile on Sam's face or the subtle head nod of denial.

"Sam, that was so thoughtful! Thank you. What a difference the lampshades make!"

Sam's eyes opened wide with a feigned look of innocence. Katie's eyes narrowed as she looked at her husband.

"Oh, no, my dear. Sorry, but I didn't provide them," Sam denied rather skillfully. "And, I'm not allowed to tell who did. It's supposed to be a secret."

Sam's wife looked more confused now. Camille saw that she had to help smooth this over, too. "Oh—you're right. Well, I think I have an idea anyway, don't you?"

Sam smiled conspiratorially. "I do," he agreed.

Katie seemed satisfied.

"Well, come Katie. Camille looks fairly busy here."

Katie was happy to leave, and was out the doorway before Sam finished his sentence. With his wife already halfway down the sidewalk, Sam paused as he started out the door. He glanced back at Camille, giving her a knowing wink.

Camille grinned. "Sorry about that. Thanks for the lampshades, Sam."

Camille climbed back up the stairs again. She took a welcome shower and then exchanged one long outfit for another. The workers were just finishing the first floor.

"Y'all are doing a terrific job."

The workers stopped for a moment and showed toothy, appreciative grins. "We start upstairs now."

"Uh—it's almost sundown. Why don't you paint upstairs tomorrow, while I'm at work?"

"You sure? We told you wanted painting very soon."

"Tomorrow is soon enough. You may clean and store your brushes on the patio."

"OK. We clean up. We come back tomorrow very early."

A knock at the front door appeared to signify an end to the discussion.

Charles was standing in the doorway. He was wearing a crisply starched white business shirt and a dark red designer tie. His suit coat was slung casually over his shoulder.

"Charles."

"Sorry I had to work a bit late. Let's get this *abaya* business finished before the next prayer call."

"Uh, sure. I'll just get my money."

Camille walked quickly into the living room. Charles followed. His eyes drifted to family pictures on the table, then suddenly fixated on one particular picture. He raised his eyebrows as he instinctively picked up the framed silver photo.

"My God," he asked in a suddenly serious tone, "who is this?"

"Oh, that's Ashley, my sister."

"Your sister? Is she married?"

"Once upon a time, but no more. But she's back in Biloxi."

"Too bad. She's lovely."

"Of course she is." Camille flipped her hair back, then realized. "You know, Charles, you just may be seeing her yet..."

Camille stepped out into the sunset with Charles. He helped her into his car, and they drove to a large shopping mall.

"This is the shop where all the upper-echelon Saudi women buy their *abayas*. Of course, you'll be requiring a designer *abaya,* if you're going to do this thing. And naturally, it will cost quite a bit."

"Naturally."

Camille walked through the stores with Charles. "I read the Koran before I came here," she reported. "There isn't anything in the Koran about hot, black, and ugly. It just states that women should dress modestly and cover their adornments. But—I guess it's become an unwritten custom now, hasn't it?"

"Yes, it has," Charles agreed. He guided Camille into an elegant shop.

"The lady requires an *abaya,*" Charles requested in his melodic Welsh accent.

The Arab salesman bowed slightly, and visually sized Camille for length. He walked to a rack and quickly pulled out a plain black shroud.

"Oh, no, that won't do at all," Charles continued. "We'll need something a little more—stylish, you see."

The shopkeeper nodded and walked to a different section. He returned with an *abaya* edged subtly in golden threads of Greco-Roman design.

"Perhaps your husband would approve of this one?" the shopkeeper asked.

"Perfect," Charles stated with finality.

"Good thing I think so, too," Camille sarcastically agreed.

"Madame would like to try it on for length?"

Charles took the *abaya* and helped Camille slide her arms into the sleeves. The shopkeeper looked back and evaluated the length of the robe.

"Yes," he approved, "it appears to be the right length."

"Appears to be the right length?" Camille questioned. "Why doesn't he just measure it?"

"He can't touch it," Charles explained.

"He can't touch my hem?"

"Of course not. He can't touch it if you're wearing it."

Camille shook her head in disbelief.

"The gentleman approves?"

Camille rolled her eyes.

"Yes," Charles looked at her, obviously enjoying his role, "the gentleman approves."

"Very good. That will be 720 riyals, or 127 dollars."

"Dollars!" Charles commented disapprovingly. "It's not like real money, you know!"

"Like—the British pound, perhaps?" Camille chided. "At least it's not your dollars."

She handed the shopkeeper the money. The shopkeeper walked over to his cashier's till and walked back to the couple. He handed the change to Charles. Charles flashed a wide grin as he took her change.

"Hey!" she protested.

Charles laughed appreciatively.

"What a strange feeling," she commented to him. She flipped the scarf of her gold-encrusted designer *abaya* around her neck. "How paradoxical," she continued. "Instead of feeling subjugated, I suddenly feel empowered. It's as if—before I had just a regular body. Now I possess a body that would drive men into a frenzied passion if they were privileged to view it. Just imagine..."

Charles took Camille by her elbow and guided her out of the store. "Just imagine how hungry I am now," he replied.

Charles and Camille walked up a flight of stairs. Camille had to occasionally stop to pick up her long, loose robes. Wearing an *abaya* obviously required some training.

They entered a large Oriental restaurant. Three waiters immediately descended upon them. Once seated, a fourth waiter appeared. "Would you care for cocktails?" he asked in a crisp, formal manner.

"No thanks," Charles replied tongue-in-cheek, "I'm driving."

The waiter looked perplexed, but nodded. "Very good. Some iced tea then?"

"Yes, tea would be fine."

"Cocktails?" Camille was surprised.

"Oh, they're not real cocktails, of course. Just fancy fruit juices."

"Oh, I get it."

After a good meal, Charles deposited Camille back on her villa doorstep.

"Goodnight, Charles."

"Goodnight," he replied abruptly, and walked away.

Camille was glad the workers hadn't painted the upstairs yet. She slipped into a long cotton nightgown, pulled the covers over her, and contentedly fell asleep.

Later in the night, she was awakened by a cold warning chill coursing through her body. She didn't move, but opened her eyes ever so slightly. There was someone in the room. She sensed the presence by the side of her bed. Her eyes slowly took the information in. A tall man, she could smell faint liquor on his breath, mixed with a signature men's cologne. She tried to place the scent, but couldn't.

Camille stayed immobile in bed, pretending to sleep. The man stood there, gazing down. Several more minutes passed. Camille realized the man wasn't there to hurt or molest her. She sensed he was confused and lonely. She saw him turn to leave. He quietly descended the stairs, and she heard the lock turn in the front door.

Camille sat up in bed. After a few minutes, she drifted back to sleep, wondering how many more people had keys to her villa. Yes, getting new locks would be a priority.

The next morning, Camille was sitting at her desk at work when the phone rang.

"Camille, there's someone named Shelby Hansen on the line for you..."

"Shelby! How are you? Where are you?"

"I've had some trouble tracking you down. I can't believe you actually left the coast to come here."

"You're here, too? I haven't seen you since graduate school, and then we both show up here? What are the odds?"

"I'm dying to catch up on old times. Do you want to have dinner with us this week?"

"Well, why don't I cook dinner for you at my villa?"

"Sure, that'd be great."

"How's tomorrow night?"

"Alright."

"And Shelby, bring the whole family. I want to see how your boys have grown."

Camille happily took a few stolen moments of clinic time to plan a dinner menu. The problem was getting a limo to take her grocery shopping. That evening, she gave a cursory wave to the compound guard as she entered the gates.

"Doctora, Doctora! Wait, please," he called after her.

Camille stopped and turned toward him.

"I found you good maid."

"Maid? I didn't order a maid."

"Oh, but must have maid. Samantha her name. She come round soon, OK?"

Camille chuckled. The word "OK" had somehow become a mainstay in the Arabic language.

"OK."

Within minutes, a very attractive, petite Filipino woman knocked hesitantly at her door. "Doctora? Hallo. My name is Samantha."

"Well, Samantha, come in."

Samantha entered the villa. As the young woman looked around, Camille was amused to see her obvious disappointment at the furnishings. But, she appeared as if she could rise above it.

"Doctora, I do good job for you. I be here at two o'clock every day. I clean, I cook dinner, I get groceries..."

"Get groceries?" Camille interrupted. "How do you get to the grocery store?"

"Oh, my husband drive me. You give list, money. I bring back food. Give you receipt from store," Samantha concluded, proud of her business presentation.

Camille leaned forward. "How fortuitous your timing is, Samantha."

The Filipino woman looked puzzled. "Is that good?"

"Good? Yes. You may start this afternoon if you want. I happen to have my grocery list right here in my hot little hand."

Samantha's face burst into a wide grin. "Oh, yes. One moment, please. I get husband."

Within two minutes, Samantha was back with her husband in tow. "Eddie, this is Doctora."

Eddie took off his hat and bowed his head. "Very nice to meet you."

"Nice to meet you, too, Eddie. Thanks for driving Samantha on such a short notice."

Camille was impressed by the efficiency of this maid and the Filipinos in general. They were smart—most spoke two or three languages. They were also direct and to the point.

Within the hour, Samantha had returned with the exact groceries and receipt, as promised.

"Good job," Camille acknowledged as she reviewed the receipt.

"Thanks. Uh—Doctora? You friends with Mr. Charles, yes?"

"Yes."

"He have no maid. He need maid. You talk to him for me?"

Camille sighed. "Well, Samantha, he seems to have done fine without a maid..."

Camille saw the disappointment on Samantha's pretty young face. "Alright. I'm not promising anything, but I will talk to him about it."

Arrested

Camille very much anticipated dinner with her old friends. At seven o'clock p.m., Shelby and her family arrived at the gate.

The guard buzzed her villa. "Doctora, OK to let them in?"

"Yes, Tawfi. Please let them come in."

Shelby, her friend from college, was a slender woman with long, natural white-blonde straight hair and large cornflower blue eyes. Camille noticed that she wore her *abaya* with an uncharacteristic detachment. Most women, she had discovered early on, had strong feelings toward their *abayas*. There was usually even a litany that accompanied the donning of the black robes.

Dan, her husband, had black curly hair and a friendly grin. "Cammy!" he hugged her. "This is such an interesting coincidence!"

Three tow-headed boys circled around Shelby's legs. Camille laughed at the boys' exuberance and Shelby's unflappable calm.

"Cammy, you remember Tommy and Jack, but you haven't met the baby of the family—Teddy."

Camille watched as Teddy explored the dirt in the large potted palm and laughed. "Wow, girl, you've sure enough been busy."

The women happily exchanged stories as dinner progressed. Dan seemed content to eat and chase his sons around the patio. Samantha, the new maid, was happy to demonstrate to her new employer how efficient she was at dinner parties.

The pleasant mood dissipated with an abrupt, demanding pounding on Camille's door. She crossed the room and opened it.

"Is Dan Hansen here?" Two tall, serious Arab policemen looked around the room.

"Yes? I'm Dan Hansen."

"Your car has been hit. You will come with us to the police station."

Dan appeared more concerned about his car.

"All cars are very bad. You come now," they insisted.

Camille had read that this was the usual Arab way of dealing with traffic accidents. Everyone was hauled to the police station, and sometimes thrown in jail until it could all be sorted out. Shelby, Dan, and Camille walked out to the gate.

"Oh, my God. I'm so glad the kids were out of the backseat. They would have all been killed!" Shelby exclaimed.

The car trunk had been smashed in and the back seat was now in the front. In fact, all the cars parked on the street by the compound had sustained damage.

The three Americans pieced together the information that a drunken Arab had lost control and smashed his Mercedes into a line of parked cars. Rather than staying, he'd left the Mercedes and walked away. Several other neighborhood men were openly scavenging the Mercedes tape deck, car phone, and other expensive accessories, while the Arab policeman watched with indifference.

Dan calmly turned to Camille. "Cammy, do you mind if Shelby and the boys stay here for a couple extra hours? If it takes longer, I'll call our compound for one of their limo drivers."

"Of course, Dan. I'm just so sorry this happened at my compound."

Shelby looked at her husband and waved goodbye as he got into one of the police cars.

"You know," she began, "this should bother us more. Why doesn't it?"

Camille thought for a moment, then laughed with the realization. "Could it be because we're from—"

"Mississippi?" Shelby finished, laughing with her.

The next morning, Camille had barely gotten her *abaya* off when an anxious, professional-looking Arab approached her.

"Doctora Camille? How do you do? I'm Hamad. I've been hired to be the business manager for the clinic."

Camille's look of puzzlement increased the newcomer's anxiety. "I thought we were going to wait another month." Camille looked toward Gerald. Gerald continued to move his computer mouse around, ignoring her.

Safiya poked her head out from behind the screen.

"Oh, he just dropped into our laps. Hamad has a master's degree in Business Administration from Wharton. He's Jordanian, so he's just barely legal. I'd love to have a Jew or two—they're so smart," Safiya continued, chuckling. "but then we'd get into real trouble."

Camille shook her head and laughed in amazement at Safiya's candor. She looked back at Hamad, and extended a hand. "Well, welcome, Hamad. You sound exceptionally qualified."

Some more whispers came from behind the screen. Camille was growing tired of that. Safiya's head popped out again.

"Camille, come here. We need to speak to you."

Camille walked to the other side of the private screen.

"The clinic is progressing faster than we expected. We need someone who has a master's degree in deaf education and is fluent in sign language…"

Safiya looked expectantly at the blonde American.

"Yes, I can see that…"

Safiya and Naomi looked at each other. Camille wasn't getting the connection.

"Uh, Camille," Naomi started again. "We received an application from your sister, Ashley."

Camille sat down in an empty chair next to Safiya. "Yes, Ashley told me she might apply. I didn't think she really would."

"Well, it makes sense to hire your sister. We've already completed the family background check, and we can save money on extra housing, since she can stay with you."

Camille winced. She'd have Ashley underfoot. Here she flew thousands of miles to get away from home, and her little sister would be right there in the same house. Camille sighed out loud. She knew she didn't have much choice. "Well, alright."

"Good. Let's consider it done, then," Safiya agreed. "Hamad can work full-time on completing the arrangements. We can have her here within a few weeks."

Safiya turned to Hamad. "Oh, Hamad, this afternoon I want you to take Camille along with you to our different business vendors. She can show you the equipment we need for the clinic."

Camille stood up and numbly walked back to her table. Hamad joined her.

"I'll make the appointment calls for this afternoon. Then, we need to look over the clinic budget figures before we go."

A Fax from God

⎿⋏∨Ь·⎮⎮⎟⎟30

Camille found it easy to work with Hamad. "The Arab and English numbers look so similar..." Camille mused as she looked at the budget pages spread across the table.

"They should be," Hamad answered with some pride. "The Arabs developed the first number system, you know."

"No, I didn't know."

"When you Westerners started copying our alphabet and numbers, we decided to make changes so you wouldn't understand them."

Camille tilted her head and frowned. "Why? Wouldn't it be easier if we all had one number system?"

"Privacy," Hamad answered. "Now, Doctora, I'll go and finish making the calls for our business appointments this afternoon. That doesn't mean the business people will be there. They may or may not, as they choose. It's just something you have to work with in this part of the world."

Hamad took out his appointment book and made notes. "We'll leave before lunch so we can get one appointment in before prayer call."

Camille nodded happily. It would be nice to get out of the clinic for a change.

The first appointment, as Hamad had warned, was a "no show." Hamad glanced at his watch. He pulled up to a bay of pay phones near the entrance of a shopping mall. "I have to call our next business appointment before prayer call."

He jumped out of the car, deposited coins, and quickly dialed. Just then, Camille heard the familiar prayer call chant begin from the loudspeakers. Hamad was talking furiously on the phone, nodding, one hand clapped over his ear to hear the telephone conversation despite the loudspeakers. Camille saw a matawain out of the corner of her eye, and sucked in her breath. Sure enough, he was headed straight for Hamad, stick raised.

"You! Go and pray! Go and pray!" he screamed. "Mohammed said you must not use the pay phone during prayer call!"

Hamad looked both peeved and defiant. "And...how did Mohammed tell you this? Did he send you a fax?"

The matawain stopped short in his tracks, then regained his composure. "You go and pray now!"

Hamad shrugged and hung up the phone. The matawain charged inside the shopping mall to check on the shopper's prayer compliance.

Camille had draped her *abaya* over her face to cover her laughter. Hamad made it back to the car, and started the engine.

"What a comeback!" Camille said with some admiration. "Thanks, Hamad, I needed that."

"If it weren't for my new job," Hamad answered seriously, "we'd be back in the States. My wife has a master's degree in computer science from Stanford, and she can't get a job over here."

After a few more appointments, Hamad and Camille returned to the clinic. A pretty, petite young Arab woman was sitting very properly at the clinic table.

"Doctora Camille?" her small, sweet voice asked. "I'm Hala, the new therapist."

"Oh, yes...I heard you were coming. Glad to meet you, Hala."

"It's H(k)ala," the young Arab woman pleasantly corrected.

"Sorry. H—ala? *Eewa* (yes)?" the American woman tried again.

Hala laughed gently. "In Riyadh, they say 'eewa'; in Jeddah, they say 'iwa'."

"Oh, now I have to learn the regional dialects, too. Will you help me?"

"Yes, I will. Doctora Camille? I just got married last month."

"Congratulations."

"I brought my wedding pictures. Would you like to see them?"

"Sure, H—ala."

Camille picked up the ornate wedding album and opened the first page. "Hala, that's a beautiful dress." Camille turned toward the other side of the room. "Gerald, did you see these pictures?"

"Oh, no, Doctora Camille. He can't."

"He can't?"

Gerald turned for a moment from his computer. "Not allowed."

"Not allowed? I don't understand."

"Males that are not in the immediate family are not allowed to see wedding pictures," Gerald explained, then resumed moving pictures of furniture around on his computer.

"Really? Huh…"

Camille paged through more photos, then stopped on what appeared to be a familiar scene. "Wait, this looks familiar. Is that—Disney World?"

"Yes, we went there for our honeymoon."

"That's you on the spinner ride? In your *abaya?*"

"Oh yes, that's me. When the ride turned upside down, my *abaya* went over my head. It was a little embarrassing."

Camille laughed. The door opened, and one of Safiya's young female cousin, Dalal, sauntered in. Camille tried to stifle a groan. She had to work with these super wealthy, bored "volunteers."

"Camille," the young woman arrogantly flipped her glossy dark hair back, then adjusted her tight designer jeans hiding under the *abaya.* "My chauffeur is waiting for you. Safiya said you were to go with me to pick out the clinic file cabinets."

Camille gave the woman a cold stare. The woman stared back, equally coldly.

"I'm sure we'll work together very well, Hala. We'll talk more later."

The chauffeur wound the Jaguar through the complicated street system, then pulled in front of a large office supply warehouse. The two women got out and walked into the sprawling office building. Two salesmen immediately descended on them.

"We need to see file cabinets. Show us something that will last!" Safiya's young cousin demanded in Arabic. The women were respectfully ushered up the stairs. After inspecting several models, they agreed on a style.

"We'll need six of these. And you will give us a discount for our clinic."

The salesmen looked at each other. They knew they had little choice. Camille followed the Arab woman to the checkout counter. Dalal pulled a wad of bills out of her designer purse. As she handed over the money, Camille curiously watched the young Arab woman's movements. The Arab men continued to act very respectfully, apparently aware of Dalal's powerful family connections. The beautiful young Arab woman understood this. Yet there was an element here of testing the limits. Dalal had left her *abaya* casually opened. Underneath, she wore a tightly knit, low-cut red top. Dalal nonchalantly bent down and gave the male clerks full view of her cleavage.

Camille watched the clerks' faces. There was no leering here. Not with this powerfully connected woman, and not as employees. The clerks continued to act formally.

As the two women were driven back to the clinic in Dalal's chauffeur-driven Jaguar, Camille wondered if this woman's behavior stemmed from normal experimentation of youth, frustration, boredom, or an unfathomable mixture of all these elements.

As the Jaguar entered the palace gates, the women saw excited guards running toward the palace gymnasium. Safiya and several of her female relatives were standing at one corner of the gym, *abayas* on, but hair still dripping wet.

As the women wailed something about "a voyeur—an intruder," the men were busily searching the grounds. Suddenly, a frightened Arab man bounded from an upstairs window.

"There he is!" Safiya screamed in Arabic. "That man was watching us take our showers!"

Four guards pounced on him, wrestling him to the ground. The men carried him to Safiya's husband for dispensation.

"I should beat you to death!" Sami screamed in anger.

"Sami, don't—don't kill him!" Safiya pleaded.

Several police cars arrived on the scene. The voyeur was handcuffed and thrown roughly into a squad car. Sami got into the front seat of the car.

Camille turned to Naomi. "What will happen to him?"

"Don't ask. Oh, by the way, the new clinic bus arrived today. It's out front. The driver is ready to take you home."

That evening, Camille felt relieved to reach the sanctity of her villa. As she plunked herself into a chair, the phone rang.

"Have you had dinner?"

"Who—?"

"Oh, sorry. It's Charles. I brought home a lot of food from the company party today. Would you like to share some?

"Sure. Give me a minute, though, OK?"

Camille leisurely made her way down the sidewalk to Charles' villa. She looked forward to some pleasant company. But Charles appeared to be on edge about something.

"Yes, Camille, do come in."

"What's up?"

"What do you mean?"

"I don't know. You just seem...out of sorts."

Charles laughed sarcastically. "Could be." He turned around with a serving spoon in his hand. "I was told today I had to hire three more American engineers."

"So?"

"So? Do you know how much more you cost? We could hire five Brits for that price. But we have to deal with the American corporations here."

"Charles, I don't get it. If Brits are cheaper, why not hire them?"

"You didn't know, did you, that in the American corporations here in Saudi, Brits are categorized as Third World employees?"

"No," Camille shook her head, "I didn't know."

"Just imagine," Charles continued, "the British Empire brought civilization and the English language to the world. And now we're treated like a Third World nation by your corporations."

Charles reached over and slapped a piece of cake onto a plate in front of Camille. She didn't have the heart to tell him she wasn't hungry for dessert.

"And do you know," he continued, "that if I tried to immigrate to the States, other countries have priority over Britain?"

Camille tentatively touched Charles' arm. "Charles, you're a very fine person. I can't think of anyone or any corporation that wouldn't want you."

"Is that right, Camille? Is that why—" Charles looked at her coldly, "—you wouldn't tell me your own sister is coming here to Jeddah? Am I not good enough for her?"

"Charles!" Camille was stunned for a moment. She stood up and threw the linen napkin into her plate. "First of all, I just found out myself. And, if you want to meet my sister, you're more than welcome. But I warn you, she is one very emotionally repressed woman." Camille headed to the door, then turned. "Come to think of it, she ought to get along splendidly with both you and this country. Thanks for the dinner."

The next morning, the new clinic bus picked Camille up right on time.

"Good morning, Fatma!" Camille grinned at the new Lebanese clinic secretary. Camille liked her. Fatma had a great sense of humor and helped lighten the somber clinic atmosphere.

Camille pulled out some budget figures from her briefcase as the bus proceeded toward the palace. Suddenly, the driver started shouting nervously. "*La! La!*"

A car pulled in front of the bus, cutting it off. The driver slammed on the brakes, and Camille's papers went flying. Two matawain brandishing their sticks screamed at the driver to open the bus door. He was reluctant. The matawain continued to scream at him, and warily, he slowly opened the bus door halfway.

Camille sat quietly reading what was left of her papers as the two matawain continued to scream at the hapless driver. The driver flailed his hands and screamed back at them. Camille appeared to pay no attention, which was rather difficult given the noisy scene.

The matawain boarded the bus and strutted down the aisle, looking at the two female riders. Both were properly covered, and there were no male passengers present. The matawain approached the driver again, and screamed a question.

"Doctora! Doctora!" he answered, pointing to the blonde American. Two religious police scrutinized Camille for a moment, then apparently decided they'd completed their harassment duty for the morning. The bus proceeded the last ten blocks without incident.

Camille felt sorry for the distraught driver. As she readied herself to leave the bus, she put a comforting hand on his shoulder. "You did good," she soothed.

The driver looked at her with his eyes wide open, bewildered and fearful.

"Doctora!" Fatma screamed. "Don't touch him!"

"Oh, I forgot. Geez—I'm sorry..."

The head chauffeur watched the scene from the gatehouse. He waited until the two women went into the palace, and approached the bus driver.

"What happened? Why are you late?" he demanded.

The driver, now terrified, tried to explain about the matawain.

As she entered the building, Camille tossed off her *abaya* and headed straight for her computer. The Arabic prayer call, as usual, was the sound effect in the booting-up process.

"Does that sound bother you?" Hala asked.

Camille smiled as she listened to the haunting, melodic strains. "Naw, actually I kind of like it."

Keep Her Out of Trouble

As Camille was entering data into her computer, she caught Jack Daniels, the personnel director's voice.

"I'll keep her out of trouble. I'll take her with us tonight."

"Whatever you think is best," she heard Safiya reply.

Jack emerged from the inner office. "Well, Camille," he said in his crisp British accent, smiling politely. "I'd appreciate you joining us on a company dinner boat trip tonight. I'll pick you up at your villa at six."

Camille nodded her head in acknowledgement, knowing this was an order rather than an invitation.

After work that night, the bus was in its usual pick up spot. Camille and the secretary climbed in.

"Where's our regular driver?" Camille asked in English. Fatma asked the same question in Arabic. The driver shook his head, muttered something, and threw his hands into the air.

"He knows nothing," Fatma explained. "He was just hired today."

"Oh," Camille realized.

Fatma looked over toward Camille. "Maybe this one, Doctora, you won't touch."

Camille was grateful to reach the sanctuary of her villa. She showered off the day's sweat. As she combed through her damp hair, she heard the phone ring.

"Camille, how was your day?"

"Charles. So...are you finished being angry with me?"

"Yes. So sorry about that. Actually, I just finished talking to your sister."

"You—talked to Ashley? Just now?"

"Why, yes."

"But—I've been trying for weeks, and haven't been able to get ahold of her."

"Not surprising."

"What do you mean, not surprising?"

"It's the way things work around here," he answered cryptically. "You'll learn soon enough. Try her after we hang up. You'll probably still be able to reach her."

"I will. But, why were you talking to her?"

"I'm helping with the arrangements, actually. And, your sister doesn't sound anything like the cold fish you described. In fact, she sounds rather...intriguing."

Camille laughed. "Intriguing? Ashley?"

"Yes. But we can discuss that over dinner. There's a new Lebanese restaurant with great beef shwarmas, and—"

"Oh, I can't," Camille interrupted. "Jack Daniels came to the palace today and talked to Safiya. He said he was going to 'keep me out of trouble', whatever that meant. I was told I would go with him on a company boat trip tonight."

There was a hesitation on the other end of the line. Then Charles' voice took on a hard edge. "I wonder what he's playing at."

"I don't have a clue."

"Do me a favor—call me tonight when you get home. No matter how late it is."

"Alright, I will."

Camille hung up the phone. She sighed once, and then tried Ashley's number.

"Hello?" The voice on the other end sounded far away.

"Ashley? Is that you?"

"Camille? I've been trying to reach you for weeks."

"Me, too. Girl, are you sure you know what you're doing?"

"You mean Jeddah?"

"Of course I mean Jeddah."

"Well," Ashley's voice took on a defiant tone, "if you can go, then why can't I? I think I've earned it."

"But, hon," Camille reasoned, "it can be dangerous over here."

"Well, not too dangerous to have Beau come over. And, I'll be staying with you in the compound."

Camille sighed again. She couldn't fault her sister's reasoning. "Alright, but there's some things I really need to tell you right now before—"

Camille looked puzzled as the phone connection went dead. She shrugged and put the phone receiver down, not yet realizing that the timing of the disconnection was more than chance. She finished dressing.

There was a knock at her door. As Camille opened it, her face registered surprise as she looked at Jack and then the woman standing next to him.

"Well, hello!"

"Camille, this is my wife, Anne. She's here from London for a while. Anne, this is Doctor Camille."

"Anne, I'm very pleased to meet you," Camille said genuinely.

As they drove through the city, Camille casually studied Jack's wife—probably in her early forties, she was still very much a stunner. Peaches and cream complexion, natural red hair, and soft blue eyes, Anne was a very attractive woman. The two were attentive, giving the other small, secret looks. Jack obviously adored his wife, and she in turn adored him. So, why was there such a dark stream of anger in him just below the polite surface?

Their car pulled up to a large boat at the Jeddah docks. Several people waved from the stern.

"Jack! I see you brought Anne. How nice!"

The three boarded the boat, and Jack introduced Camille.

"This is Ben and Sybil—he's the manager at DuPont here. They're originally from Denver. This is Dr. Ernst and his wife, Kat—they're from Munich. Dr. Ernst runs the company clinic. This is Sun Yang. He's in charge of one of our computer divisions."

Camille smiled and formally shook hands with the Chinese man.

A lanky, bushy-haired, bearded young man presented himself. "Hallo, I'm Jamie."

"And, yes," Jack added, "our Jamie. He's an English professor at the university."

The boat set sail, and food was brought out.

"Camille, do you know any engineers that'd be interested in coming over?" Ben asked.

"No, not offhand. Wouldn't it be easier logistically to hire Brits?"

"Umm, well..."

"What he means is," Jack interrupted in a superficially pleasant tone, "the American corporations would rather hire Americans. You know—we being a Third World nation, and all." The sarcasm was not lost on the group.

"So—it is true?" Camille appeared thoughtful.

Jamie, the young professor, seemed eager to ventilate on the subject. "I mean, really. The American economy is strong. Why would someone who's doing well in their own country want to come over here and deal with all this rot?"

Camille looked at Ben and Sybil, then shrugged. The young professor realized what he was saying, and his anger turned to embarrassment. "Oh, of course, I understand in your case, Camille. Setting up a new clinic and all. But I mean, other Americans..."

Camille again looked at Ben, and both chuckled.

"Most likely to have some different experiences. Don't you like to have different experiences, Jamie?"

"Certainly. But, that leads to another matter I've been wondering about—" Jamie seemed intent on making a point. "After you won the Gulf War, why didn't you just take over the whole bloody country? Then you could have all the oil you wanted!"

The three Americans on board broke out into simultaneous peals of surprised laughter. How could they explain the American psyche?

Ben decided to try. "Jamie," he started softly, "Americans have been there, done that, and got our T-shirt. It's called Manifest Destiny."

"I—I don't understand."

Sybil joined in. "We're not interested in having the sun rise and set on our Empire, like—ahem, some countries," she chided gently.

Humorously, Camille took up the explanation. "Yeah, we're all pooped out from driving those covered wagons across thousands of miles. We're more interested in developing start-up computer software companies in our garages." She smiled warmly at Jamie. "Is there anything else you'd like to get off your chest?"

The tension seemed to melt, and Jamie seemed less troubled. "Ben," he turned back to the American, "did I tell you about almost being arrested because of my fountain pen?"

"No, Jamie, you didn't. Tell us."

"Well, I have this Mont Blanc pen, you see. I'm quite proud of it." He reached into his pocket and held it up. He looked at Camille. "Mont Blanc means 'white mountain' in French—"

"Well, duh!" Camille responded sarcastically. "Ever heard of 'the Quarter', as in French?"

Ignoring the sarcasm, he continued. "When I lecture to my Arab students, sometimes I inadvertently point with my Mont Blanc pen. Two of the young Arabs thought the design represented the Star of David and that somehow I was subliminally trying to convert them to Judaism— which is strange since I'm not even Jewish. Well, the two students went to the dean, and I was grilled for two hours. They took away my Mont Blanc pen. I asked them, 'do you know how much that costs?' They were trying to decide whether to arrest me for subversion or just fine me, when a French professor stepped in and explained the pen's history."

A defiant gleam shone in Jamie's eyes. "I never did get the bloody pen back. But I did go out and buy another one, so I could use it to point to those same two Arab students during my lectures. That's my only consolation in this incident."

The German doctor seemed to get into the spirit of the topic. "That reminds me of my shower curtain. I bought a shower curtain that had an imprinted map of the world. When I came into the airport at Riyadh, the customs agents unrolled it. They cut out the country of Israel and gave it back to me. Oh, I still use it, but of course Israel is in a strategic location on my shower curtain, and I have to wipe water off my bathroom floor when I shower. I had to laugh at the agents while they were busily cutting, it was so ludicrous."

Ben gazed out over the water. "You even have to watch out who you laugh at..." he remembered.

"Oh, yes," Sybil recalled. "Did you hear about how Ben got arrested?"

"What were you doing, Ben?"

"Oh, nothing much," Sybil continued. "We were at the shopping mall. One of the sheiks lost his balance and fell against a shoe exhibit. He looked so funny, lying in a pile of shoes, and I laughed. The sheik's pride was hurt, so he had Ben arrested for not being able to control his wife."

"That's borders on extreme," Camille commented. "How long did they keep you in jail?"

"Not too long—three or four hours. Just long enough to miss dinner."

Everyone chuckled and sipped on soft drinks.

Jack stood up. "I'm going for a little swim. Anyone care to join me?"

Everyone laughed as Jack stripped down to his boxer shorts and jumped in.

"Is that a 'Brit' thing?" Camille laughed.

"Of course it isn't," Jamie responded. "We're not generally known for running around in our boxer shorts. Oh—that reminds me of another good story. Did you hear about the Frenchwoman who refused to remove her necklace with a cross on it when she was coming into the Riyadh airport?"

"You know, I heard something about that," Sybil responded. "She kept refusing, so, didn't they, like, give her a 'full' exam?"

"Full—exam?" Camille was trying to catch up.

"Yep, you know—everything."

"Ugh," Camille groaned. She stood up and walked over to inspect the remaining food.

"Well, if you think that's bad," Jamie continued, "last year a planeload of French landed in Libya. Before they let the women off, the officials threatened to give each woman on board a gynecological exam."

Camille was running out of food, and was still hungry. She humored the young professor, who was trying to amuse them with provocative stories. "They didn't give them the exams, did they?" she hoped.

"No. The French government had a Libyan plane landing in Paris about the same time. They informed the Libyan government that if they proceeded to give the French women exams, then all the Libyan women would get the same kind of treatment. The Libyans immediately changed their minds, and didn't bother the women anymore."

Jack had climbed back onto the boat, dried himself, and was fully dressed again. "We must go back in now," he explained as he took the helm.

"We must?" Camille asked. "We're not even out in open sea yet."

"One needs a special visa to go beyond the harbor."

"You're kidding, right?"

"No. The Saudis have problems with expatriates who get over here and don't like it. The expats charter boats to take them across the Red Sea into Egypt, and fly home from there. In fact, one of your fellow countrymen did just that less than a year ago."

"He was that unhappy?"

"Apparently. He'd only been here a month. He was from Green Bay, Wisconsin. He said Saudi was nothing like Green Bay. I can't imagine."

Camille was suddenly wistful. She thought of Hans and the many times they'd been to Packer football games at Lambeau Field. "Oh, I can imagine," she said softly. "Green Bay—a clean, orderly city, well-planned roads, good schools, low crime rate, creators of the 'Lambeau leap,' and home of the legendary late Vince Lombardi..." Her voice trailed off.

"Did you actually get to some Packer games?" Ben asked.

"Oh, yes." Camille shivered at the memory. "And froze my behind off in twenty degrees below wind chill...but, y'all understand that, with the 'Mile High' stadium and all..."

Camille stopped, realizing that the Americans were the only ones who understood or cared about what she was talking about. "Sorry. Guess I was getting a little homesick myself. Maybe it's good we're turning around."

Jack and his wife said pleasant goodnights as they left Camille at her villa door. She unlocked the door and threw her *abaya* on the chair. She plunked herself down in a chair and kicked her shoes across the floor.

"Charles," she remembered. She picked up the phone and dialed his villa.

"Hallo?" his cool, precise Welsh voice answered.

"Hi."

"Camille, how was it?"

"Alright."

"How was Jack?"

"He was fine. He brought his wife."

"She's in town? Oh...I see now."

"You see what?"

"I think he just wants to get you away from the compound when he can. I'm sure he feels we're getting too close."

"But, Charles, you're the most honest of my friends—sometimes, brutally, but at least you tell it like it is. Can't they understand friendship?

"Not here, my dear."

"Well, they'll just have to—I don't know what I'd do if I didn't have you to explain things to me."

"Don't worry about it. Get some sleep."

"Good idea. Oh, with all the excitement I forgot. My maid, Samantha, wants me to talk to you. She is really eager to do some work for you. I think they need the money."

Charles sighed. "Well, I'm quite capable of managing my own villa."

"I know. Your villa is always spotless. But, just talk to her, alright?"

"Well, alright. I'll give her a call tomorrow."

"Thanks, Charles. Goodnight."

Ubiquitous Tuna Fish Sandwiches

At the clinic the next morning, Camille was deeply absorbed in a trial computer software program.

"Camille?" Naomi tentatively interrupted.

"Yes?"

"Would you meet me in my office? I have a favor to ask."

Camille walked over to the corner where Naomi had constructed her makeshift office. Camille could hear the hesitation in Naomi's voice.

"Uh, Gerald and I are new in Jeddah, like you. We were wondering… when we go back to the States next week…" Naomi paused, "would your mind watching our daughter, Talia for us?"

"Sure. Of course I will."

"Good. That's a relief for us."

Naomi peered out at the clinic room. "Where's Hala?"

"I don't know."

"Hasn't she called?"

"Naomi, no one has called."

Camille saw the exasperated look on Naomi's face. Both heard the clinic door open, and the small, demure Hala appeared.

"Doctora Camille, Doctora Naomi, good morning."

Naomi's face turned angry. She walked back into her office and closed the door. Hala looked frightened as she glanced toward her former professor's office.

"Doctora Camille, my husband just agreed to bring me now," she pleaded in her small voice.

"Well, I guess the men make sure you have to depend on them around here…"

Gerald leaned back from his computer screen and shot Camille a disapproving look.

"Oops, sorry. Guess that's something else I'm not allowed to say. Put your things away, Hala, and come here. You can organize the first part of the database."

Hala obediently picked up the stacks of files from the computer desk. She looked around carefully, leaned close to Camille, and whispered, "We just moved into our new house, you see. I would have called you, but the phone lines aren't in our area yet. It will take many months…"

"That's not an easy situation, is it?"

"No, it's not." Hala seemed relieved, and went to work.

After several hours, the Filipino maids interrupted them with trays of sandwiches and fresh fruit. Safiya's nanny for her children followed behind.

"Hallo. Thought I'd join the good doctors for my lunch break."

The nanny pulled a silver cover off one of the trays. Camille groaned inwardly. It was the twelfth workday in a row of tuna fish sandwiches.

"Ah!" the nanny exclaimed cheerfully, "the ubiquitous tuna fish sandwiches again!"

Camille laughed appreciatively, ignoring the disapproving looks of Naomi and Gerald. She was grateful for any humor to lighten these tense lunch periods. "Ubiquitous. I wonder what the exact meaning of that is..."

"Let's look it up in the dictionary," the nanny suggested.

"Yes, let's!" Camille was enjoying this. She walked to the bookshelf.

"Let's see—u-b-i—ah, here it is. From the Latin, existing or being everywhere at the same time. Hmm, not quite right. Omnipresent? No, that's about the same..."

"I suggest we eat," Naomi replied icily.

"But of course," Camille acknowledged in a feigned British accent, grinning at the nanny.

Safiya appeared in the doorway. "Martha? What are you doing here?"

Martha seemed unconcerned. "Just socializing a little."

"Well, finish your sandwich, and then get back upstairs."

"Alright." Martha leisurely finished her sandwich and rose to go. "Can't say for sure, but I know one thing..."

"What's that, Martha?" Camille asked.

"Tomorrow, it certainly won't be tuna fish sandwiches."

Camille laughed again. "I'm so blasted healthy now from this diet. I'd love to clog up my arteries again with some pizza and French dressing."

"French dressing?" the nanny questioned.

"Yes, ma'am. It's an old Biloxi tradition. When you call for 'take out', they ask if you want French dressing on the side."

"Then let it be done!" the nanny pronounced, throwing her arms in the air as she disappeared toward the stairs.

"We're not to fraternize with the servants," Naomi said pointedly.

"Servant? Martha isn't a servant. She's responsible for the guidance and instruction of Safiya's children. Personally, I like her spirit." Camille chomped down on a carrot. "I've just never had so much health food in my entire life."

Hala laughed. "I ate pizza at Disney World. But I didn't dip it in French dressing." Hala looked over at the inanimate faces of Gerald and Naomi, and decided to change the subject. "Doctora Camille, I heard you had some problems with the matawain on the bus the other morning."

"Yes, Hala. It's a little difficult for me to understand their logic sometimes."

"Us, too," Hala boldly confided, her chin rising with some defiance. "We don't like the matawian, either. They constantly harass us, even more than they do you. Just last month, when my husband was still my fiancé, he was driving me back to class after lunch. The matawain stopped us on the road and made us come to the police station. Even though all our papers were in order, he screamed at us for almost an hour. I was so late getting back to school, I missed my final exam."

Hala's story seemed to strike a sympathetic chord with Naomi.

"During the Gulf War," she confided, "the matawain kept bothering the female American troops as they were trying to drive their trucks or perform their regular duties. Finally, the general told the women, who were trained in combat, to get the matawain out of their way in whatever manner they chose. Matawain ended up flying over trucks and into hospitals with broken arms and legs. So—the Saudi government moved most of the matawain away from the troops, and decided to bring them to Jeddah. That's why we seem to have more here lately."

Camille took a sip of tea. "What happened to the women who tossed the matawain?"

"Nothing—why?"

"Oh, I was just curious."

"This is just a theory," Naomi reached for a banana, "but it would be hard for a matawain to admit that an inferior woman physically overpowered him."

Camille tried to hide a small grin. She continued chewing on her carrot as she stored this information. It might come in useful.

"Well, in the States, there'd be some blasted lawyer slapping the women with lawsuits. We have more lawyers than any country in the world. Hala, have you ever heard this joke about lawyers? It was lunchtime in heaven. God was hungry, so he went to the front of the cafeteria line.

This one man came rushing in, and God let the man go before him in line. 'Who's that man?' everyone wanted to know. 'That's our only lawyer who made it to heaven'," God explained.

Hala chuckled. "Funny," she said, "we have the same exact joke here, only it's about architects."

Camille was thoughtful. "You know, that's one good thing about seeing patients in Saudi. You probably don't have to worry about medical malpractice all the time."

The clinic door opened. Safiya walked into the room and casually sat next to Camille. She leaned toward her in a conspiratorial manner and said in a low voice, "Pizza tomorrow, with French dressing."

Camille laughed appreciatively. "Thank you so much, Madame Safiya."

Safiya seemed to be in good spirits. "I know Hala is a newlywed..."

Hala grinned at the recognition.

"In some ways, Saudi marital laws are more fair than American laws."

"Really? In what way?" Camille wanted to know.

"Well, when a woman marries, she keeps her own property. Even if she later divorces, she never loses the property she brought into the marriage."

"That's fair."

"And, before a man can marry, he must pay in cash for everything— the house, the furniture; we don't believe in credit."

Camille sat back as she sipped her tea. "You know, Safiya, that would save a lot of hardships in a relationship."

"Well, I'm keeping you from your work." Safiya stood up to excuse herself.

The outside door opened and Fatma, the Lebanese secretary, jangled in with her shopping bags.

Safiya gave her a mild frown. "Fatma, when our clinic is open to the public, you're going to need to tone down your jewelry." Safiya gave her one last look and exited.

Camille chuckled at Fatma's appearance—big hoop earrings, heavily frosted hair, bright red lipstick, and at least a dozen bangles on each arm. "Fatma, doesn't all that jangling jewelry bother you when you type?"

"*La*! (no) It's like merry music! What does Safiya mean by 'tone it down'? This is the latest style! Oh, Doctora, by the way—I stopped off at the Salon Farrah in the Galleria on the way back. Your hair appointment is for six o'clock."

"Thanks, Fatma. But how will I get home?"

"Oh, no problem. They have a limo service. When you finish, you just tell them at the salon, and they'll call one for you."

"Great. I appreciate that."

Everyone rose from the table.

"Gerald and I will be out for the afternoon," Naomi informed them. She gathered her briefcase and walked toward the door. After five years in the Kingdom, Naomi still refused to put on an *abaya* or learn the language.

Hala waited. After a few minutes, she rose from her seat and looked out the window to make sure the couple had gone. Satisfied, she walked back toward Camille. "Doctora Camille," she said in her small, sweet voice, "I made a special treat for you."

Hala carefully brought out a large bag. Then, she cautiously extricated an elaborate silver coffee set. "I know you like coffee," she explained. "I wanted to make you some of our special blend..."

Hala busied herself at the sink. After the pot began brewing, she ceremoniously brought out another container. "I know you don't get fresh dates where you are from."

"Hala, I've never had fresh dates in my life."

"Well, that's why I brought you these." She pulled out an aromatic display of dates. "These are our very best. I picked them up at the Jeddah Fruit Market last night."

Camille savored the coffee and fresh dates, which to her surprise, were delicious.

"Hala, I'll remember this kindness. Thank you."

"Thank you, Doctora," Hala responded. "You make our work easier."

Stranded

The bus came a little earlier that afternoon. Camille wasn't finished with her computer program, but had learned not to question the scheduling. The bus driver obligingly dropped her off at the Galleria Shopping Center, and Camille quickly found the Salon Farrah. Fatma had assured Camille this salon was the best in all of Jeddah. It certainly looked fancy enough. What time was her appointment scheduled? She thought she remembered Fatma saying six, but she'd better check just in case.

She stepped up to the receptionist. "Excuse me. My secretary made a hair appointment for me. Do you have the time it was scheduled?"

Several of the Arab hairdressers stopped talking and looked at the blonde American.

"What is your name?" the receptionist demanded.

"Camille Kohl."

The receptionist scanned down the list, then frowned. "Yes, here it is. Doctora Camille!" she seemed to spit the words out.

"Yes, that's it. I thought my appointment was for six, but I'm just checking—"

"Excuse me," the receptionist cut her off. She walked over to a hairdresser working on another client. They exchanged words in Arabic, and the hairdresser became upset. She left her client in the middle of a haircut.

The receptionist roughly grabbed Camille's arm and led her to the beautician's chair, then pushed her down in the seat.

"You don't understand! I just wanted to check on my appointment time..."

"So, what is it you want done, Doctora?" The hairdresser was openly hostile.

"I—I just wanted a little trim, that's all." Camille was becoming concerned about the kind of haircut she'd receive. But there was no stopping the Arab woman now. The hairdresser sprayed her hair with water, then roughly pulled it into layers. After some yanking and cutting, the hairdresser produced a surprisingly decent haircut.

Camille, ready to cry, got up from the chair. She tipped the hairdresser, who grunted at her in return. She approached the counter, and here several women hissed at her. She paid the receptionist.

"I hate to ask, but my secretary said you could call a limo to take me home."

"We do not do that anymore. Not since last week."

"What? You don't have limo service anymore?"

"No we do not."

"But—how am I going to get home?"

The receptionist walked away. Camille was left alone in her confusion. Numbly, she started toward the door. She heard one angry woman comment loudly to another in Arabic, "these demanding American women..."

Camille turned and looked at the hostile group. With great effort, she found the words to address them in Arabic. "We are all women. There is no difference between us."

The women continued to stare angrily.

At a loss for an Arab equivalent, Camille broke into English. "We are all harassed and put down. Why can't we just help each other?"

Tears blurred Camille's eyes as she headed for the elevator. Maybe she could find a taxicab, or try to find a phone and call someone. The elevator opened and she got in. The doors closed, and the elevator started descending. A hard jolt brought the elevator to a halt. The lights flickered, then went out.

"Now what?" Camille's fears rose as she frantically pushed the elevator buttons to no avail. She remembered she had a small medical exam light in her briefcase. She pulled it out and looked at the instructions on the emergency panel.

"They're in Arabic! Why didn't I learn to read some Arabic?" She slammed her hands against the door. *"Musa'di! Musa'di!"* she called for help. No answer. She studied the doors again, then tried to wedge her hands between them. "If I had something metal—my ruler, it's metal!"

Camille groped in her briefcase and pulled out the ruler. She slid it between the doors and pushed. The doors reluctantly yielded. Camille slowly wedged herself out. She sighed with relief. Level Three. Only two more floors to go, this time by stairs.

She walked out to the mall entrance. It was starting to get dark. Taxis were usually thick on every major street. Why wasn't there a single taxi at this shopping mall?

Camille frantically looked around for a pay phone. There were no pay phones here, either. Two men in a large van drove up, blatantly motioning her to get in.

Tired and afraid, tears streamed down her face. Even if she did find a taxi, she only knew the name of her villa complex, which was in an obscure part of town.

Just then, a limo slowed to a stop in front of her. The power window came down, and an attractive Arab woman stuck her head out the window.

"Do you need help?" she asked in English.

"Yes—yes I do."

"Where do you need to go?"

"To my compound, but..." Camille put her head down sadly, "I doubt if you've ever heard of it."

"What is the name of your compound?"

"Montoya," she answered dejectedly.

"Montoya? I know it well. I play bridge there twice a week. Come, my driver will take us."

Camille gratefully climbed in the car. "Hi, my name is Camille."

"I am Aida."

Camille detected a difference in Aida's accent. "Are you from Jeddah?"

"No, I am from Beirut. We had to move until things improve enough to go home."

"Wow! And I'm crying because I had a bad day. I can't imagine having to leave my country like that."

The lady smiled graciously. "We are all a lot stronger than we think."

The limo pulled up to Montoya. Camille took the woman's hands. "Aida, how can I thank you? Would I insult you by giving you money?"

"No thanks are necessary. I know you would do the same for me."

Camille climbed out of the limo, then turned back. The limo was already pulling away from the curb. *"Assalamu aleikum* (peace be with you)," she said quietly to Aida as she disappeared from view.

Camille gratefully reached the sanctuary of her villa. She made herself a sandwich and flipped through a few TV channels. An old episode of "Star Trek" was on. In this episode, a young blonde woman crewmember in a short skirt appeared on the bridge, and the station went blank. The censors had obviously just caught it. Camille shrugged and flipped to another channel. It was a rerun of pilgrims circling the stone at Mecca. She stared at the screen, transfixed by the movement of the masses. The ringing phone jarred her.

"Hello?"

"Well, I finally got through!" Hans' angry voice announced. "Why haven't you called me?"

"Honey, it's nice to hear from you, too," she answered somewhat sarcastically. "Hans—I have tried to call you every day for the past three weeks. I just can't get through."

"Come on. What do you mean, you can't get through?"

"I don't want to sound paranoid, Hans, but I think long distance calls here are sometimes put through in a selective way, if you know what I mean."

Hans paused for a second. "Nah," he decided, "that's all in your head."

"Whatever," Camille answered, now feeling insulted.

Hans' voice softened. "Hon, I just miss you."

"I miss you, too, Hans. This is hard on all of us. Where's Beau?"

"He's at school."

"Oh, that's right. Tell him Naomi and Gerald are leaving for the States tomorrow. They said they'd call you as soon as they arrived and make the final arrangements for Beau. He should be here next week."

"Good, he'll be glad to hear that. Well, this call is costing money. I'm just glad you're safe."

"Hans, I'm fine."

"Alright, then. I'll talk to you soon, Cammy. Goodbye."

"Bye, hon."

Camille put the phone down and took the dishes to the kitchen. The phone rang again.

"Camille," Charles' assured, crisp British voice greeted.

"Yes, Charles."

"Your phone line's been busy."

"Yes, my husband called."

"Oh...so he was finally able to get through?" There appeared to be some mild surprise in his voice.

"Yeah—what's up with this bad phone connection, anyway?"

"Well," he answered cryptically, "there may be a reason for it, but I'm not sure." Charles decided to change the subject. "Have you been home all this time?"

"No. I had another exciting adventure, though."

Charles chuckled. "Why don't I fix you a cup of tea, and you can tell me about your adventure."

Camille brightened. "That sounds good. I'll be right over."

Camille grabbed her house key and walked the hundred feet to Charles' villa. Charles opened the door, still looking business-like in his starched white shirt and tie.

"Charles, did you work late?"

"Yes. We work a lot of twelve-hour days. Ready for your tea?"

"Uh-huh, and may I have some lemon, too?

"Yes, you may," Charles chuckled.

Camille sat cross-legged on Charles' floor.

"So," he started, "tell me about your latest adventure."

"Well, my secretary made a hair appointment for me. And I got there early, so I went up to check on when my appointment was—"

"And, they thought you wanted to go ahead of everyone else," Charles finished.

"Yes, that's it exactly. Then they insisted I go ahead. That was the roughest haircut I've ever had, and the Saudi women were even hissing at me. When I finished and tried to call a limo, they told me the limos didn't come to the Galleria any more."

"What? You went to the Galleria?"

"Yes, why?"

"Haven't you been told?"

"Told what?"

"The young Saudi women were sneaking off to the Galleria to meet their boyfriends. So the matawain won't let the limo companies or taxis service that shopping area anymore."

"Now I find out. Well, then I got stuck in an elevator and I had to pry my way out."

"How did you get home?"

"A wealthy Lebanese woman appeared in a limo and asked me if I needed help. She actually plays bridge at Montoya twice a week."

"How fortunate for you. Next time, you must ask me first."

"Ask you—first?"

"Camille, I'm sure you're quite self-sufficient in your own country. But—you don't know the dangers and nuances of this country. I don't mean to be assuming. I'm just trying to help you."

"Oh."

Charles decided to change the subject. "By the way, I interviewed your maid, Samantha, just before you got here."

"How did it go?"

"Oh, she was fine." Charles suddenly seemed agitated. "It's her husband that really has a nerve!"

"What about her husband?"

"He actually came with her. He was brazen enough to ask me questions about my habits, as if I were the one being interviewed!"

"Charles, I think he's just being smart."

"Being smart? He just doesn't know his place."

"Here we go again with people's 'places'...Charles, is Samantha pretty?"

"Why yes, she's quite attractive."

"Do you think her husband loves her?"

"Of course. That was obvious."

"And, go with his scenario a moment...what would happen if you raped or abused Samantha?"

"It's not a viable scenario. I would never do such a thing."

"I know that, Charles. But, the Filipinos seem to think more like Americans. What would happen to you?"

"Nothing. I doubt that there would be much of a consequence for me."

"You see what I mean?" Camille asked gently.

Charles nodded.

"Boy, I'm tired." Camille took the last sip of her tea. "And, I have to get ready for my son."

"Oh, that's right. Do you want me to drive you to the airport to pick up Beau next week?"

"Sure. You don't mind?"

"No, it'll be interesting to meet him. Now, off you go. Get some rest."

Camille stood up and walked toward the door. "Bye, Charles. You know, you're actually pretty useful to have around..."

"Y'all go home now, hear?" Charles tried to drawl.

"Close, but no cigar," Camille commented Then she closed the door.

Charles stood staring at the door. "Now I wonder what that means?"

CHAPTER 5
When Can I Come?

The next morning at work, Naomi and Gerald were busy with preparations for the convention in the States.

"Now, here's a list of phone numbers and schedules," Naomi instructed, "and here's Talia's school schedule."

"OK, Naomi. And here's a copy of Beau's phone numbers and airplane schedule."

"Oh." Naomi looked at the paper as if this were something new.

"Naomi, Beau is very excited and anxious about this trip next week. You did remember you're going to bring Beau back with you, didn't you?"

"Yes, of course I am," Naomi answered with irritation.

"Doctora Naomi—your limo is here to take you to the airport," Fatma, the secretary, announced as she hung up the phone.

"Oh, alright. Let's see—have I forgotten anything?"

"C'mon, Naomi," Gerald chided with his usual lack of patience. "We always go through this."

"And you'll call Talia tomorrow night?" Camille reminded her.

"Yes, yes, I'll call."

The couple disappeared out the door. Camille breathed a sigh of relief and stretched back in her office chair.

"Doctora—Doctora?" Fatma touched her shoulder.

"Fatma, you may call me Camille when patients aren't around."

"Okee-dokee, Camille. There's a phone call for you."

"Phone call?"

"Yes. Someone who says they're from...it's called Biloxi?"

"Biloxi? I wonder who?" She picked up the phone.

"This is Camille Kohl—"

"Cammy..." her sister, Ashley, interrupted. "Listen, I'll be arriving on the fourteenth. Here's my flight numbers and times. Could you have somebody pick me up?"

"Of course I can. Uh, Ashley?..."

"Yes?"

"Sis," she said in a serious tone, "are you sure you really want to come here? There are..." she paused, looking around the room, "...problems."

"Yes, Cammy. Why do you keep trying to discourage me?"

Camille rolled her eyes to the ceiling and sighed.

"Right. Be seein'ya."

The phone range again.

"Doctora!" Fatma held the phone out as she blew on her freshly manicured nails.

Camille cautiously took the phone from between Fatma's still wet, bright red nails. "Hello?"

"Camille, is that you?"

"Yes..."

"This is Lou."

Lou had been an Air Force colonel who'd worked with Hans when he was in the Air Force. Lou had been head of engineering and had helped oversee the electrical installation upgrades at Keesler Medical Center.

"Lou? Colonel Lou? How are you?"

Lou chuckled. "I've been in Jeddah for two years now. My villa is about a mile from yours."

"Is it? This sure is old home week."

"How's Hans?"

"He's fine. A little cranky that he isn't over here yet."

"Well, I'll give Hans a call later. Listen, I'll call you next week and get you over for a meal, alright?"

"Sure, that'd be nice, Lou," Camille began. "I want to ask you something about my villa—"

"Uh, not now. This isn't a secure line."

"It isn't?"

Lou chuckled. "You haven't figured that out yet?"

"Well..."

"We'll talk about it soon. Gotta go."

Lou hung up. Camille noticed soft breathing on the line. "Who's this on the line?" she demanded. The phone clicked, and the dial tone came on.

Camille was so glad to hear a friendly voice from home. She grinned as she started singing while shuffling back to her desk. "Old black water, keep on rolling, Mississippi moon, won't you keep on shining on me— just keep on shining your light...gonna make everything, pretty mama make everything alright..." She plunked down in her chair, chuckling with satisfaction.

"Fatma!" she called across the room to the secretary.

Fatma had resumed painting her fingernails dark red. "Yes, Doctora...I mean, Camille?"

"You know what I would really like to eat right now?

"No..."

"Some homemade chocolate chip cookies with walnuts in them, and a big glass of cold milk."

"That's nice," Fatma answered, still leisurely blowing on her wet fingernails.

Camille became absorbed again in the clinic budget figures.

"Doctora," a gentle voice interrupted. Camille looked up at a pleasant Filipino woman, then at her watch.

"Man, time flies."

The servant put a silver tray of cookies and a glass of milk next to her. Camille smelled the aroma.

"Hmm...Christine, these are fresh baked!" Camille bit into one. "And still warm!"

The servant grinned, bowed quickly, and left.

"What a nice way to test a hypothesis," Camille commented as she stuffed her face. She doubted seriously that Safiya was this unwitting. Much more likely, she made no pretensions that whatever clinic business was conducted in her palace was also her business.

She's Egyptian

The glass doors from the pool area slid open. It was Jack Daniels, the ever-hovering personnel director.

"Good afternoon, Doctora," he greeted formally.

"Mr. Jack! Good afternoon."

"I need you to go with me to the airport and pick up the new therapist from the States."

"The new therapist?"

"Um, yes…Safiya gave her permission."

Camille sighed and put on her *abaya*. "It would be nice," she commented as the two walked out, "if they'd tell the clinic director these little details."

Jack drove through the traffic.

"Tell me a little bit about this therapist," Camille prompted.

"Very well. She's Egyptian. But, she was raised in an American school and received her advanced degree in New York. She's a little older, has grandchildren, and is married to an American, who is retired."

"Oh…that's some background."

Jack parked. They walked into the terminal. Camille stopped and looked at the white pillars surrounding the Jeddah airport.

"Beautiful architecture, isn't it?"

"Yes, it is."

Jack pulled out a sign with a woman's name on it. They made a game of trying to guess which woman was the therapist. Two hours and six plane loads later, the game wasn't funny anymore. Jack pulled out the flight information once again.

"That's odd. It shows her plane landed over two hours ago. Would you sit here for a few minutes, Camille? It looks like I'm going to have to talk with the officials."

"Sure, Jack. Good luck."

Jack walked over to a glass-partitioned office. Camille could hear him address the officials in fluent Arabic. The officials gestured angrily. Jack kept his cool, continuing in a calming tone. Camille had learned to appreciate how the Brits interacted with the Arabs. Never directly confrontational, the Brits usually handled potentially volatile situations with diplomacy.

After ten minutes, Jack nodded. He motioned Camille to come with him. Following the two Arab officials, they walked into a small room. Sitting at the table was an Arab woman. She was dressed in a tight, short skirt and a form-fitting sweater. Above the neckline of the sweater was a large gold cross.

Jack addressed her in Arabic, trying to defuse the situation. Camille understood the delay now. Here was an Arab woman, flaunting her

Christianity, and dressed in clothes nowhere close to the country's female clothing requirements.

The woman was tired and seemed defiant. "Are you Mr. Daniels?" she asked in English.

The closer Arab official became visibly upset. "Speak Arabic! You are Arab. You speak Arabic!"

The woman countered, "I am an American citizen!"

Jack waited a moment, until the woman realized that she wasn't helping the situation. In Arabic, Jack quietly asked, "Are you ready to go now?"

The woman looked at the two officials. "*Iwa* (yes)."

Jack nodded at the officials, and they roughly pushed her luggage toward her. He summoned for one of the many porters hovering around. Three appeared. Jack pointed to two, who immediately loaded the luggage onto carts. The trio crossed the parking lot and Jack tipped the porters. The two women settled in the back seat of the car.

"Hi, I'm Camille."

"I'm Layla Farida Zaynab-Owens. But my American friends call me Lilly."

"Lilly. That's a pretty name. Do you mind if I call you that, too?"

"Lilly," Jack interrupted, "I know you're tired, but Camille's villa is only minutes away. I'll drop her off, then get you situated, alright?"

"That's fine with me, Jack." She crossed her arms and huffed a few times. "Crazy bastards."

Camille and Jack exchanged glances.

"Thanks, Jack, that's very thoughtful."

Jack smiled graciously. He actually didn't seem to mind that he still had a few more hours of work left.

Camille cheerfully greeted her maid, Samantha, at the door. Samantha was in tears.

"Oh, Mum, so sorry—so very sorry!"

"Samantha, what's the matter with you?"

Samantha ran quickly into the other room, then returned with one of her silk blouses. The maid held up a tell-tale iron burn mark on the bottom edge of her blouse. Samantha's lip trembled. As Camille held the blouse up for inspection, Samantha burst into tears.

"Mum, I was ironing, and the workmen came to put in your new doorbells."

Camille was puzzled. "Doorbells? I didn't order any doorbells."

"Yes, the work order is right here."

Camille inspected the paper. A man with an Arab name had signed it.

"Huh…something's not quite right here." She looked around the villa.

"Samantha, how long were the workmen here?"

"Oh, all afternoon. They were all over the villa, Mum, not just the doors. They keep getting in my way."

Camille frowned. Bugging devices? She'd check later.

"I will buy you a new blouse, Mum."

"Huh? No—uh—I always tuck this blouse in, so you can't see the burn anyway. Just, next time, Samantha, turn off the iron if you get interrupted."

Samantha backed away, relieved. "Yes, Mum. I finish dinner now. Oh, I forgot. Miss Talia is here."

"Oh, OK. I'll go check on her." As Camille climbed the stairs, she wondered aloud, "What did Samantha think I was going to do? Beat her?"

Naomi's little daughter, Talia, met her at the top of the stairs. "Camille! Come and play a game with me!"

Camille laughed. Talia was a happy, upbeat child with an infectious laugh. She would take Camille's mind off her own family.

Three days passed. Naomi still hadn't called. After school on the fourth night, Talia came and sat down on the sofa next to Camille. "My mommy didn't call?"

"No, honey."

The little girl broke out crying. "Why hasn't my mommy called?"

"I don't know, sweetie. I'm sure she's very busy."

Talia ran sobbing into her bedroom. Camille sighed. She picked up the phone, and dialed the number for the state-side hotel.

"Yes, Dr. Naomi Ryals, please. She's in Room 346." Camille waited. "She's not in? Would you leave her a message, please? Tell Dr. Ryals that her daughter wants her to call home. Make sure she gets the message… Thanks."

She rose to find Talia. The little girl was lying on the bed, slowly leafing through a picture album.

"Hey, Talia! Wanna take a walk and get an ice cream cone?"

Talia sat up, grinning. "Sure!" She jumped off the bed and grabbed Camille's hand.

After work the following day, Camille was putting dinner on the table. "Talia! Come to dinner!"

Talia skipped in.

"Did you wash your hands?"

Talia was about to answer when the phone rang.

"Mommy!" Talia shrieked. "It's Mommy!" Talia rushed to the phone.

"Hello? Mommy! It's you!...Yeah, I'm doing a good job in school. I'm doing my homework...Mommy, I got invited to a birthday party!" Talia's mood quickly shifted from brightness to loneliness. "Mommy, when are you coming home? Tuesday? OK. Love you, Mommy. Goodbye."

"Wait!" Camille ordered. She took the phone.

"Naomi?"

"Oh. Hi, Camille."

"Have you made the final arrangements for Beau?"

"What? Oh, no. I'll get to it. I've been very busy."

"He's been waiting patiently," Camille reminded her.

"Yeah, OK. I've got to go now. I've got an interview."

"Alright, Naomi." Unsettled, Camille hung up the phone.

The next few days, Camille helped Talia pick out a birthday gift and get her to the birthday party. Talia's spirits were lifting again.

"My mommy's coming home tomorrow!"

"Yes, I know, sweetie."

Beau Forgotten

On Monday afternoon, Naomi and Gerald returned to the clinic. Camille waited patiently for the first hour, until Naomi had returned phone calls and settled in.

Finally, Naomi approached her. "Camille, these are the new computer programs. I want to get these catalogued and online in the next few days." She started to walk away.

"Naomi!"

Naomi turned around, apparently aggravated by Camille's abrupt summons.

"Naomi, where's Beau?"

"Beau? Oh—yes. I didn't have time to get him."

"You what? You didn't have time? He was waiting for you, Naomi. He's out of school, and all packed."

"Well, I just didn't have time."

"You didn't even call my husband and tell him?" Camille was incredulous. "My son must be devastated. What am I going to do now?"

Naomi let out an inpatient sigh and put her hands on her hips. "Well, why don't you take a Saudi expediter to the embassy and get the paperwork changed tomorrow? Just call Jack Daniels to set it up."

Naomi turned to leave.

"By the way, Naomi, Talia is fine."

Naomi shot her an angry look, and then disappeared back into her office. Camille looked at her watch—two a.m., Central Time. Hans would still be asleep.

She dialed Jack's office number. "Hello, Jack? Oh, I'm so glad I caught you..." She explained the situation as best she could, trying not to let the anger and bitterness into her voice.

"Yes, I can help you set that up tomorrow," Jack said affably. "By the way, did you ever get new living room furniture?"

"No..."

"Well, we can't have our clinic director with that sort of situation. I'll put a written request into Safiya this afternoon."

"Jack, you're great. Anytime I can help you..."

"Yes, maybe sometime."

Camille dreaded getting home and calling her husband. She didn't have to call. The phone was ringing incessantly as she walked down the sidewalk to the door.

Hans was furious. "Just what the hell is going on over there? Why didn't Naomi bring Beau over? Do you know how bad Beau is feeling right now?"

"Whoa, Hans—Hans—I know, I know. I'm just as upset."

"Why? Why didn't she even call?"

"She said she was too busy."

"Haven't you been watching her daughter all week?"

"Yes."

"Hans, the personnel director is getting a Saudi expediter to go with me tomorrow morning to the Saudi embassy. We're going to get Beau's paperwork completed."

"Good. But when can he come over? He was already checked out of school, just waiting..."

"Hans, I don't know! I'll find out tomorrow and call you at this same time."

"Well, OK. Here—Beau wants to talk to you."

"Mom—why can't I come over?"

Camille felt her heart wrenching from the sound of Beau's unhappy, confused voice. "Oh, honey, I'm so sorry. Tomorrow I'm going to the Saudi embassy. I won't leave there without a date for you to come. You'll know by this time tomorrow, sweetie."

"Mom, I'm really sad. I've never been this sad before."

"Beau, I'm sad, too. Please know that I'll be working on this all day tomorrow, if necessary."

"OK, Mom. I love you."

"I love you, too, honey."

Get Out of Our Embassy!

True to his word, the next morning, Jack Daniels had a limo and a Saudi expediter waiting at the clinic.

"I'm leaving for the embassy now," Camille called coldly to Naomi.

"Fine," Naomi barely acknowledged.

The tall, professional-looking expediter smiled at her, and Camille relaxed. The laws in Saudi were complicated and at times needed diplomatic intervention from a professional to "expedite" the system. This expediter was obviously used to American women; he'd probably graduated from an American college. She could relax, and let him take care of matters very efficiently. They entered the Saudi embassy.

"You may sit over there, Doctora," he pointed to a wooden bench in the lobby. Camille nodded. The expediter addressed the desk clerk in Arabic.

"I'll be handling a situation for the American doctora. She'll be waiting in the lobby for this time."

"*Iwa*," the desk clerk nodded with some hesitation. The rules in Saudi Arabia seemed to change as quickly as the nation's shifting desert sands. The desk clerk realized that a family of great influence employed the expediter. The clerk was afraid to tell him that the rules had again changed. This week, no women were to be allowed in the embassy. "Oh well," he thought to himself, "it will probably be alright."

Camille made sure her *abaya* was straight and her head completely covered before she sat down. As inquisitive as she was, she remembered to keep her head lowered. Averting the curious glances from males passing by, she pulled out a small book entitled, *How to Speak Arabic*, and busied herself with another lesson.

Thirty minutes passed, yet Camille sat demurely on the wooden bench, keeping her head in her book. A loud voice, screaming in Arabic, broke her concentration. Camille couldn't pick up every word, but pieced together the gist of his curses.

"You whore of the Satan West! You defile our sacred building!"

Camille looked up to see a scrawny matawain with wild eyes waving a stick, and approaching her from the foyer. She sized him up. He was an inch or so shorter than she, and all skin and bones. She doubted he'd had any extensive combat training.

He continued to approach, wildly waving his stick. "You will take a beating for your arrogance!" he continued in Arabic.

Camille doubted he knew much English—he certainly hadn't been the recipient of any advanced education concerning the outside world. Camille gently put her book down, then stood up. Eyeball to eyeball, the two were now less than ten feet apart.

She began to address him in English. "You little piss ant, ratty-looking old fart—" Camille pointed to a wall behind him. "I've got a spot on that wall where your raggedy ass is going..." The American woman motioned for the crazed matawain to come forward.

"C'mon. Come and get it." Camille threw her headcover back, and positioned herself. Those karate lessons were finally going to come in handy.

The desk clerk watched, frozen in horror. "*La!* American Doctora! *Wakkif* (stop)!"

The matawain stopped, stick in midair. He looked at the desk clerk, then Camille's stance. Something was different here. The matawain changed directions, and headed for the hapless desk clerk, screaming at him about guarding the sacred halls.

The Saudi expediter emerged about this time. He approached the desk clerk and made a formal announcement. "Our business is finished here. The situation is resolved."

Camille saw the expediter's look of amusement as he walked toward her.

"Ready?" he asked.

"Sure."

Safely back in the limo, the expediter turned to Camille. He tried to stifle a smile as he asked, "Did you enjoy yourself?"

Camille sat back with a Cheshire grin. "Why, yes. Yes, I did."

The expediter handed her a large packet.

"All the paperwork is complete. Your son will be leaving the States this Thursday morning. The airline tickets will be at the counter in Gulfport. And, we've arranged for an airline employee to escort him on all his transfers."

"I don't know how you accomplished these arrangements so quickly. You have made one boy very happy," Camille said gratefully.

He smiled. "That is what I do."

Camille was transported quickly back to the clinic.

"Camille." She looked up to see Naomi standing above her. Naomi's eyes seemed to soften. "I'm glad Beau is coming...I really am. There are— things..." Naomi hesitantly looked around the room, then stopped.

Camille waited expectantly for a moment. No other explanation was forthcoming. Naomi was back in business mode.

"Safiya wants you to test Sharif. He's upstairs finishing with his with tutor."

"OK. Where's Hala? She could get some training on this."

"She didn't show up for work."

"Didn't she call?"

"No, she didn't. If we did that, we'd be fired. But they get by with it." Naomi walked away, obviously irritated.

As Camille gathered up test materials, Naomi approached her again. She looked around then lowered her voice.

"That's why I don't want you to get too friendly with the Arabs. They'll take advantage of it."

Camille nodded and walked upstairs. She heard a young boy's muffled sobs. As she drew closer to the room, she realized it was Sharif. His elderly male tutor was screaming at him in Arabic.

"Why are you so stupid? Why can't you learn this? Now, write it again!"

Sharif pleaded that he was trying, but his pleading was interrupted as the tutor hit his hands with a ruler. Sharif screamed in pain.

"Oh! I get nowhere with you, you silly boy! All you want to do is play!"

The boy continued to sob. Sharif was a year younger than her son, Beau, yet they were alike in so many ways. Both of them were loving children with big, soulful eyes. Neither liked the regimentation of the standard scholastic environment. Sharif's sobbing only reinforced Camille's pain of the separation from her own son.

Camille knocked abruptly on the door then entered the room. "Lesson finished," she stated flatly.

The instructor looked disconcerted, but left. Sharif's sobs subsided as the American sat down next to him.

"Sharif," she asked, "when do you get to play?"

"Never!" He put his hands over his eyes and sobbed again. "I want to play sometime!"

Next to a silver beverage set, Camille saw a box with straws wrapped in paper covers. She walked over and grabbed some, then sat back down.

She tore the tip off one paper straw, then blew the paper cover through the air, hitting Sharif in the cheek.

"Ow!" Sharif laughed, touching his cheek.

"Tell you what, Sharif. We'll do our testing, then we'll practice with these straws so you can get your brothers and sister at meals, OK?"

A glint of mischief appeared in Sharif's eyes. "OK!" he agreed.

The monthly clinic meeting was set for late that day, after Safiya's husband, Sami, had finished his regular business day. He grinned at the staff as he entered the room. "Hamburgers! Hey, we actually get junk food tonight?"

"I call him my Saudi hick," Safiya joked. "When we got married, all he ate was fat and cholesterol."

Sami led the meeting efficiently. Camille read the minutes from the last meeting, and then Naomi gave an update.

"I'm going to give this clinic one year to become self-supporting," Sami announced.

"Well, we have enough *zakat* for six months, without any other contributions—" Safiya responded with some hesitation.

"Excuse me, what's *zakat?*" Camille asked.

"That's ten percent of a business's earnings that goes to charities or other public needs," Sami explained.

Naomi looked at her, smiling. "It's kind of like our church tithing."

"Can you count on friends who were going to give you donations?" Sami asked Safiya.

"Well, they said they'd help," his wife answered with some uncertainty.

"There are alternative sources of revenue..." Camille began.

Sami looked interested. "Like what, Camille?"

She held up computer pages of the clinic equipment list. "I've been going over the products we'll need to order on a regular basis. If we get an exclusive distributorship for even two of these replenishable items, we'll cut our ordering costs by forty percent. These two items are ones clients can also purchase for home use. And, as other clinics open, it would be easier and cheaper for them to purchase directly from our clinic rather than pay overseas shipping costs. Here are some tentative figures..." Camille pushed the printout between Safiya and Sami.

"I can see where this might work. Do you have an extra copy?"

"Sure, right here." She slid the duplicates across the table. "I know two of the manufacturers on this list, and gave them a tentative call. They're quite willing to work out an agreement."

"I'll have the accounting department look over the figures tomorrow."

Safiya looked confused. "I don't understand this..."

"Well, Safiya," Naomi said soothingly, "if you don't understand it, we certainly don't have to do it."

Gerald grunted and crossed his arms over his chest. "I don't think that would work in a medical clinic. Safiya, are we going to actually charge our patients for their supplies?"

"There's any number of ways to resolve that problem, Gerald. We could include the supplies in the clinic bill, for instance. Hospitals have been doing it for decades."

"It won't work," Gerald decided. "It's not even worth the effort."

"Still..." Sami said, looking at the figures, "I might run this by accounting."

It was dark when the meeting ended. Camille was glad to get back to her villa. She called back to the States, knowing that Beau was waiting.

"Hello?" Beau's voice was hopeful.

"Hi, honey."

"Mom! Am I coming?"

"Yes, hon. Today is Tuesday for you, right?"

"Yes."

"Well, guess what? Your tickets are at the Gulfport airport. Beau, your plane leaves Thursday morning."

"Really? For sure?"

"For sure."

"Oh, Mom, I'm so happy!"

"Me too, sweetie. I've got to hang up now. I've got to catch Dad at work."

"OK...Uh, Mom?"

"What, hon?"

"I've been missing you..."

"Me too, Beau. See you in two days."

Camille punched in Hans' clinic number. "Yes, I'm calling from Saudi Arabia. Could you get me Dr. Kohl, please?"

"Hans?"

"Yeah. Cammy?"

Camille could hear static on the line.

"Cammy, I can barely hear you."

"Hans!" Camille shouted over the noise, "Beau is leaving Thursday morning. His tickets are at the counter at the Gulfport airport."

"Where?" The static was getting louder.

"Call the Northwest ticket counter." By this time, she was shouting.

"The ticket counter, OK. Look, the static is getting too bad. Hang up and call me back," he shouted.

"OK." She hung up and redialed.

"All circuits are busy, try again later," came the recording. She started to get up from her seat when the phone rang again.

"Hans? Oh, hi Sybil...You're having a what? A party? It's nine o'clock, and I'm really tired...What?" She sighed heavily. "Well, I'm trying to get through to the States...Alright, I'll try to make it over."

Camille dialed ten more times, only to get the same recording, "All circuits are busy. Try again later." The frustrated woman threw her hands up in the air. She grabbed her house key and walked toward Ben and Sybil's villa.

"Camille, how are you?" Sybil gave her a hug.

"Fine. How're you doing, Sybil?"

"Going stir crazy. There's nothing for most of us women to do here..."

"Well, there are lots of malls around, what about shopping?"

"Sure, beautiful malls," Sybil agreed, "but, with the import restrictions, the shelves aren't even half full."

"What about movie theaters?" Camille thought.

"Try to find one..." Sybil answered, starting to wiggle to the music.

Camille laughed. The silliness was catching. "How about... bowling?"

Sybil burst out in peals of laughter. She turned the Middle Eastern music up louder, and two women dressed as belly dancers gyrated past. Sybil threw off her robe and jiggled her bells.

"We're having a belly dancing class! There's an extra costume in the bedroom. Join us!"

Sybil flung her arms in the air and went twirling around the sofa.

Camille looked at Ben, who handed her a beer. "Uh—I can't see it happening, Sybil. I'll have a quick drink, then I'm out of here."

An Arab woman approached her. "Oh, Cammy—" Sybil introduced. "This is Nahla. She's Lebanese. She's a flight attendant for Saudia Airlines."

"Nice to meet you." Camille shook her hand.

"We're just working off a little angriness," the Arab woman explained.

"Angriness?" Camille laughed.

"Yes. Saudia Airlines just changed the rules again! Now we're supposed to have our head covered while we're trying to work—very inefficient!"

"Nahla, come on! Show me the next movement!" Sybil called.

"Got to go..." Nahla whirled off.

"Lots of energy here." Camille lifted her glass and finished the drink. She handed the glass back to Ben. "Thanks, Ben. I'd better get back to my villa and try to phone my husband again."

"OK. Thanks for stopping." Ben saw her to the door.

"Thanks, y'all! I needed a little light-hearted respite!"

Camille walked back to the villa. She punched in Hans' clinic number again. "Yes, I'm calling from Saudi—Oh, hi, Hans."

"I've been waiting for you to call for thirty-five minutes! Why didn't you call me back?"

"Hans, I did. I tried ten times, and got the same recording. There just aren't enough phone lines in Saudi Arabia."

"Well, I'm sure you could've gotten through before now!"

"Hans, do you want the information?"

"Yes, go ahead."

"Beau's on Flight 5411 at nine a.m. Thursday. His reservation number is JQ8689234. Now, Hans, would you please go ahead and call the ticket counter right now, just to make sure? If there's any problems, I want to know right away."

"Alright. Do you want me to call you back?"

"Only if there's a problem, Hans. It's ten p.m. here, and I've had a rough day."

"Well, I've had a rough day, too, Camille."

She ignored his terseness. "Goodnight, Hans."

The phone rang again.

"Camille? This is Lou."

"Hey, Lou..."

"Do you need a ride to get Beau Thursday night?"

"How did you—never mind. I have someone here at Montoya to give me a ride."

"Well, if it doesn't work out, I'll pick him up."

"Thanks. I appreciate that."

"Cammy? Don't make any plans for tomorrow night. You can come to my place for dinner."

"Uh, I guess...sure."

"I'll send my driver to pick you up at six-thirty."

"Alright."

Camille heard the phone click. She waited. She heard the sound of faint voices through the receiver, as if people were talking in the distance.

"Did you hear enough?" she asked icily. There was another abrupt click, and then the dial tone returned.

The next morning, Camille woke with early prayer call. Now that Beau's problem was resolved, she felt a surge of positive energy. She put on her jogging clothes, preparing for her daily run around the small compound. She was actually looking forward to her work in the clinic.

At work, Fatma greeted her. "Camille—" the Lebanese woman glanced around and saw Safiya. "I mean, Doctora—Doctora Naomi wants to see you right away."

"I'm sure she does," Camille commented, remembering last night's clinic meeting. She knocked on Naomi's door.

"Come in."

"Good morning, Naomi." Camille waited.

"I thought we had this clear. You need to go through channels."

"What channels? We're not exactly a Fortune 500 company."

"I'm the executive director. You're the clinical director. All ideas get passed through me, and I pass them along."

"If you're talking about the distributorships, I sent you three memos about it over the last month."

"I mean about anything. That includes your research projects."

"My research projects? You've already approved them. We're just waiting on the equipment."

"No, they're not approved. Gerald is now head of the research department. He'll decide whether your research is approved or not."

"What? Naomi, this is really frustrating. We had an agreement worked out before I came over here, and...Gerald isn't even in the same field of expertise."

"That's the way it's going to be."

"Naomi, it can be that way, but you know Gerald hasn't liked me since day one. How's it going to help the clinic if Gerald vetoes projects because of personal feelings?"

What This Place Needs

Camille sat back. Without trying, she could read Naomi's frustration and insecurity. A realization came to her.

"Oh, Naomi—this isn't about the clinic. This is about you and Gerald establishing your careers here…"

Naomi's anger flashed through her at Camille's understanding of her situation. "And what's this about the personnel director calling Safiya about furniture for you?" she retorted.

"He's just trying to help. I have a collection of animal urine-soaked, cast-off dirty furniture—"

"Well, Safiya will be here in a few minutes. She's actually going to spend her valuable time driving over with us to look at your furniture."

"She doesn't have to do that."

"She wants to—she can't understand what the big deal is…" Naomi put her face close to Camille's and lowered her voice in reverence. "Safiya is a billionaire! She could BUY New York!"

"Well, then," Camille stood up, "she can BUY me some furniture!"

Naomi looked disgusted. "Just go and give the therapists their daily assignments. And try not to be so friendly with them!"

A few minutes later, Safiya appeared. From across the room she called, "Camille, would you please come here?"

Camille got up, ready for Round Two.

"I got a call from Jack Daniels. He said it was standard procedure for company personnel to have new furniture. I don't know what all this bother is about—"

"Safiya, the former tenants in my villa kept two cats indoors. They relieved themselves over most of the furniture. It's not only dirty, but it smells bad."

Safiya sighed haughtily. "I knew I'd have trouble with a white American woman. When I was volunteering at the school, the American headmistress said I should have every experience possible, so she made me scrub toilets!"

Camille caught herself laughing. "Safiya, as Naomi said, you're a billionaire. Nobody can make you scrub toilets if you don't want to—"

Safiya gave a little "harump."

"Well, let's put on our spook outfits and get this over with!" She threw on her *abaya* and head cover. Safiya, Naomi and Camille entered the Rolls Royce. Safiya's chauffeur, who was normally relaxed and friendly with Camille, was today very formal.

The three women soon arrived at Camille's villa. Safiya strolled in. She briefly checked the downstairs rooms, then turned to Camille. "What this place needs…" she said in a high voice, raising a finger, "is decorating! Get some plants, get some pictures—"

Camille looked around, amazed. "At least can we get the furniture steam cleaned so we can get the urine smell out?"

"Do what you want on your own. I have other, more important things to be concerned about!"

Camille, now disgruntled, wished she didn't have to spend the twenty minutes in the car with the two women on the way back to the clinic. She gazed out the car window, trying to focus on her son's upcoming arrival.

Returning to the palace, Safiya tossed her *abaya* on her office chair and dialed the personnel director's phone number. "Jack, I don't see what the problem is with Camille's villa. It's perfectly adequate. She just needs to do some decorating!"

"Well, it is your clinic, Madame Safiya," Jack reasoned on the other end. "But for the past twenty years, company policy has provided officers with new furniture. Naomi and Gerald received new furniture…"

"That's different!"

Jack knew better than to continue. "Very well, then. Will you at least let the compound manager come by the clinic this afternoon for an hour or two and take her shopping?"

"I will think about this!" Safiya slammed the phone down.

After lunch, Sam, the compound manager, appeared at the clinic door.

"Doctor Camille," he smiled formally. "Mr. Jack asked me to take you shopping for some decorative items."

"Sam, how nice! I don't have much time with my work schedule, and my son is coming in two days."

Camille picked up her purse and *abaya*. She knocked on Naomi's office door. She could hear Safiya and Naomi talking, but no one answered.

"Fatma," she called to the secretary, "tell Doctora Naomi I went with the compound manager."

She gratefully walked out into the warm sun with Sam. "How's Katie doing?"

"She's fine."

Sam skillfully drove through the maze of streets, parked, and escorted Camille into a large store. He helped her load her plants and inexpensive pictures with Arab scenes into the car trunk.

"You know," Sam began, "Charles has been one of my best friends for a very long time…"

"I know, Sam."

She could see Sam's hesitancy.

"May I ask?"

"Ask what?"

"Is there anything serious between you two?"

"Oh, come on, Sam," she laughed. "Charles is a great help to me, but I'm married, remember?"

"How disappointing. I was hoping for a bit of hot gossip."

"Besides," Camille chuckled, "I like 'em big and bossy—" Her voice trailed off as she realized she was talking about her own husband. She missed him.

Sam looked at Camille as she tried to explain.

"Sam, Charles is very good looking, but he's not my type."

"That's funny," Sam grinned, "he said the same thing about you."

Arriving at the compound, Sam seemed in a hurry to get Camille's boxes into her villa. "My, my look at the time. I can't stay for long, you know."

Sam looked up from the boxes for a moment. "There's a lot of frustrated women in the compound with nothing to do but talk."

Camille smiled. "Sam, you didn't tell Katie you were helping me, did you?"

"No, it's better that way…don't you think?"

"Unfortunately, yes."

"Oh, by the way, the work crew wants to steam clean your furniture this afternoon. Is that alright with you?"

"Sam!" She impulsively hugged his neck. "Thanks!"

Sam appeared embarrassed. "I'd better go."

Camille's maid, Samantha, arrived at the same time as the work crew.

"Samantha, don't try to clean the villa today. Here's a grocery list of my son's favorite items. Just get groceries, OK?"

"Very well, Mum."

Camille's spirits had brightened considerably. Her villa was getting attention, her son was coming, and she was actually off work early. She decided to lay by the pool in the warm Jeddah sun and relax.

He Speaks No Language

The next morning, the clinic bus was late. Lilly, the new Egyptian-American therapist, was on the bus. She'd haphazardly thrown her *abaya* over her tight skirt and sweater outfit to signify her begrudging compliance. The new driver, not quite as bright as the previous driver, looked agitated.

"You're late!" Camille scolded him in English.

"He speaks no English," Lilly grumbled.

"Then tell him in Arabic."

Lilly hook her head again. "He speaks no Arabic."

"Well, what language does he speak?"

"No language. He speaks no language!"

Fatma, the Lebanese secretary, giggled.

"That's why we were late. The dummy couldn't find his way from my villa to yours because it's not his usual route."

"Then how did he get here?"

Lilly held up a map. "I have a street map! It's my second day in Jeddah, and I have to help this dummy do his job!"

The driver's eyes shifted back and forth. He didn't like the abuse he was receiving in any language.

Camille chuckled, in spite of herself. "Lilly, if he speaks no language, how are you giving him directions?

"Get in and I'll show you."

"Alright." Camille sat in the front right seat.

Lilly sat in the left front seat, directly behind the driver. She slapped him hard on his back, then pointed her finger straight past his nose. "Go!" she commanded.

Camille put her hand over her mouth, trying hard not to laugh. The bus driver stomped on the gas pedal, and the bus lurched forward.

"Lilly! I thought we couldn't touch the drivers."

"I'm not touching him. I'm hitting him. Big difference!"

Lilly held up the map for study. She reached out and slapped the driver's right arm, then stuck her finger by his nose and pointed right.

"Turn right!" she screamed.

The bus driver swerved right, knocking Lilly back into her seat. The jolt from the bus pushed Lilly's shiny new wig over her eyes. Tears welled up in Camille's eyes, she wanted to laugh so badly. Lilly unabashedly straightened her wig.

"I'll have to use more bobby pins on my wigs if we keep this driver!"

The bus driver made angry noises in some as yet unidentified language.

Lilly was following the street signs and checking her map. "Let's see—two more streets—No! One!" She excitedly smacked the driver's left shoulder. Her outstretched finger hit the corner of his left eye.

"Yeow!" he cried, holding his eye.

"Left! Turn left, now!" She continued smacking his left shoulder. The bus driver made a wide swerve to the left, sending two cars into the sidewalk. Camille was laughing so hard now, tears were rolling down her face.

The gates to the palace were ahead. The bus driver, confused and humiliated from Lilly's less than gentle guiding hand, throttled full steam between the gates. Two of the regular palace guards jumped out of the way and cursed the driver in Arabic.

Undaunted, Lilly took her fist and slammed it into the driver's back.

"Stop!" she screamed.

The driver slammed on the brakes. The front tires came to a rest on the third step leading to the front door of the palace. The women jolted backwards into their seats. Lilly's wig also went flying backwards.

"Oh-h-h!" she groaned angrily, pulling the wig back down tightly.

Camille was laughing so hard now, she couldn't catch her breath. "I'm sorry..." she said to the driver. She hoped he understood—she wasn't intentionally trying to hurt his feelings.

"Doctora Camille! Remember, don't touch him!"

"I know, I know, Fatma." Camille wiped the tears from her eyes.

The two palace guards had caught up with the bus. The driver sat in his seat, terrified.

"Open the door!" they screamed in Arabic. He was too frightened. "Out! Out!"

One guard pried open the bus doors and grabbed the hapless driver. He was pulled by his arms, heels dragging, toward the guardhouse.

"Well," Camille sighed, looking at Lilly, "scratch another bus driver." She jumped off the bus steps onto the sidewalk, reflecting on how callous she was beginning to sound.

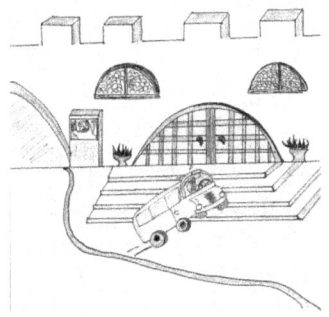

Camille was surprised that Naomi and Gerald weren't at the clinic yet.

"They're at some special meeting with the architects," Fatma read the message on her desk. Fatma analyzed her fingernails. "Time for a touch up..." She pulled the nail file and polish out of her large purse.

Lilly walked briskly over to Camille. "Well," she said in a business-like tone, "where should I start?"

Camille didn't have a clue. She hadn't even known about the therapist's arrival until the day before. She looked at the different piles of work projects. She scooped up one pile and handed it to the new therapist.

"Here, Lilly. We've already started receiving equipment orders. Check the invoices to see which orders are completely filled, and which are back ordered. Then write me a list of both. Any questions?"

"Nope! Got it!" Lilly charged off happily.

Within an hour, Lilly was back. She dropped the papers on Camille's desk. "Now what?"

The American realized she only had two more days of busywork, tops. And Lilly didn't look like the type of worker who'd be happy sitting around, filing her fingernails. "I hope the clinic building will be completed on schedule," she told her.

"When's it supposed to be ready?" Lilly asked.

"Three weeks. Then you'll be very busy."

"Good! I like busy!"

Just then the clinic doors opened. Naomi and Gerald appeared.

Lilly grinned. "Hi, Naomi! Hi, Gerald!" she called across the room.

Gerald ignored her.

Naomi glanced coolly toward the new therapist's direction. "Oh," came the lukewarm response, "hello, Lilly."

Lilly looked hurt and confused. Camille knew the feeling. She remembered how friendly Naomi had acted in the States, and what a sudden transformation she made on Saudi soil.

"What's wrong with her?" Lilly asked through clenched teeth.

"Well, for one thing, in the clinic, Naomi wants us to be more formal. The staff is supposed to address them as Doctora Naomi and Doctor Gerald."

Lilly huffed and pulled herself up. "That'll be a cold day in hell," she commented.

Camille stifled a chuckle. She handed Lilly another batch of work. "Here's our computer program inventory. Do the same with it."

"Right!" Lilly brightened, tottering off in high heels.

"This is gonna get interesting…" Camille commented under her breath.

"Doctora Camille?" Naomi called from her office. She looked at Lilly to emphasize the point of protocol. "Would you come here, please?"

Camille walked into Naomi's office. Naomi picked up a file folder. "We haven't ordered the clinic research equipment yet. That will take

146

a while to get from the States. Here's the information from the Jeddah distributor. Call them to come over here for a meeting." She handed Camille the file.

Naomi appeared tired and distressed. "The CEO of the company is Safiya's cousin," she continued. "You handle it all."

Camille called and set up a meeting.

After work, a new driver, the third in a week, greeted them. This one spoke a smattering of English. "Hallo, hallo," he greeted the women. "Doctora home first," he stated. He obviously had gotten his orders.

"Well, of course," Lilly huffed, "even though my villa is six blocks closer."

"Oh, Lilly, give it a rest," Camille ordered.

Samantha, her maid, greeted her at the door.

"Sam, you didn't burn any more clothes..."

"No, no, Mum," Samantha giggled, "I buy new things for your son. Look!"

Samantha led her employer upstairs to Beau's new bedroom. On his bed was a bright pink floral bedspread. Matching pink flowered curtains graced his windows. Samantha beamed proudly. "I even got matching garbage can!"

"Uh, thanks, Sam," Camille tried to keep the disappointment out of her voice. She saw her maid's smile start to fade. Camille gave the petite woman a hug of reassurance. "It was thoughtful of you, thinking of Beau. I'm sure my son will notice right away..."

Samantha's head went up with pride again.

"I'm going to take a shower now. A limo is picking me up in thirty minutes. Bring me the receipts and I'll pay you."

The limo driver was right on time. A pleasant, intelligent-looking Filipino man greeted her. "Doctora, Dr. Lou is waiting."

The chauffeur drove carefully through the traffic. Occasionally at stop signs, he glanced back. "Doctora, I'm not looking at you," he explained. "Eighty percent of all accidents in Jeddah are caused by rear-end collisions. I try to allow two car lengths as a cushion. But I also look in the rearview mirror just in case the car behind doesn't stop."

"I'm impressed. Do you do a lot of work for Dr. Lou?"

"He requires my services two days a week. I also have," he said with some pride in his voice, "my own taxi service."

"That's great. You're quite an entrepreneur."

"Our generation won't be rich," he said wistfully, "but, if we work hard enough, we'll be able to put our children through college. Then they'll have a better life."

Camille sat back in the seat, impressed with his work ethic and vision.

"Here we are !" the chauffeur announced.

"Wow!" Camille exclaimed. In front of them was a huge white building with high stone walls. The chauffeur drove into the courtyard, and opened Camille's door. A large, muscular man with white hair and matching white beard approached her.

"Lou. It's been a lot of years."

The large American gave her a hug, and kissed her cheek. "Well, Cammy! Off on an adventure, I see. Come in."

Camille looked in amazement at the spacious foyer and inside fountain. "Wow!" she repeated again. "You rate..."

"Yeah," he laughed. "I heard about the condition of your villa."

"Is there anything you don't know?"

His eyebrows raised for a moment. "I was hoping you could meet Heidi, my girlfriend. You speak some German."

"It's required in the family I married into."

A servant appeared and took her *abaya* and purse from her.

"Hey!"

"Oh, don't worry. Your belongings will be very safe."

Lou led Camille into a large dining hall. "Heidi had to work late at the hospital tonight. She's a nurse."

Another servant appeared with two pitchers.

"I have iced tea and lemonade. Which do you prefer?

"You never did drink, did you?" Camille remembered.

"No, it just never excited me much."

A third servant whispered something in her boss's ear.

"Dinner's ready."

"How many servants do you have, Lou? I've seen four so far."

"I started with one. Then one brought another family member, and another. The longer you're here, the more you seem to acquire."

One of the servants pulled Camille's chair out for her.

Camille raised her glass in a toast. "Seeing you makes me a little homesick." She thought for a moment. "So, are you going home for Christmas?"

"No...but I'll miss the Christmas boat parade."

Camille smiled. "How about 'Christmas in the Pass'?"

"I'll miss that, too." Lou put his hands behind his head and laughed. "This year, though, I hope I have my staff trained not to bring me home any more special Christmas presents."

"Special presents?"

Lou chuckled and glanced at the Arab standing by the door. "Last Christmas, Abbas thought I must be lonely, so he went out and procured a hooker. He wrapped a big red bow around the hooker, and presented her to me."

Camille laughed. "What happened?"

"Well, the poor thing wiggled around, trying to be appealing."

Camille stirred her lemonade. "I know this isn't nice to ask, but I heard it's shaved?"

"Smooth as a baby's bottom. However," Lou slowly peeled a jumbo shrimp, then leisurely dipped it in the sauce, "she had one hairy set of armpits."

Camille laughed at the disparity.

"Well, I thanked Abbas, but said I wasn't interested. I told him he could have her."

"And he did?"

"He did. Of course, when my girlfriend Heidi found out, she went ballistic. She scrubbed down the bedroom and actually burned the mattress."

"I hear that," Camille picked up another shrimp. "Must be a German thing. My husband has a fetish about toilets. He keeps them all 'sterilized'."

"Heidi, too. You could perform friggin' brain surgery in my toilets."

"I thought there weren't any prostitutes in the Kingdom."

"Not many. However, I was sitting on a bench with Heidi one day when a woman came and sat down across from me. She pulled her *abaya* back enough to expose herself. Then she did some muscle movements, I guess to show me her special skills. I replied, 'not interested, but thanks, anyway'. The prostitute shrugged as if to say, 'so what—no sale' and moved on. Heidi, however, was highly insulted that the woman would proposition me while I was sitting with her."

"But, that's a fairly rare occurrence, isn't it?"

"Pretty much. It's not a big problem. The Saudis are more worried about the growing number of expatriates in their country. They have cause for concern. Foreigners outnumber Saudis. Saudi women are denied birth control and urged very strongly to have children. There's still quite a bit of intermarriage, though, and that results in higher levels of birth defects. Hence—your clinic. Safiya has the right idea—" He broke off as cheesecake was placed on the table.

"One more thing you need to remember..."

"What, Lou?"

"Saudis don't like it when you complain." He looked at her pointedly.

Camille winced. "Yeah, I found that out."

"Dessert?" Lou asked.

"No thanks. I've been doing good lately."

Lou patted his belly. "I'm not, but it's one of my few pleasures. So, Beau will be here tomorrow?"

"Yes, he's so excited. I saw an amusement park close to the Red Sea. I'll take him to it first thing."

Lou interrupted with a headshake.

"What?"

"You can't take him."

"I can't? Why not?"

"He's too old. You can't take him in public places; not without a man along."

"What? I can't go out in public with my own son?"

"Not without an escort. Now, if you had a daughter..."

"Oh, man!" Camille was disgusted. She sucked on her lemonade straw while thinking about the places that she couldn't take her son.

Lou softened. "Hey, I hear Ashley's coming here soon. How's she been?"

"Still withdrawn. I didn't realize the head trip Jimmy did on her." Camille took a thoughtful sip of lemonade. "Lou, do you know a Brit in Sami's company named Charles Morgan?"

"Charles? Sure, I know him. He's become somewhat of a hermit after his wife died. Why?"

Camille smiled. "Do you think it would be alright if he took Ashley out once in awhile?"

Lou titled his head and thought about it. "She's going to be in the same compound anyway—they're like fishbowls. You know, they're both sort of introverted. Maybe they could help each other get out of their shells a bit…"

Lou looked up to see his chauffeur signaling him from across the room. "But enough of this introspection. It's time to get you home." He got up from the table. "Max, time to take Doctora back to Montoya."

Lou walked Camille to the door. "I know you're anxious to get a good night's sleep, so you'll be fresh when you pick up Beau."

"Thanks, Lou."

"Don't mention it."

"Lou? You've got a Ph.D. in electrical engineering—can you stop by my villa sometime and show me where the bugs are hidden?"

Lou chuckled. "Sure. I'll call you next week."

CHAPTER 6
He Certainly Looks American

Lilly, the new therapist, started in immediately at the clinic the next morning. "Is this all you have for me to do?"

"Lilly, will you chill?"

"But I'm used to working. I go crazy if I don't have something to do all the time."

"Well, then, that'll be two of us. Look, finish what you have, and I'll work on another project to give you."

"OK."

"Giving her work is just making more work," Camille muttered under her breath.

Lilly came back thirty minutes later. "Now what do I do?"

"Here!" Camille handed her worksheets, trying to be patient. "I want you to make some handouts for the clinic patients. Pick out the salient features of different dysarthrias, simplify the wording, and translate it into Arabic."

"Dysarthrias? There's only one kind."

"There are several."

"No," she argued, "there's only one."

Camille couldn't envision another five months of creating busywork. Frustrated, she crossed over to the bookshelves and pulled out a book.

"Here!" she said, tossing it on Lilly's desk. "Mayo Clinic Guide. Read up!"

Fatma was busy smacking her bubble gum and listening to music on her headset, while she happily pecked away at her thirty words per minute on the keyboard. The phone rang. Fatma continued to peck her typewriter keys to the beat of the music.

"Fatma! Answer the phone!"

"Huh? Oh—hallo?"

Lilly stormed off to her desk.

"Doctora, it's for you."

Camille walked over to the phone. "Hello?"

"Hallo, Doctora Camille?"

"Yes, who is this?"

"This is Yehya from Montoya."

"Who?"

"Yehya. I work in the front office. You did not order a limo for your son's pickup?"

"No need. I already made arrangements."

"Who, please?"

"Charles Morgan," Camille blurted out. A warning bell suddenly went off in her head.

"Thank you," the voice responded with a satisfied crispness.

Camille frowned and slowly replaced the receiver. She realized she'd just made a strategic error, although she didn't know why.

At lunchtime, Lilly was still petulant. Naomi and Safiya joined them.

"What's up with Lilly?" Naomi asked.

"Oh, she just wanted to have a discussion about dysarthrias."

Naomi picked up a carrot. "I told you not to get too close to her."

Late in the afternoon, Camille noticed Lilly hadn't been bothering her. She walked over to Lilly's corner, and found the Egyptian woman had her head bent down. She was crying.

"Lilly, are you that upset about our discussion?"

"No, it's not that. Today is my birthday."

"Oh, Lilly, we didn't know."

"I'm all alone over here," she sobbed, "and I don't have a phone in my villa yet. They said I'd have a phone." She was glancing toward Naomi's office. "My husband was going to call me tonight and wish me happy birthday."

Camille went back to her desk and wrote a note to Naomi. 'Lilly is crying. It's her birthday and she doesn't have a phone yet in her villa. May she use the clinic phone this one time to call her husband?'

She knocked on Naomi's door. Safiya and Naomi were in the middle of a discussion. Naomi read the note, cast her eyes upward, and said "What next?" She handed the note to Safiya.

Safiya read the note then made a hand movement as if to dismiss the problem. "I suppose…"

The two women went back to their discussion. Camille closed the door and walked over to Lilly. She put her head close to Lilly's and said quietly, "Safiya said it would be alright if you called the States from here, since it's a special occasion."

Lilly wiped her tears and burst out with a big grin. She jumped out of her seat and zeroed in on the phone. "Hello...hello...Hi, honey! How are you? I'm fine. I still don't have my phone yet..." she glanced disparagingly at Camille. Camille sighed and looked up at the ceiling.

Later, as the women boarded the clinic bus for home, Lilly seemed intent on making a point. "You yelled at me in front of the secretary."

"Fatma wasn't even listening."

"That isn't the point. You yelled at me in front of the help. You have to learn. I'm an Egyptian." Lilly held her head up. "I have my pride."

Camille sighed and stared out the window. "Yes, Lilly, you have your pride."

Lilly's anger dissolved. "I'm trying to work as hard as I can. You're my boss. I don't want to be fired."

Camille smiled. "Lilly, you're Arab. You know the customs. You speak and write Arabic. I don't. Who do you think they'd fire first?"

Lilly was quiet for a moment. The driver slowed as they approached Camille's compound.

"Camille?" Lilly asked in a quietly pleading voice. "Are you real mad at me?"

"No, Lilly. I'm not mad at you."

"But you think I'm a pain, right?"

"Lilly," Camille smiled as she prepared to step off the bus, "I think you're one of the most delightful pain-in-the-asses I've ever met."

The Egyptian woman looked proud again. "Thanks!" she smiled happily.

Camille unlocked her villa door. She took a shower and changed clothes. Then she picked up the phone.

"Hey, Charles. Camille."

"As if I didn't know. Ready?"

"Yep."

"Meet me outside the gate."

The couple drove toward the Jeddah International Airport.

"You know, Charles, I hope they don't give Beau any grief getting through Customs."

"They won't. You know, the Saudis have made some remarkable progress in the past few years."

"Such as?"

"Oh...they've cleaned up their water supplies, built modern roads. They even have dairy farms where there was once desert. Some expats used to take advantage. They'd repeatedly break traffic laws. So, now the Saudis have a central computer bank. If someone violates laws and doesn't pay fines, the computer will pick this up. They'll have to settle before they're allowed to leave the country."

"Huh. I guess you have to compare a country to its own past, rather than judge it against other countries."

"That's a rather heavy speculation for tonight, Camille."

They parked the car and walked inside the airport.

Charles listened to the announcements. "We're in luck. Your son's plane just landed at Gate Three."

Camille peered anxiously past the glass wall at the deplaning passengers. All she saw were adults. "Oh," she said, disappointed. "I don't see him."

A young, blonde man with a crew cut, wearing a leather jacket, grinned at her and waved. Camille cocked her head. "Who...? Beau? Charles, that's Beau!"

Charles studied the boy. "Well, he certainly does look his nationality."

Camille was puzzled. "That nationality is that?"

"Why, American, of course."

"Charles, how does one look American? We're the melting pot—all colors and nationalities.."

Camille looked at her son again. With his new crew cut and leather jacket, he did remind her of someone. "Oh...I know the American you mean."

"Sorry? Who'd that be?"

"Why, Arnold Schwarzenegger, of course."

Charles cast his eyes sideways at the sarcasm.

"He looks like a seasoned traveler, picking up his bags," Camille commented with some surprise. She watched in awe as three porters descended on him.

Beau looked confidently around. "One!" he held up a finger then looked at the porters. "You!" he pointed to one.

The rest left.

Charles and Camille looked at each other, somewhat surprised at the boy's confidence. Beau and the porter approached the couple.

"Stop!" Beau put his hand up to the porter. "Mom!" he grinned and gave her a hug. The porter looked around uneasily, hoping no matawain saw the open sign of affection. The porter was counting on a big tip from this young American in the expensive leather jacket.

Beau turned and looked at Charles. "Hi!" he said, extending a hand, "I'm Beau!"

Charles shook his hand. "I'm Charles."

"Nice to meet you, Mr. Charles."

The group started toward the car. As the porter completed stuffing bags in the car. Camille motioned to him. The porter looked at Beau, confused.

"She'll pay you. That's my mom."

Camille tipped the porter 50 riyals. They left the airport and blended with the downtown traffic.

"Nice weather for December." Beau rolled down his window. "Is that a statue of a boat?"

"I never have figured that one out." Charles replied.

"Look, Mom!" Beau laughed, "Pizza Sheikh!"

Camille chuckled.

"Look at that bumper sticker. It says 'I LOVE JEDDAH'!" He laughed again.

"He has the same sense of humor as you," Charles observed.

They slowed for a red light. A beggar approached the car and stuck his stump in the window next to Beau's face.

"Aaaa—No!" The horrified American boy rolled up the car window. "He didn't have a hand!"

Camille covered her smile. "Now remember, Beau, I told you about them…"

"Yeah, yeah. But it's different when you actually have a stump jammed in your face."

"Oh, by the way," Charles remembered, "Sam wanted us to bring Beau up so he and Katie could meet him."

"Well, just for a few minutes. I'm sure Beau is tired."

"No, I'm not. I'm too wired to sleep."

Charles parked the car and the three dropped Beau's luggage in the foyer of Camille's villa.

"Are you sure you're ready to meet more people tonight?" Charles asked him.

"Yes, sir."

They walked upstairs to the manager's apartment and knocked. Sam came to the door. "Camille! This must be Beau! Well, Charles, bring them in." Sam was always pleasant and easy going. Katie appeared formal and stiff.

"How do you do, Beau?"

"Nice to meet you, ma'am." Beau shook her hand.

"Do sit down."

The two men joked with Beau while Katie sat brooding.

"My, he's tall, isn't he?" she finally commented.

Sam brought out a pitcher of beer.

"Well, Beau, how about a toast?"

Beau's eyes widened. "Sure!"

Camille put a hand over Beau's mug. "Sam, he's just twelve. He's never had alcohol before."

"Sure I have, Mom."

Camille narrowed her eyes, but decided against pursuing the subject at the moment.

"Just a taste," Sam assured her. "It will make the boy sleep after his long trip."

"Well..."

Sam proceeded to pour Beau a full mug. Beau picked up his mug and grinned at his mother. Camille rolled her eyes in resignation.

Katie's Siamese cat emerged from the bedroom, curious to see what all the noise was about. Katie had never borne children. Rubbles, the Siamese cat, was her surrogate baby.

"Kitty!" Beau laughed and bent down to pet the cat.

"Don't touch him!" Katie shrieked suddenly.

Katie's outburst stunned the rest of them. Charles frowned and put down his beer. "Well, now. Guess we'd better be going."

They rose to leave. Sam ushered them to the door. "Sorry," he said quietly, "I don't know what got into her."

Beau waved it off. "Aw, she's probably on the rag—"

"Beau!" Camille was shocked at her son.

Sam and Charles looked at each other, and laughed in spite of themselves.

As they walked down the steps, Charles apologized again. "I'm sorry, Beau. I don't know what Katie's problem is with that cat."

"That's OK."

"Well, thanks, Charles, for picking up Beau." She gave him a quick hug.

Charles face cracked a grin. "Next week, you'll let me pick up Ashley, won't you?"

"Sure. Mind if I tag along?"

Charles cocked his head in a mock haughty expression. "If you must."

Camille laughed and playfully hit his arm. "Right, then. Goodnight."

She turned toward her son. "C'mon, kid...just wait 'til you see how the maid decorated your bedroom."

As Camille unlocked the door, her son looked at her. "Mom, he's nice, isn't he?"

"Who?"

"Charles."

Camille smiled. "Yes, honey. He's helped me a lot here."

Beau considered this. "He's a good guy."

Camille helped her son carry his bags upstairs. "Want a sandwich?"

"Sure. Mom..." Beau came and sat on a chair, "When Dad put me on the airplane, he cried—right in the middle of the airport. It kind of surprised me."

"Yeah, I'm sure."

"Sometimes, I think he doesn't care. But then he goes and cries..."

"It's—kind of the way he grew up, honey, in a stoic German family and all. It's hard for him to show his emotions."

Beau chewed on his sandwich. "I guess you're right."

"Getting tired?"

"Yeah, a little."

"Well, I've got some towels laid out for your bath. You can unpack tomorrow."

"Mom, I see what you mean about my bedroom—the pink flower stuff."

"Can you live with it until we go shopping?"

"Oh, it's alright for now." Beau finished his sandwich and took his plate to the sink. He went upstairs. She heard the bath water running. A while later, he called down. "OK, Mom, I'm done."

Camille climbed the stairs. "You're almost a teenager now," she rubbed her hand over his crew cut, "and taller than I am now. Still, goodnight, son. Sleep tight."

Beau smiled, tired but happy. "Love you, Mom."

The next morning, Camille arose as usual to the first prayer call. She put on her jogging clothes and slipped quietly out the door.

"Good morning, Mom!"

Startled, Camille turned to see her son dressed in a T-shirt, shorts, and jogging shoes.

"Beau, it's only six a.m. Aren't you tired from your trip?"

"Naw! I feel great! Let's go!"

The two took off jogging around the compound. Finished, they walked back to the villa.

"I'll take a shower, then make you breakfast."

"OK, but—" Beau threw open his arms, "I'm ready to see Jeddah!"

Camille laughed. "I used to feel that way."

After breakfast, Camille handed Beau 500 riyals. His eyes opened wide.

"Wow! Five hundred riyals? Mom, can I go shopping and pick up a stereo?"

His mother smiled. A riyal was a fraction of a dollar. "Whatever. Now, son, listen to me very carefully." She sat him down. "Jeddah is beautiful, but it can be dangerous, too. Take the American compound bus only, do you hear?"

Beau rolled his eyes. "Yes, Mom."

"Here's our compound address, phone number, my work phone number, and the address. Make sure you take it. You can go over to the big American compound…there's a bowling alley, movies, and restaurants. But only ride the compound bus. It will be at the front gate at eight o'clock. Do you understand?"

"Yes, ma'am, I got it. I'll be fine."

She looked at her blonde, blue-eyed son. "I love you, honey." She gave him a kiss on the forehead.

Camille heard the familiar honk of the clinic bus. "Gotta go. Be home by four."

At work, it was another tense day. Naomi or Gerald didn't ask about her son's arrival. She had hardly expected it. Hamad, the new business manager, and she decided a color-coded patient file system would be effective for the clinic. They were busy trying colored markers when Naomi walked into the room. She frowned.

"What are you doing?"

"Coloring," Camille answered with some sarcasm before she could catch herself.

"I can see that. Why?"

"Naomi, we're looking at a color-coded system. It's used in a lot of hospitals and clinics. We thought it might be helpful, especially with the language problems we're going to have."

Naomi glanced at the table. "We don't need that." Then she walked back into her office.

"You made her angry," Hamad seemed concerned.

"I know. It just…came out."

Lost

The clinic phone rang.

"Hello," Fatma answered. "Camille Kohl? Yes, just one second, please."

"Hello, this is Camille Kohl—Beau? Where are you?"

"Mom—I don't know! I took a cab, and the driver can't find the palace."

"Didn't you give him the address?"

"Yes, but he still can't find it."

Lilly jumped up. "Let me talk to the cab driver."

"Hallo—hallo—" Lilly got out her Jeddah map and gave directions in Arabic. She finished, and put the phone down. "It's OK, Camille. He's Egyptian! His honor is at stake. He will get your son safely back."

Naomi had come out of her office. "What's going on?"

""Beau—he got a cab, and they're lost."

"Oh, by the way...don't let him take a yellow cab," Naomi advised casually.

"A yellow cab? Why not?"

"Well, sometimes the people in the yellow cabs don't make it back from their rides."

Camille was incredulous at how dispassionately Naomi delivered this message. Did she realize how truly cruel this was? "Now you tell me?" she asked.

Camille felt a building nausea deep in the pit of her stomach. She doubled over from the feeling. "What have I done to my son?" she asked aloud. "Why did I bring him here?"

Naomi walked back into her office and closed the door. The rest of the staff stood speechless.

Fatma recovered first. "Camille, you and I will go to the corner and look for the cab."

Camille hesitated.

"Come on, Camille, It's better than sitting around here."

"I'll stay by the phone in case the cab driver calls back," Lilly volunteered.

Camille and Fatma gathered up their *abayas* and headed toward the front gate. The guards approached.

"Where are you going?" the tall guard asked Fatma in Arabic.

"Her son is lost. The cab is in this area."

"Very well. But stay in sight at all times."

Camille and Fatma stood on the corner, covered in their *abayas*. Cars passed. Men called out to them. More time passed. A carload of men drove slowly by, then turned around and stopped in front of them. The palace guards watched nervously from the gates, ready to intervene.

Fatma threw her hands up, and her many bracelets jangled as she talked. "Go away, you crazy men!"

The palace guards decided this was enough. They approached the car.

"Fatma, I think we'd better go in."

"Yes, I think we must."

As Fatma and Camille entered the clinic door, they saw Safiya sitting at the table.

"I hear your son is lost."

"Yes, Safiya. His first day here!"

Safiya smiled gently. "He'll be alright. Lilly tells me he is with a good cab driver." She changed to mock sternness. "Now, how do you think it looks...you two women standing out on the corner of my house?"

Camille put her hands up to indicate her bewilderment. The ringing phone startled her.

"Camille, it's your son again!" Fatma said excitedly.

Camille rushed to the phone. "Beau! Where——?"

"Mom! I'm alright! I'm back at the villa. And the cab driver...he said he wouldn't charge me, because it was his duty to bring me back safe."

"Oh, Beau! You don't know how relieved I am! Now, stay put! I'll be home in less than an hour."

"OK, Mom. Your maid is making me some dinner."

Camille put the phone down and sighed deeply. She looked around the room, tears in her eyes. "Thanks, everyone. You were all great."

Camille was especially happy to get home that night. "Beau!" she burst into the door.

"Hi, Mom..." Beau was sitting cross-legged on the living room floor reading a comic book.

Samantha came down the stairs. "Oh, Mum, your son is so handsome."

"Thanks, Sam. Right now, he's also dog meat."

"Dinner is ready for you."

"Great. You can knock off early."

Samantha looked confused.

"I mean, you may leave early."

"Oh, OK. Bye, Mister Beau."

Camille sat cross-legged on the floor with her son.

"OK, Beau, tell me what happened."

Beau grinned sheepishly. "Well, Mom, I got on the American bus just like you said. I checked out the American compound—big deal. So I walked out the gate, and caught a city bus."

"You did what?"

"You know, one of the regular busses. I got to see the downtown, and the docks by the sea. Gad—you should see all the hundreds of scrawny cats by the docks. What's up with the cats, anyway?"

"Beau," Camille continued questioning, trying to be patient, "how did you get the cab?"

"Well, I got off the bus when the driver asked me for some kind of change—he didn't like my bills. He let me ride for free, but I think he was glad when I got off."

Camille's patience was wearing thin. "Bottom line, kid."

"OK, OK. I started walking toward some cabs. One waved me down. He said, 'American?' I said, 'Yes, why?' He said, 'I take you wherever you want to go—500 riyals. I said, 'You'll get 100, or you'll get nothing.' He decided to take 100, but I decided not to trust him.

"The next cab driver pulled up, and he seemed better. I gave him directions to the palace, but he got lost. He said something about being Egyptian and honor—that he'd get me back no matter how long it took. Someone finally gave him directions to our compound. Then, Mom, he wouldn't take any money."

"Did you get his name or phone number?"

"No. Why?"

"To thank him."

Camille got up off the floor and sat in a chair. "Beau you do the usual kid stuff, but you've never disobeyed me about something important. What possessed you to go off the American compound?"

"Mom, I was just so excited to be here. I just wanted to see it all—" he threw his hands out expansively, "in one day."

She regarded her son. Beau looked hesitant.

"You...you're not going to send me home, are you?" he asked.

Camille put her hands on her son's shoulders and looked into Beau's eyes. "Beau...do you promise to listen to me, and not take those kind of chances any more?"

"Mom, I promise. I'll stay right here in the compound tonight. Your American friends—their kid Jeremy is my age. He asked me if I could watch some videos with him."

"That's fine. They're in Villa Seven. Just be home by nine-thirty. It's your first day of school tomorrow."

Beau grinned, returning to his usual carefree self. He jumped up, then stopped at the door. "See? I even remembered to take my key."

The next morning, Camille knew there was a problem when she had been told "Beau's schooling is all arranged." She and Beau waited at the designated corner at the allotted time. No bus. Twenty minutes later, Camille was now fuming.

"Chill out, Mom!" her son laughed.

"Well, Beau, I'm tired of waiting. It looks like you're going to be a little late this morning. Maybe I can get our clinic driver to take you."

Camille and Beau walked to the back of the villa. A few minutes later, her buzzer rang. She picked up her briefcase. "C'mon, Beau. Plan B."

The clinic bus driver, who spoke fair English, looked at Beau.

"Mofi, this is my son, Beau. Beau, this is Mofi, our driver. This is Beau's first day of school, and his school bus didn't come. Could you please take him?"

"No problem, Doctora. I drop Doctora Naomi's daughter there."

Mofi looked at the blonde, gangly twelve-year-old American. He broke into a wide, semi-toothy grin, and patted the seat next to him. "Mr. Beau, please to sit up front!"

Beau looked at his mother and put his nose up in the air, and laughed. "Men up front!" he chortled.

Camille climbed behind Beau. "Don't get any ideas, kid." She looked at Lilly and mumbled, "Eight years of college, and my twelve-year-old son gets to ride in the front of the bus."

Lilly shook her head. "I was visiting one of my old friends last night. Now that her son is older, he's taken over all of her money. He's even put her on an allowance, and tells her whom she can see. Last night, he threatened to beat her because she had me over for dinner. He doesn't approve of me."

Camille looked out the window. "Can you imagine...carrying a child for nine months, raising him, and loving him for years—then he turns around and abuses you? Under those circumstances, why would you even want to have children?"

Lilly shrugged. "Because you don't have a choice. Birth control is banned."

The two women were introspective until they reached the clinic.

Camille looked at her son as she got off the bus. "Now, Beau—you have all the phone numbers and addresses. Please call me the minute you get to school."

The women walked in the clinic door.

"Doctora Camille, Doctora Naomi wants to see you," Fatma greeted.

Camille took a deep breath and knocked on Naomi's door.

"Oh, hi, Camille. Look, I'm way behind here. The equipment people will be here at nine. You'll have to meet them. Pick out what equipment we need for the clinic."

"Sure." Camille turned to leave.

"One more thing," Naomi cautioned, "this is Safiya's cousin. Don't say anything too out of line, alright?"

"Alright, Naomi. I'll be the perfect lady."

Camille was impressed when the two gentlemen arrived precisely at nine a.m. Even though dressed in the customary white *thobes*, they spoke English with an American accent. Camille relaxed somewhat.

The two Arab businessmen brought out folders. They discussed equipment and wiring specifications.

"My first choice is the C-arm 360 model," Camille stated. "As a back-up, we could look at the stationary arm, but that's more cumbersome."

"Very good, Doctora." The older man wrote the model numbers down.

"Oh, one more question. We want the personnel to be safe, since they'll be using the equipment daily. What are the scatter rates on these machines?"

The younger man looked at her intently. He appeared to be studying her. He took his time, unembarrassed by his open interest.

"Ah—" he finally said, "I'll fax you that data. It's in the technical specs back at the office." He paused. "No, I think you should see an actual model of the C-arm. I will have my driver take you to my office tomorrow." He opened a leather appointment calendar. "Shall we say eleven o'clock?"

Camille hoped the look on her face didn't belie her concern. She looked up and saw Naomi watching, and gave Naomi a questioning look. Naomi hesitated for a moment, then nodded.

"Uh, sure. Eleven o'clock."

"Very well." He extended his hand for her to shake. "It was very nice meeting you, Camille."

The American woman hesitated. This Western business custom was a little risqué for the setting, and Safiya's cousin knew it. She slowly extended her hand.

He grasped it firmly. Then, looking into the American woman's eyes, he gave her hand a subtle, yet firm squeeze.

A jolt of energy traveled up Camille's arm, and she reflexively pulled her hand away. The Arab man had communicated his intentions clearly to her, and it wasn't about equipment. Flushed, she lowered her head. She could sense this handsome, wealthy Arab businessman was powerful in his world. She felt some concern, guessing that this man was used to getting pretty much what he wanted.

"Goodbye, Camille," he said softly. "I look forward to our meeting tomorrow."

"Doctora Camille?" Fatma interrupted, "Phone call. It's the school."

Relieved, Camille walked over to the phone.

"Hello? Beau, please tell me—"

"Yes, I'm at the school," Beau interrupted. "Miss Sally wants to talk to you."

"Miss Sally? This is Beau's mother, Camille."

"Hi, Camille. Sorry about the bus mix up. We didn't get the new schedule entered into the computer until eight-thirty. The bus will be there tomorrow morning at seven-thirty. If it's more than ten minutes late, call me office, will you?"

"Great. Thanks, Miss Sally."

Camille poured a cup of coffee and settled down to work. She looked at the equipment brochure. "Neat!" she said happily, "a new C-arm!"

Hala approached. "Doctora Camille?"

Camille looked up and smiled. She liked the sweet, gentle voice and demure ways of this young professional Saudi woman.

"Well, good morning, Hala. How are you?"

Hala's smile was cryptic. "Good. I have some news..."

"Yes?"

"I'm going to have a baby."

Camille quickly calculated. Hala had been married three months now. "Hala, congratulations!"

Hala lowered her head and blushed slightly. "Thank you."

Naomi's office door opened. "Camille, have you got the equipment figures?"

"Yep." She picked up the folder and walked into Naomi's office.

"Close the door," Naomi ordered. "You heard?"

"About what? Hala? Yes, she told me."

Naomi leaned back. "You know how much work we're going to get out of her now?"

"No, how much?"

"Well, now we've got morning sickness. Next, she'll take off days at a time because her husband won't want her to work too hard. Then, she'll be out a month or so for the delivery. We may or may not get her back after that."

Camille sat for a moment. "You know, Naomi, I see your point. It's hard to operate when staff attendance isn't reliable. But...does Hala really have any choice about being pregnant?"

"I suppose not."

"Then, we might as well try to be happy for her. Is that all?"

"For now."

Safiya joined the staff for lunch. The mood was light, and the staff seemed more open.

"The Gulf War was pretty scary," Hala ventured.

"Oh, yes." Fatma jangled her bracelets and flipped her hair back in agreement.

"We didn't know if or when the chemical weapons would be used," Hamad, the business manager, added.

"Gee, it's hard for me to even comprehend being that close to a war," Camille thought aloud.

Looking for a Wife

A servant respectfully approached Safiya and whispered in her ear. Camille caught the name; it was Safiya's cousin. The rest of the staff went back to their workstations. Safiya glanced toward Camille with a puzzled look, then rose from her seat to take the phone call. Fatma was merrily listening to music from her headset and pecking slowly away at her keyboard.

Camille's desk was only five feet from the extension. Safiya picked up the extension phone. Camille tried to pretend she wasn't listening, but clearly this was a matter concerning her.

Safiya's family spent time in France. She knew Camille was learning Arabic, so she turned her back and started speaking in French. What she didn't know was that Camille came from a long line of French settlers in New Orleans.

"*Oui?*...Yes, she has a husband...No, he's only coming for a short visit. Why are you so interested? Yes, my brother is married to an American woman, but this is different. Besides, I don't think she's that special..."

Camille was pretending to be absorbed in a book, but made a face at Safiya's back about her apparent assessment.

"She's very independent," Safiya continued in French.

Camille looked nonchalantly toward the door, concentrating on blowing a huge bubble from the large wad of bubble gum she'd stuffed into her mouth.

"I don't know if she is even trainable..."

Camille had been concentrating on blowing a large, pink bubble of gum, and it was now a healthy eight inches around. When she heard Safiya's words, the bubble made a large "pop" all over Camille's face.

Hearing the noise, Safiya glanced her way. Then she turned back to her conversation. "OK—if you want some time. Yes, I understand. You can stall his entrance visa." Safiya hung up the phone. Her back still turned, she stood there for almost a minute. Then, turning, she brightly said, "There now! Enough business for one day. I think I'll go see what my children are up to."

Camille marveled at Safiya's self-composure as she gingerly pulled the mass of bubble gum off her face. A wave of reality hit her suddenly. She could be stuck in this country forever. The color drained from her face.

Hala walked toward the clinic director with a stack of papers. "Doctora Camille, are you alright?"

"Wha—? Oh, I guess I've just got some cramps, or something. You know, it's that time."

"I'll make you some herbal tea. I brought a special blend," Hala volunteered.

It's Not *Real* Money, You Know

After work, an eager son greeted Camille, ready to share his new-found discoveries.

"Mom! What a great day!" Beau looked around. "Where's dinner? I'm starved."

"Honey, remember I told you Charles was fixing dinner?"

"Oh, yeah. I forgot."

"I told him you like shrimp."

"He made shrimp?"

"That's what he said." Camille looked at her watch. "In fact, we're supposed to be over there already."

Camille watched as Beau skipped ahead and arrived at Charles' door. "Mr. Charles! Thanks for making us dinner!"

Charles was carrying a silver serving tray of hot rolls to the table.

"Not a problem, Beau. Sit here, please...now, what do you want to drink?"

"Coke."

"But of course," Charles commented sarcastically.

Beau looked around. "This place is really nice. It looks better than my mom's villa."

"Yes, I know. Quite a point of contention with her." Charles put the tray on the table, then switched on the stereo. Soft strains of Tina Turner filled the room.

"What's love got to do, got to do with it? What's love, but a second-hand emotion..." Charles sat down and listened for a moment to the song. He chuckled with some bitterness at the words. "Right. Now, Beau, tell us...how was your first day of school?"

"It was great! You should see the girls!"

"They're attractive, are they?" Charles asked, grinning.

"The Swedish girls, the Norwegian girls...they're...goddesses!"

"Goddesses?" Camille burst out laughing, surprised by such exuberance.

"Yeah. This one Swedish girl...I went up to her and asked if she'd ever date anyone besides someone from her own country..."

"What did she say?" Charles encouraged.

"She just looked at me. Then she said 'What for?' And...getting to school this morning was fun..."

"It was?"

"Yeah, we had to wait a little while. There was a sixteen-car pile-up!"

"Beau—no!" Camille became alarmed as she remembered about the traffic problems.

"Yes! I've seen some pile-ups in New Orleans, but sixteen cars? I counted 'em!"

Camille winced.

"But we had the most fun on the school bus coming home."

"Oh, really? How's that?" Charles was getting into this. He poured more Coke for Beau.

"Jason, he's my friend; he's from England...well, he brought a copy of *Playboy* magazine. We held the fold-out of the naked lady up to the window of the back seat."

"Beau!" Camille burst out.

Undaunted, her son continued. "The bus driver started gibbering 'give me that, give me that.' Jason said, 'Speak English, I cahn't understand you.' The driver said, 'But I am speaking the English, I am, I am!' It was great!"

Beau laughed and heaped more shrimp on his plate. "Jason said to the driver, 'You just want the pictures yourself'." Beau broke off and looked at Charles. "You're from England, right?"

"Wales, actually."

"Wales? Isn't that next to Australia?"

Charles sat back, deeply offended. "Bloody hell!"

Beau threw back his head and laughed at Charles' reaction.

"Honey, Wales is a part of Great Britain." Camille looked at Charles apologetically. "It's a deficit in American schools. The emphasis is more on memorizing fifty state capitals."

"Test me! I know all fifty!" Beau beamed.

"Not now, honey."

"Oh, Mom, I've got a field trip coming up. Can I trade you my dollars for more riyals?"

Charles handed Beau the serving dish of shrimp sauce. "Why would you need to trade?" she asked.

"For spending money."

"You can spend your dollars anywhere; the two currencies are tied together—dollars, riyals." Charles lifted his chin in displeasure at the perceived slight. "But not the British pound! It's not like *real* money, you know!"

Beau laughed delightedly. "That's a good one, Mr. Charles. I'll have to remember that."

"Where's your field trip, honey?"

"Oh—out in the desert."

Charles raised his eyebrows. "The desert? You'll enjoy that. Just be careful of the camel spiders."

"What are camel spiders?"

"Well, they actually won't be much of a problem if you don't fall asleep," Charles teased. "You see, they're big spiders that eat flesh. They inject anesthetizing venom while the victim is asleep. Then the spider can leisurely eat away at the flesh, and the victim doesn't feel a thing."

Beau was fascinated. "Really?"

"Really. I know of a fellow who woke up with half his cheek chewed off."

Beau's eyes were big with wonder. "Cool!"

"So, Beau," Charles looked toward the kitchen, "you want dessert?"

"What you got?"

Camille frowned. "Beau, we'll have to work on your manners some."

"Actually, it's fresh lemon torte. Quite good."

Charles brought the dessert to the table.

Beau wasn't convinced, but he wanted to be polite. "Well, let me try a bite." He swallowed the torte and made a face. His eyes wandered to the TV set. Charles had turned the volume down, but the picture was still playing. "May I be excused?" he asked, jumping up from the table.

"Yes, you may be excused," Camille commented sharply, hoping to make a point.

Beau ignored her. "What's this?" he asked Charles. "It looks like a comedy, but everybody's wearing Arab clothes."

"That's an Egyptian comedy," Charles explained. "The Saudis are not allowed to be actors."

Beau's eyes widened again. He was enjoying this. "They can't even be actors? Bummer..."

"Well, if you're not going to finish your dessert, you can help with the dishes," his mother decided.

"Sure." Beau picked up the dishes and started towards the kitchen.

"Leave it. The maid will be here in thirty minutes." Charles looked at Camille. "I was planning on going shopping for a Persian rug tonight. Would you two like to go along?"

Beau lowered his head, then looked pleadingly at his mother. "Uh, Mom? Jeremy just got some new video games today..."

"Son, I thought you wanted a genuine Persian rug for your bedroom."

"I do. But—could you pick it out for me, please?"

Camille grinned mischievously. "I have an idea, Charles. Why don't you take Ashley with you when she comes next week? She'd love the experience."

Charles thought for a moment. "You're right. Anyway, there's a party going on over at Cedric's villa. Would you like to join it? They're most likely fairly pissed by now."

"Pissed?" Beau asked. "Are they mad at you?"

"Mad? Uh, no, Beau, they're not angry."

"But, you said they were pissed."

"Yes, pissed."

"Then they're mad."

"Oh...no, that means drunk."

"Hmm, that's a funny name for it. Do you mind if I go now, Mom?"

"No, go ahead. Just be home by–"

"Nine-thirty," Beau finished. Beau turned to leave, "Thanks, Mr. Charles, for the dinner and all." Beau was out the door.

Camille put her hand on Charles' arm. "Charles—"

Charles looked at her hand, then her face. "What?"

"One of Safiya's cousins owns a medical equipment company in Jeddah. I met him today about our equipment orders."

"So?"

"So...this is too strange...He—he likes me, Charles. He called Safiya about me."

Charles leaned closer. "What did Safiya say?"

"Oh!" Camille laughed. "She tried to discourage him. She said I wasn't much of a prize."

Charles laughed. "Well, you are rather...shall we say, strong willed?"

Camille gripped Charles' arm tighter. "Safiya couldn't seem to dissuade him. He said something about holding up my husband's entrance visa. He can't make me stay here in the country, can he?"

Charles pulled back. He looked upwards for a moment, then sighed. His words had the chilling effect of blunt reality. "Oh, yes. Yes, he can."

Camille sat in her chair, unable to move with their import.

Charles stood up, grabbed Camille's hands, and pulled her up off the sofa. "But this is a problem we can't solve tonight, can we? I'm going to go join the others before they get any more 'pissed'. Come along for a few minutes. It will take your mind off more serious matters."

Camille walked numbly with Charles to Cedric's noisy villa.

"Look! It's Camille!" The group broke out into song, "New Orleans ladies…"

"Oh, not again," Camille laughed. She looked at her watch. "Oh, I have to call my sister." She calculated the time. "I'd better hurry before it gets any later. Bye, y'all!"

The men stopped singing. "Bye, y'all!" three of them shouted in unison.

Camille started the next workday in carefree spirits. Then she remembered…she had an appointment with Zayad, the owner of the medical equipment company. She threw herself into an ambitious, computerized inventory system to keep her mind off the upcoming meeting.

At precisely eleven o'clock, an Arab man entered the clinic and approached the American. "Doctora? Mr. Zayad sent me. You will come with me now."

Camille glanced around the clinic, as if looking for help. No one seemed aware of the drama unfolding. She picked up her briefcase and *abaya*. "Very well."

The chauffeur opened the door to the black Mercedes and she got in. The chauffeur drove without conversation across the city. He pulled in front of a large, modern office building and opened her car door. Another Arab man was waiting in the foyer. He opened the door, then escorted her to the elevators. Without words, both entered the elevator. The Arab pushed some buttons, and they ascended to the top floor.

The doors opened, and Camille cautiously stepped out onto white polished marble floors. She looked around. The spacious office complex was understated, yet elegant…expensive Persian rugs, large palms, and designer furniture. The Arab escort motioned seriously toward a large sofa. Camille sat.

Fifteen minutes passed. Camille picked up an Arabic newspaper and leafed through it. Although the words were in Arabic, she could at least look at the pictures.

Another Arab finally approached her. "Come with me, please. You will see the machines."

Camille followed the man down the hall and into a room. An Arab in a white technician's coat greeted her. "Welcome, Doctora. You have questions for me?"

Camille inspected the equipment, and the technician expertly explained the system details.

"I have copies of all the specifications right here. And here is my card. If you have more questions, please call me."

The technician picked up the phone and dialed. "She's ready," he stated in Arabic.

The first Arab appeared at the door. "Follow me, please."

He led her down the hall to another office, and knocked on the door.

"*Dakhal* (enter)," a voice from within said.

Camille walked into the room alone.

Zayad was on the phone, talking in Arabic. "Yes, she's here now. I'll be taking her to lunch. She won't be back until..." he glanced at the woman, "later." He hung up the phone.

"So, Camille, did you like the C-arm?"

"Yes. And your technician was very knowledgeable."

"Of course." He paused for a moment to write a brief note, then looked at her. "I'm taking you to a restaurant which very few Westerners ever see. You will get specialty dishes that you can't get in...Biloxi."

Camille stood and looked at him without comment. She hadn't recalled being asked if she wished to have lunch with this man. For a brief moment, her unresponsiveness seemed to unsettle him. But he quickly recovered his overpowering self-assurance. Zayad picked up the phone again.

"Bring my car around," she heard him order in Arabic. He walked toward the office door. "After you," he said, sweeping his hand toward the hall gallantly.

The chauffeur drove them into a part of Jeddah which was unfamiliar. Zayad was quiet. He nodded to the chauffeur as they alighted at the restaurant, and the chauffeur drove off. They walked past the canopied entrance into a lush entryway.

Camille looked around. The fair-skinned blonde with her *abaya* thrown on haphazardly was a stark contrast to the group she faced. The Saudi women were not only totally covered in their black *abayas,* but many were also wearing facemasks. Camille watched in fascination as the women discreetly lifted their face shields from beneath to eat and drink. This was definitely the conservative upper crust of Saudi society.

The men cast curious glances at Zayad; the women cast disapproving looks at the only Westerner in the restaurant. Camille looked at Zayad. She could tell her escort was enjoying the reaction.

The waiter quickly and reverently seated them.

"I'll order for you," Zayad stated. He quickly rattled off foreign-sounding items to the waiter.

Camille had been studying him. This man was tall, well built, and remarkably attractive. He possessed a casually regal bearing.

The Arab now placed his full attention on his dinner guest. He looked directly into her eyes. Camille was surprised to see that his eyes were a tawny, golden color. There was no apparent malice in them. In fact, she was startled to sense a loving, sensual nature saddened by a trace of loneliness.

"Well, now, Camille," he broke into her thoughts, "tell me why you're in the Kingdom alone."

Camille was caught off guard by his question. "Uh…why?" She fought for composure. "Well, I wanted to help set up the first clinic in the Kingdom."

"Your husband…why is he not with you?"

"He's a doctor. He has his own medical practice."

Zayad sat back in his chair and crossed his arms. "A husband would not do this."

Camille did not answer immediately. She knew the stories of Westerners disappearing in the Kingdom, yet also knew Zayad's family was quite honorable. Undoubtedly, Hans' frustrated phone conversations with her had been reported to him in detail. Zayad appeared to be an astute business man sensing an opportunity.

Camille carefully weighed her need for self-preservation with her need for defending her freedom, and decided to risk being honest. "A husband would not do what exactly, Zayad?"

"Leave his wife unattended in a foreign country. You are his responsibility."

"I'm my own responsibility," the American bristled.

Zayad's eyes showed amusement. He was actually enjoying her resistance.

Camille sensed his readiness for a challenge, and decided to switch tactics. "Zayad, do you have a wife?"

Sadness stole across his glistening eyes for a moment. "Yes, I had a wife," he held up his glass for the waiter. "She died in childbirth."

Camille's face softened for a moment. "Oh, I'm sorry. But you're a very attractive man. With your looks, wealth, and influence, I'm sure you're considered quite a catch in your circle."

"Maybe," he leaned forward, "I don't want to look in my 'circle', as you say."

Camille glanced down at her plate.

"You have only one child, don't you? A boy..." Zayad continued.

"Yes, just the one."

"This is somewhat unusual. Were there—problems?"

"No. No problems. I only wanted one child."

"Ah, interesting. But you could change your mind..."

Camille raised her water glass, sure she finally had the upper hand. "Nope," she said with some satisfaction, "I'm fixed." She was quite certain this would quell any more budding romantic interest.

He grinned. "Fixed?"

"Yes, sir, fixed. But I hear the Kingdom is filled with fertile women."

Zayad turned his head away for a moment. Then he put his hand down hard on hers. A disapproving gasp came from nearby tables. Camille tried to pull her hand away, but Zayad held it firmly.

"I'm not looking," he said evenly, "for a fertile woman. I have enough children. I'm looking for companionship—someone to keep me company in my travels." He let loose of his grip. "Camille, life could be so much easier for you..."

The regal Arab paid the waiter, then stood up. Camille stood, but he blocked her way for a moment.

"Your husband—he has made a grave error." Then Zayad let her pass.

As they walked out into the warm sunshine, Camille tried not to show the confusion Zayad had so keenly brought to the surface. Why had

Hans so easily let her go halfway across the world? Why wasn't he in any hurry to take a leave of absence from his practice, and join her?

The chauffeur opened the car door for them. Zayad looked at his watch. "It's too late for you to go back to the clinic. My driver will take you to your villa."

Camille spent a quiet night in her villa, contemplating her potential fate. Thankfully, tomorrow started the weekend. It would give her time to sort through her emotions.

Swimming in *Abayas*

At eleven-thirty the next morning, Beau was still in bed.

"Beau, c'mon, honey...get up. Looks like you're over your initial adrenaline charge of being in a new country."

"Huh? What? Mom, let me stay in bed."

"Well, I'm going to my seamstress's house. I'll be gone an hour. Then you need to get up, because I have a special surprise for you."

Beau's head came off the pillow. "What surprise?"

"When I get back, we're going scuba diving in the Red Sea."

Beau jumped out of bed. "Neat! I'll fix myself something to eat, and be ready."

Camille hailed a taxi. She knew her seamstress's house was only six blocks away, and she could easily walk it. But, not in this city. She wouldn't make it one block without constant harassment from men on the street and in cars. And, Camille knew from the reports, if she got hurt or raped, it would be considered her fault for "enticing" the man.

The taxi driver pulled to a stop.

"Sixteen Al-Hamra Street." He nodded. She got in. Camille studied the fabric samples as they drove. Five minutes. Ten. Fifteen. Camille looked up.

"We only had to go six blocks. Where are you going?"

The taxi driver shrugged. "No Anglise, no Anglise..."

Camille became angry. She wasn't going to play this game today. "Six blocks! That's all!" she shouted in Arabic.

The driver's eyes squinted at her. He immediately turned and headed back. She saw her seamstress's compound.

"Stop!" She got out.

The driver held out his hand. "Fifty riyals," he demanded.

"Oh, so now you speak English. Here's ten. Go screw yourself."

She walked into the gates of the compound and knocked on a door. A beautiful Egyptian woman answered.

"Camille, so nice to see you. Come in, come in. Would you care for some coffee?"

"No, thanks, FiFi. Sorry I'm late. The cab driver decided to jack me around."

"Do what?"

"Oh, I'm sorry...he tried to take me for a ride around the city instead of six blocks."

FiFi threw her hands up. "What can I say? These crazy men! After we're finished, I'll walk back with you to your villa."

"That's nice of you, FiFi, but then how will you get home?"

"These cabdrivers know me. And, they know my husband."

"Well, thanks. Did you finally get your new pattern books?"

FiFi threw up her hands once again, even more agitated this time. "I had beautiful pattern books from Paris. But, when I came to the airport here, the inspectors took them all away from me except one."

"Why? Why would they take your pattern books?"

"Because they said I had pictures of improperly clothed women. I pleaded with them—'it's for my business; only ladies see them'—but it didn't matter." She picked up a large pattern book, threw it on the table, and opened it.

"Here! This is what they did to my pictures!"

An airport inspector had meticulously and liberally used a black magic marker to cover the arms and legs of the models.

Camille sighed. "Gheez," she said finally, "I can at least get an idea of what I want."

FiFi took out her tape measure. "Camille, you've lost weight!"

"Yeah. It's all the healthy fresh vegetables and fish Safiya feeds me. What can I say?"

"But you look very good. Now...which materials would you like?"

The American woman held up a solid, light gray silk swatch.

FiFi looked puzzled. "You want a suit made out of–that?"

"Yeah. What's wrong with it?"

"It's–it's just so…dull! You need color, a bright pattern…This!" FiFi held up a bright orange and pink flowered silk. "Much more interesting!"

Camille laughed. FiFi looked confused.

"FiFi, that would look wonderful on you. You have such a deep, beautiful coloring. But I'm pale…this strong print would overwhelm me. Besides, I don't think corporate America is quite ready for this."

FiFi shrugged her shoulders. "Well, OK, if you want to use this dull material."

"Yes, I want the dull stuff."

"This will be finished for you in two weeks. I will call you when it's ready. Now…I walk you to your villa."

The two women enshrouded themselves in their black *abayas* and head covers. They walked out into the midday sun. Cars honked. Men waved and yelled rude suggestions. Within three blocks, a car with four men pulled up. One got out.

The two women kept walking. The man walked toward them, with the others following in the car.

FiFi glanced at Camille. "I hate this—I really hate this," she said through gritted teeth.

Camille saw the man stalking her from the right rear. She prepared herself. He grabbed the right sleeve of her *abaya*. Camille turned swiftly, jabbing her knee into his groin. Surprised and in pain, he doubled over. Camille turned to the three open-mouthed men in the car.

"LEAVE WOMEN ALONE!" she commanded in English.

FiFi stood grinning jubilantly. Her head rose with dignity. "Go bother someone else!" she said in Arabic.

The two women walked the last few blocks. Camille turned to FiFi.

"Here's some money for the cab back, FiFi. And…" she pressed a metal cylinder into the Egyptian woman's hand, "here's a spray can of mace. Use it wisely in the name of all harassed women!"

FiFi laughed. "Goodbye, Camille. It's been fun."

Camille opened her front door. Beau was sitting on the floor with three other boys.

"Hi, Mom! We're playing Monopoly."

She frowned. "Beau, you didn't ask…" Her words were interrupted by the doorbell. She opened the door to find a small Arab man with a big pizza box.

"Iz thees the villa of a Beau Stud-a-Muffin Kohl?"

All four boys broke into guffaws of laughter. Camille sighed. "Yes, it is."

"Forty riyals, please." Camille shot her son a disapproving glance.

"Mom—would you mind?"

Camille slapped 50 riyals into the man's hands. "*Sukran* (thanks)."

Beau opened up the pizza box. "Oh, I forgot…"

Camille opened the refrigerator door and took out the French dressing. "Here".

"Thanks, Mom."

Beau went back to his game. "You landed on Boardwalk, Stewart. You owe me 200 dollars."

"Dollars? I'll pay you in pounds!"

Beau jokingly put his nose up in the air, imitating Charles. "Pounds?" he exclaimed, feigning the Brit's accent. "It's not like—**real** money, you know!" He threw his head back, laughing manically at his own wit.

"Beau, I'm glad you're enjoying yourself, but we're going scuba diving. You gentlemen put the game up, eat your pizza, and we're out of here."

"Oh, alright." Beau passed around slices of pizza.

The doorbell rang. Camille opened it to find her American friends, Shelby and Dan.

"Are you ready?"

"Sure—OK—everybody out!"

A group of lanky, teenage boys filed out, munching on slices of pizza.

It was a mellow, bright blue afternoon sky with puffy white clouds. Dan parked the car in the lot at Hoda Beach.

"Mom! The water is so beautiful! Is that the Red Sea?"

"Yes, it is, Beau," Shelby answered. "Just wait until you see all the different colors of fish."

The boys eagerly put on their scuba gear and headed toward the water.

Camille and Shelby changed into baggy shorts and T-shirts.

"We're lucky we won the war…" Shelby mused.

"Why?"

"Because the Saudis temporarily relaxed the Western women's dress code for swimming. Normally, we'd be trying to scuba dive in *abayas*."

Camille's laugh was one of incredulity. "You are really, really kidding, right? How in the world could one swim in an *abaya*?"

"Well, I guess they didn't take into account water sports. At least on Hoda Beach, they usually leave us alone. But, you'll see some women out today at other beaches, trying to swim."

Still contemplating the sheer mechanics of trying to swim in an *abaya*, the women waded into the warm December waters.

"Look at the gorgeous colors of the coral!" Camille exclaimed. She followed Shelby out farther into the clear, blue waters. Shelby expertly continued her dive, exploring even further. Camille hesitated. "Uh...this is far enough for me. You go ahead."

Shelby smiled. "You're afraid, aren't you?"

"You got that right."

"But, you swim laps, don't you?"

"Yes, I do. And I know my feet can always touch the bottom of the pool."

"C'mon," Shelby encouraged, "remember...you're here for a little adventure."

Still with some trepidation, Camille followed her friend out into the deep azure water. She was surprised to find herself entranced with all the colorful species of fish. Camille glanced toward the shore and saw a man waving his arms.

"Shelby, isn't that your husband?"

"Yes. We'd better go in."

The two paddled leisurely to shore.

Camille was relaxed and pleasantly tired as she reached her villa.

"Mom," Beau announced, "I'm going to Charles' place."

"Why?"

"He told me he'd show me how to boil shrimp his special way. I made a deal with the guys. If Jimmy's dad got the shrimp, I'd fix it."

"Well, OK. But if Charles is busy, don't bother him now."

"I just called him. He told me I could get the shrimp and come over."

"Beau—" Camille was a little exasperated, but her son was already out the door. Camille saw people she knew sunning themselves around the pool. She quickly changed into her swimsuit and threw on a beach robe. As she was pouring herself iced tea to take to the pool, the doorbell rang.

Camille opened the door. Zayad, the Saudi businessman, stood there, replete in his white *thobe* and *gutra*. Camille's jaw hung open. It was an inviolate rule, she thought, for Arab men to come into Western compounds to socialize. She closed her surprised mouth and swallowed hard.

"Hello, Camille. I was passing the neighborhood, and thought I would stop and see your villa."

Camille allowed her laugh to contain some sarcasm. If only Zayad knew how trite that sounded.

"May I?"

"May you what, Zayad?"

"May I come in a moment?"

Camille felt a cold warning chill travel down her spine. Zayad was crossing the carefully fixed cultural boundaries. With resignation, she swept her hand toward her living room. He entered and sat. Camille casually left the front door opened slightly. She looked down and realized her beach robe was open. Even though her swimming suit was conservative, she retied the robe snugly around her.

The Arab showed the slightest hint of a smile. "So...you're happy here in Jeddah?"

Camille sighed. "It has its moments."

His face looked puzzled for a moment. "How about your son? Is he enjoying it here?"

"He seems to be, so far..."

Zayad looked too comfortable sitting on her sofa. Camille was tired of this fencing. She decided to use plain, down-home language.

"You don't want none of this," she stated flatly. "You don't have enough years left in your life to handle the grief I'd give you."

She stood across the room, waiting for the words to take effect. Then, she realized how badly she had miscalculated. This intelligent, wealthy Arab was bored. He was definitely up for the challenge, and she had just issued him a major one. His eyes gleamed like a race horse lined up at the gate.

Zayad's smile was one of anticipation. "Well, Camille, I must go now." He stood up and walked toward the door. Opening the door, he turned back toward Camille.

"I'm sure our paths will cross again soon."

Sponsor or Spy?

Camille stood at the door and watched the Arab as he walked past the group at the swimming pool. She could see their surprised eyes following him toward the gate. As Zayad disappeared through the gate, eight pairs of eyes collectively boomeranged back to the woman standing in the doorway.

"Now I have to go out there, before the gossip gets worse," she muttered to herself. She grabbed the glass of iced tea and pulled the door shut. She walked up to the group. "Mind if I join you?"

Several answered at once. "Oh, no, of course not." "Go right ahead." "Yes, do." "Certainly."

Camille pulled off her robe and stretched out into a deck lounger. Roger's Syrian wife was wearing a flowery bikini. She was just a bit heavier than what the bikini could handle, yet the woman seemed to revel in her near nakedness.

"It's so nice not to have that silly *abaya* on," the Syrian woman commented. She stretched out in a provocative way for emphasis. "Camille...your tummy is so flat. You should wear a bikini."

"Naw," Camille sipped her iced tea, "when I do laps, this is more practical."

Roger's wife looked unbelievingly at her. "You don't tell me you actually swim in your suit, do you?"

"Of course I do. Swimming is one of the best aerobic exercises around."

Camille laid back on the lounger and closed her eyes. She waited to see who would be the first to bring up the Saudi visitor. She could almost hear them thinking.

To no surprise, Janice picked up the topic. "Exercise...I've heard that word somewhere. Of course, being happily married—" the American woman glanced at Camille pointedly, then continued, "Henry and I can relax about our bodies, even if we do look like the Pillsbury Doughboy," she finished with a giggle.

"What's a Pillsbury Doughboy?" one of the Brits asked.

"It's a white, plump little dough man on a TV commercial," Camille explained.

Henry took up now, following his wife's lead. "But then, my wife's not the femme fatale of the compound…"

Camille kept her eyes closed, enjoying the warm December sun. "Femme fatale, Henry?"

"Why, yes. Everybody knows it."

"Ah…now we're getting to the crux of the matter." Camille opened her eyes and directed them at the plump American. "Everybody knows what, Henry?"

"Like that Arab who just left. He's a member of the family. Why did he come here to see you?"

Camille reached for her sunglasses. "Something about clinic equipment," she lied. "Why?"

"Why?" Henry snorted. "I'm supposed to be your sponsor, that's why. I'm supposed to look out for you."

"A job for which you volunteered. At least you got the first two letters of the job description correct."

"Whaddaya mean?"

"Sponsor—spy, I guess it's close enough." Camille closed her eyes again. She could feel Henry's anger building.

"I'm just looking out for your safety. You're an American. You've got half the Brits in the compound after you."

"They're called friends, Henry. Some of us have them."

Henry's anger boiled over into an emotional rage. He was no longer thinking about the consequences of his words. His voice became even louder and more nasal. "You're so naïve, Camille. That's why I have to protect you from yourself," he whined. "You just don't know how to handle these Brits!" he finished, booming his final words.

Janice, his wife, shifted uncomfortably in her chair. The Brits looked at each other with hurt and confusion.

Camille slammed down her glass. "That's enough! You know, Henry, you do like the Pillsbury Doughboy in that bathing suit, and I think that's the—if you'll excuse the pun—the 'meat' of the matter."

"What does that suppose to mean?"

"Look at you, Henry. You stuff yourself with food and don't exercise. My guess is that the Doughboy's dough isn't rising like it used to…"

Camille glanced at his wife, whom she knew had been gossiping about her. "So," she played with the words, "you're projecting your prurient interests on what you presume to be my passionate, private life. Well, it's all in your mind, Henry. But, hey…if that's the only way you can get your jollies…"

Henry stood up, livid, knocking his chair backward from the force. He stomped off. His embarrassed wife followed behind him.

The group watched the couple disappear into the refuge of their villa. Jamie, the Brit professor, laughed playfully.

"Let's see…" he began, "projecting, prurient, presume, passionate, private—that's quite the example of alliteration, isn't it?"

"Yes, it was fun," Camille admitted. "But I should have resisted the temptation. I know I'll be getting the payback."

"It was a good thing Charles wasn't here," Sam, the complex manager, sniffed. "He wouldn't stand for that kind of talk."

A light breeze caught the blue envelope from the chair where Henry had been sitting. The envelope landed next to Camille's feet. "What's this?' she asked. "It has my name on it."

"Oh, Henry told us he'd pick up your mail for you."

"He did, did he?" She turned the envelope over. "It's been opened!"

Camille felt suddenly tired from the back-to-back confrontations. "Y'all, I'm wiped out. I'm going to check on my son, then call it a day." She stood up and put on her robe. She walked the six villas to Charles. The door was open, and the villa was filled with the smell of cooked shrimp and spices.

"Hey, Mom, look what Mr. Charles taught me!" Beau held up a huge bucket of boiled shrimp. "Now he's making me clean up!" her son cheerily announced.

Charles looked at her through raised eyebrows.

Camille laughed. "I know…but I think Beau's adopted you."

"OK," Beau reported. "All done with the clean up. But before I go, you've got to give me an honest opinion on my shrimp."

Charles tried to pass off a stern look, but Camille knew he enjoyed the boy's open fascination with him.

"Beau, be home soon, hear? It's a school day tomorrow."

"Yes, ma'am."

Camille smiled at Charles. "Thanks." She closed the door gently, then walked to her villa and collapsed on the sofa. The tired woman carefully opened the letter. It was from Katherine, one of her friends who had recently moved to the Black Hills in South Dakota.

"Whoosh—do you feel that cool mountain air? Just thought you might need it right now...Hey, girl, how's Saudi Arabia? I hear Ashley's packing to join you. Remmy and Ashley are seeing a lot of each other. I don't know how he's going to handle her leaving, especially after losing her once before..."

CHAPTER 7
Ashley Arrives

Early winter was a beautiful time on the Gulf Coast. During the day, the warm sun seemed to gently caress one's skin. At night, the light sultriness in the air was mixed with soft, playful breezes. The gentle sunlight lazily made its way through the curtains to Ashley's bedroom. She sat on the floor, surrounded by her luggage. She had dutifully packed long, conservative outfits carefully prepared by a seamstress who was more accustomed to sewing Mardi Gras ball gowns.

Ashley lay back against her bed and sighed. What was she doing, she thought? Remmy was the only man for whom she'd ever had deep feelings. Perhaps it was the intensity of those feelings that had frightened her so much before. Now, she wanted Remmy more than ever. She was terrified of going to Saudi Arabia. Yet, she would always regret not knowing what she had missed if she didn't go. And, some small, nagging voice kept asking…"I guess I wasn't good enough for Jimmy. After all, he dumped me. How can I be good enough for Remmy?'

The doorbell interrupted her thoughts. She wiped her tears and walked to the door.

"Remmy," she greeted him flatly. She tried to push back mixed emotions as she looked at his handsome, chiseled face in the morning sun.

"Ashley…I just can't believe I'm actually driving you to the airport. Girl, I should be barring the doors."

Ashley blushed. "I…know."

The couple drove in silence to the airport. As Remmy helped the porter, each suitcase seemed to increasingly mock him, as if to say "she's going further—and further away." As Remmy heard the announcement for Ashley's plane, anger welled up inside him. What kind of fool was he, anyway?

Ashley looked expectantly up at Remmy's face. "I—I just have to go, Remmy. I want to help start the new clinic, the first for their country."

Remmy responded by brushing a perfunctory kiss close to her cheek. "That's the only reason I'm sending you off. But, Ashley, I just don't know how much more time I've got in me to wait."

Ashley turned from him and started to walk down the gantry. Her head was reeling as alternating waves of deep regret and fear overcame her. She braced herself against the wall for a moment, then, on trembling legs, managed to walk weakly to the airplane before collapsing into her seat. By the time the plane had landed in New York, Ashley's sorrow had turned to anger. If Remmy couldn't understand, she decided, then—just screw him!

The next day at the clinic was uneventful. Safiya and Naomi had summoned Camille to the office with the brief instructions, "Remember, you're responsible for giving Ashley her work assignments. And keep her out of trouble at the compound."

"How——" Camille began to ask.

"Just keep her out of trouble," Safiya reiterated.

Camille went back to her desk, mumbling. "I'm going to have to watch Ashley at the office and at the villa—lucky me."

That night, the phone was ringing as Camille walked into her villa.

"Ready to go to the airport?" asked Charles in his ever-resonant, expectant tone.

"Anxious, are we? Could I at least wash my face first? Then I'll be over."

The drive to the Jeddah International Airport was uneventful. Charles parked the car, then he and Camille searched the incoming flight information board for arrivals.

"Ah, here it is. Right on time."

Camille remembered Lilly's gut-wrenching entry into the Kingdom. "I just hope she doesn't have any trouble with Customs."

"Don't worry," the Brit assured her. "Different circumstances..." Charles stopped in mid-sentence. His lips parted slightly, and he stood as if transfixed.

Camille looked in the direction of Charles' gaze and let out a surprised gasp. A tall, slender woman of regal bearing stood waiting for her luggage. She was wearing an *abaya,* but it was of a silver color, elegantly embroidered with hand-tailored silver threading. Her long, dark hair was piled on her head, accentuating a light, cream-colored complexion and large green eyes. The guards who had been so rough with Lilly treated Ashley as if she were some delicate flower.

"Huh! Imagine that—a silver-colored *abaya.* Now, why didn't I think of that?" Camille mused.

"Sorry?" Charles asked, his mind elsewhere. He was edging toward the glass walls where passengers were filing out into the lobby. "Bloody hell. She is stunning."

Camille put her hands on her hips. "I thought you liked blue-eyed brunettes."

"Close enough..." Charles grinned.

Camille didn't appreciate the fact that Charles would "make do" with her only sister. "Charles, 'close enough' only counts in horseshoes."

The Brit looked puzzled for a moment. "Sorry?"

"Oh, never mind."

Ashley smiled at her sister. "Cammy!"

The two gave each other a brief hug. Then, the younger sister fixed her eyes on the handsome Brit, smiling coyly. "Well, Charles. Nice to finally meet you." She extended her hand to Charles, but he reflexively stepped back.

"Remember, Ashley," her older sister reminded, "you can't touch men in public."

"Oh, that's right."

Charles signaled the porters to follow him with Ashley's bags. After they were packed into the car, the porters' hands stretched expectantly toward Ashley.

Ashley grinned at her sister. "Hon, could you take care of it? I don't have any change yet."

Camille shook her head and dug into her purse. "So, what's new?"

The conversation back to the compound was pleasant, but formal.

"Sam and Katie insisted we bring her over to meet them," Charles reminded her. As compound manager, it was an unspoken tradition that newcomers were introduced to him first.

Camille thought of what Katie's reaction might be. "I don't know if she's ready for that." She turned to Ashley. "You must be tired from your trip."

"No, actually I slept a lot on the plane."

"Camille," Charles chided, "quit playing big sister. It looks as though Ashley can take care of herself."

Camille gave a little disgruntled sound. "Alright."

Charles pulled the car up to her villa door and helped unload suitcases.

"Let Ashley freshen up, then bring her round. I'll go prepare Sam and Katie."

Samantha, the maid, seemed intrigued with this new woman. "Pretty *abaya*." She looked up shyly at Ashley. "May I touch?"

Ashley laughed and pulled the silver garment off. "You may try it on if you wish."

"Oooh...thanks, Mum."

Ashley quickly showered and changed into a long, sleeveless summer dress and sandals, which she customarily wore on the coast. As the two sisters walked toward the compound manager's villa, Camille nervously briefed her.

"Katie, the manager's wife, has this thing for Charles. She was jealous of me, jealous of Beau, and she sure enough is going to perceive you as a threat, especially since you're not married."

Ashley stopped walking. "But, she's married. Why would it matter?"

Camille looked up at the night sky, sighing. "Exactly, hon. All's I know is that she idolizes Charles....and, she's got a screw loose."

A Real Singer

The two women arrived at Sam's door, which was already open. Sam stood at the door.

"Welcome, my dears!" He grabbed Ashley's hand. "Well, isn't this pleasant...to meet Camille's sister!"

Sam turned toward his wife. "Ashley, this is my wife, Katie."

Katie sat stiffly in the middle of the sofa, straightening her ever-present apron. Ashley centered her attention on the obviously distressed woman.

"Why, Miss Katie!" she gushed. "It certainly is a pleasure to meet you!"

Katie clutched her apron tightly, caught off guard by this effusive greeting.

"May I?" Ashley elegantly brushed her hand across the sofa for permission to sit.

Katie nodded numbly. Ashley sat and patted Katie's hand. "I'm sure you must know just everything that goes on in this compound. Would you be available, Miss Katie..." Ashley lowered her voice conspiratorially, "to give me some advice now and then?"

Charles turned toward Camille. "What a politician," he said under his breath.

"Training as a former minister's wife," Camille whispered back. "She had to learn how to deal with disgruntled church members." Maybe, just maybe, Camille realized, Ashley wasn't the helpless little babe in the woods she'd always projected.

Katie, who for the first time was the center of attention, seemed placated. She happily retreated to her kitchen to procure food for her guests. She quickly hid the bag of potato chips, which she'd planned to throw in front of the two American women. Now where was that special cake she'd baked just for Charles? She found it hidden in the rear of the refrigerator, cut generous slices, and put them on her best china.

Katie served Ashley first. Ashley widened her eyes in amazement. "Miss Katie, don't tell me you baked this yourself?"

Katie nodded.

"Is it your own recipe?"

"Why, yes it is, darlin'," the words rolled out of Katie's mouth.

"Cammy, just look at this...we're actually having some homemade Irish cake!"

"Why, you're right, Ashley," Camille responded, unable to match the unabashed enthusiasm of her sister.

Sam was getting into the spirit. "Let me pour you some homemade Irish beer..."

Ashley looked up. "Oh, uh, Sam...I really don't drink."

"That's true," Camille explained. "She's very Southern Baptist."

Sam looked a little hurt.

Ashley softened. "Well, I would at least like to try some genuine Irish beer...just a little."

Appeased, Sam poured her half a glass. Sam and Charles poured themselves a second glass of beer, then broke out into song. The women laughed, relieved that a tense situation had been avoided—for this night, at least.

After the third song, Sam stopped and looked at Ashley. "Sing us a song, dear."

"I don't know..."

"How about 'Summer Time'?" Camille encouraged.

"Well, alright. Just a verse or two." Ashley prepared herself, then started. "Summer time...and the livin' is easy..."

The room became quiet.

"Bloody hell," Charles commented, "she's a real singer."

Camille sat back for a moment, realizing that their reactions to Ashley's voice might begin to heal the doubts her ex-husband, Jimmy, had inflicted.

The room remained quiet after Ashley finished. Then Sam broke the silence. "Have you ever sung professionally?"

"Oh, just as a back-up singer."

"For a New Orleans group," Camille finished. She glanced at her watch. "Oh, my, look at the time. First day at the palace tomorrow, Ashley. You're going to need some rest."

The two women stood. On the way out the door, Katie gave Camille a haughty look. Katie couldn't let this encounter with the sisters be a totally positive experience. "You know, Camille, Ashley's much more Southern than you are," she declared.

This evaluation didn't seem to bother Camille. "Probably..." she responded nonchalantly.

Katie's face turned angry that her arrow had missed its mark. No one seemed to notice, however.

Charles followed the two women. Once safely outside, Ashley looked at Charles and smiled enigmatically. "We'll be seeing you."

"Oh, you may count on it," Charles answered. He was aware that Katie was watching from her balcony as they separated.

Camille tapped lightly on her villa door.

"Hi, Aunt Ashley!" Beau greeted.

"Hi, sweetie!" She hugged him.

"Beau, you've got school tomorrow," his mother started.

"Oh, Mom, I just wanted to say 'hi' to Aunt Ashley."

"OK, but bedtime soon."

"Beau," Ashley began, "I want to ask you—"

Beau's hand went up as a signal for his aunt to stop. He looked around the room, then used the sign language his aunt had carefully taught him. "Bugs…they can hear everything."

Ashley nodded. The three continued the conversation in sign language. A block away, two listening Arabs in the guardhouse looked at each other, puzzled.

"For two women," one commented in Arabic, "it is very quiet in there."

Another First Day at the Palace

Ashley's transition into the palace staff was almost effortless. Safiya and Naomi greeted her cordially, then handed her back to Camille. Camille realized that Ashley was assigned to her, so she wouldn't be bothering them much, anyway. Ashley's genteel, non-confrontational manner made the Arab staff feel comfortable. And Gerald just ignored her.

As Camille watched Ashley instruct the staff in sign language, she felt a new appreciation for her sister's professional skills.

After work, the drive back to the villa was uneventful. Mofi, the driver, was proud he now knew the way. The phone was ringing as the two sisters entered the villa.

"Ashley," Charles greeted. "I've got some take-away from the new Lebanese restaurant—beef *schwarmas*. Something new for you to try," he offered.

"Well…" she looked at her sister for guidance. Camille nodded her approval.

"Sure."

"Good. Uh…and I'm trying to find something light-hearted on the telly. I need a little comedy tonight."

Ashley looked down at the videotape Beau had rented from the local videostore. "Beau, are you finished with this?"

Beau glanced up from his videogame. "Yes, ma'am."

"I'll be over in twenty minutes," Ashley decided and hung up the phone.

Ashley was ready to knock on Charles' door, but found it already open.

"Hello, love," Charles greeted the American, now very much in charge on his own turf. He'd spread the sandwiches, along with fresh vegetables, on the dining table.

"Would you care for some wine with your dinner?"

"Uh...no thanks," Ashley said meekly. She didn't want to be figured for a prude, but she also felt uncomfortable drinking.

Charles stopped for a moment to think. "Well, how about a nice steaming cup of Ovaltine?"

The young woman nodded happily. "Yes, please. And...could you put some marshmallows in it?"

"Why, yes I will. I'll just put the kettle on..." Her request somehow made the Brit feel more relaxed.

After dinner, Charles headed over to the "telly." "Now for some entertainment."

Ashley hesitantly held out the videotape. "I brought a movie along. It's a comedy."

"What's it about?"

"It's about two singers from Chicago...they're called the 'Blues Brothers', and they're on a 'mission from God' to save the orphanage."

"Sounds boring."

"Right," Ashley grinned at the challenge. "Now it's your turn to try something different...an American cult classic." She popped in the video and began singing along with the opening rhythm and blues song. "She copped the Caddy, and left me the mule to ride..."

Charles laughed heartily at her vivaciousness. As the movie continued, he found himself singing along.

"Oh! It's Aretha Franklin!" Ashley suddenly exclaimed. She jumped up on Charles' pristine white sofa, dancing to the song. "You'd better THINK, what you're trying to do to me...THINK!"

Normally, Charles would have minded about his sofa being used for a stage platform. Tonight, however, he didn't. After all, she'd thoughtfully removed her shoes first. He sat back and watched the show.

"A little animated tonight, aren't we?"

"You betcha, babes," Ashley was surprised to find herself saying. "This is my idea of therapy." She sensed the same was true for Charles.

Work at the palace was on a smooth course for the time being. Safiya had felt comfortable enough to leave for her home in London. Everyone seemed to have settled into a routine.

Ashley and Charles became fast friends.

"Where did he say he was taking you tonight?" Camille asked her younger sister once they were safely on the clinic bus.

"Something about the Jeddah Light Opera. They're supposed to be doing a Neil Simon play."

"Oh, that's really a fun place. I think you'll enjoy it."

That night, Ashley and Charles drove through the streets of Jeddah.

"Oh, look!" she laughed. "It's a statue with car parts, and the tail lights are blinking!"

"Funny thing," Charles thought aloud, "your sister and nephew had the exact same reaction."

"Really?" Ashley seemed surprised. "I thought Camille and I were totally different."

"Oh, I think you both are very much the same."

Ashley sat and thought about this for a few minutes. She didn't know if she liked Charles' assessment or not.

The Jeddah Light Opera was an open-air theater. Mostly Westerners were in attendance, although there appeared to be a few rogue Saudis in their traditional white *thobes* in the audience. Ashley sensed there was just a slight amount of rebellion for them to be in this audience.

The play was well acted. Most of the actors and actresses were Brits, which cause some slight incongruity, since the play was about New Yorkers.

Afterwards, Charles dropped her at her villa.

"Thanks. That was fun." She gave him a big kiss on the cheek and opened her front door.

Charles grinned, touched his cheek, and said goodnight. At least three women had something new to talk about in the compound that evening.

Brits Buying Rugs

"Mom!" Beau called.

"What, Beau?" Camille was a little aggravated with her son. He'd seemed to be losing his manners over here in the Kingdom. She waited. "Beau, if you want something, come down here and ask."

She heard her son bounce down part of the stairs, then jump from the landing to the first floor.

"Yes?" Camille was busy working on a book chapter on her laptop computer, and now she'd lost her train of thought.

"Charles said there's a group of them going shopping for Persian rugs tonight. Can I go?"

"May I go, ma'am?" Camille corrected through gritted teeth.

"May I go, Mom...please?"

"It's alright with me, but it's really Charles' decision."

"I know," Beau thought. "I'll ask Aunt Ashley. He'll do it if she asks."

"Alright, Beau, ask Aunt Ashley. But you'll have to be home before the last prayer call."

"Yes!" An excited twelve-year-old bounced back up the stairs. "Oh, Aunt Ashley..."

Beau and Ashley walked across the way to Charles' villa. He greeted them at the door.

"We'd best see if the rest of the group is ready."

The three of them walked back out into the night and crossed the pool area. The villa door was open and raucous singing drifted out.

"Look! It's Ashley!" They broke into song again. "New Orleans ladies..."

Charles popped his head in the door and looked at his watch.

"Well, Charles!"

Two of the men grinned and burst into song again. "Looking for love in all the wrong places, looking for love in too many places..."

"Well, isn't that sweet of you gentlemen...a home-town song," Ashley commented, ignoring the obvious implication.

"Whadda ya mean, a home-town song?"

"Why, Wanda Mallette wrote that song. She's from Gulfport, Mississippi."

"Really?" one of the Brits asked. "Hmm..."

"We need to go straightaway before the next prayer call," Charles reasoned with the group.

The group rose and walked toward the gate to their cars, leaving the villa door wide open. Ashley sighed, walked back and closed the door.

"Hey, Ashley!" someone from the group called. "Why don't you ride with us?"

"Thanks for the offer, y'all. But I want to live awhile longer."

Three cars filled with Brits, one Syrian, and two Americans. They merrily arrived together at the rug store. Most of them giggled as they stumbled out.

"They remind me of the Keystone Cops," Ashley laughed.

Charles guided his American guests into the rug store. Speaking Arabic, Charles quickly picked out a rug for Beau, negotiated the price, and secured it in his car trunk.

The others were still walking around the store, giggling. The Syrian woman looked at Roger, her British husband. *Abaya* wide open, she had on a low-cut dress displaying lots of cleavage. She propped herself up on a rug, lit a cigarette, and crossed her legs.

"Hey, Mimi," her husband tottered over, dragging a rug. "What do you think of this one?"

Annoyed, the shopkeeper protested at him in Arabic, gesturing theatrically to make his point.

The couple ignored him. Mimi took a long drag off her cigarette, sized up her husband's rug choice, and threw her head back.

"Oh, I don't know, Ro-zhay," she responded in a thick accent. "It just doesn't say...'come to bed'...to me."

"Alright."

Her husband, Roger, tossed the rug onto a pile of neatly rolled rugs. This was more than the shopkeeper could bear. He headed toward his phone. Charles, Ashley and Beau had been watching from the entrance.

"Well, you two, I think it's best if we go next door for a cup of tea."

Ashley nodded in agreement. "I'm with you."

They had just sat down at the table with their teacups when they heard the whistles.

"Oh, oh," Charles casually commented, sipping his tea.

"Oh, oh? What's oh-oh?" Beau wanted to know.

"Just sit and watch. We have a good view from here."

Three matawain, in their usual agitated frenzy, were getting out of cars. Sticks raised, they stormed into the rug shop. Being somewhat inebriated, the Brits were a little slow on comprehending the developing situation. A look of surprise, then terror, overtook the first two Brits. They scrambled into the storeroom.

Mimi saw the large, loosely rolled rug Roger had tossed to one side. She got down on her hands and knees and crawled backwards into the rug. A slight trace of cigarette smoke drifted out and upwards into the air.

The matawain, who'd stopped at the front of the store to talk with the shopkeeper, incredibly hadn't seen the escapes. Two of the less lucky Brits were numbly debating a rug they'd rolled out onto the floor. The shopkeeper pointed to them, and the matawain approached.

"My, they're acting calm and sober all of a sudden," Ashley commented.

The Brits spoke only English to the matawain, gesturing with their hands.

"No, we don't know those other people. It's terrible how they behaved."

After a few minutes, the matawain gave up. Shouting a few angry words at the shopkeeper about "being bothered" they got back into their cars.

Roger peeked out of the storeroom. "Mimi? Mimi, darling, are you alright?"

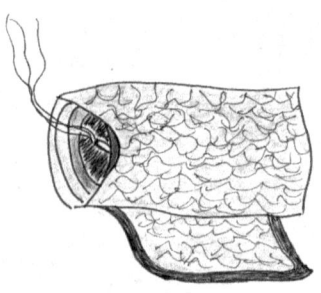

Tears streamed down Ashley's face from the laughter. Cigarette smoke was still gently wafting out one end of the rug where Mimi was hiding.

"Just follow the smoke signals, Ro-zhay," a muffled voice answered.

Beau looked at Charles. "Mr. Charles, is that what you mean by 'pissed'?"

Charles sat back with his legs crossed and took a sip of tea. "Pretty much, Beau, pretty much."

The clinic bus came early the next morning. Ashley and Camille were rushing out the door when the phone rang.

"Hello?" Ashley answered impatiently.

"Well, darlin', I finally caught you."

"Hey, Remmy. My bus is waiting."

"So, just when is a good time to reach you? I mean, Ashley, am I just pissing in the wind here or not? I need to know whether to move on."

"Remmy, I'm doing something important here. If you need to move along, then just do it. But...I love you," Ashley blurted out, and realized she meant it. Confused at her own confession, she slammed the phone down, threw her *abaya* over her shoulders, and ran to the bus.

At work, she was restless all day. Remmy was making demands, and the cultural restrictions of this country were just beginning to sink in.

That afternoon, she walked down the steps of the clinic bus and headed for the pool. Perhaps a few laps before dinner would settle her restlessness. She looked up to see a familiar figure standing over her.

"Well, Major Murray...a friendly face from home. What are you doing here in the Kingdom?"

The handsome, clean-cut American flashed a smile. "Retired Air Force now. I've been hired as an engineer at the equipment company."

"Did you just get here?"

"Just a few hours ago."

"Where's your wife, Abby?"

"She'll be here in a few weeks. She's getting the furniture packed and stored. Listen, I was just getting ready to go over to the American compound for a sandwich. Want to come along?"

Ashley scooped up some pool water. It was a little cool for swimming anyway, and it would be nice to get out of this small compound for a few hours. "Sure, David. Give me a few minutes to get ready, alright?"

"OK. I'll be waiting."

As Ashley unlocked her door, she heard the phone ringing.

"Hello?"

"Yes, hallo. It's Charles."

"Oh, hi, Charles."

"I got off early and fixed you dinner."

"Uh...dinner? Tonight?"

"Yes. In fact, it's almost ready."

"Oh, Charles. I just met an old friend from Biloxi. He invited me to the American compound for a sandwich."

"Are you talking about David Murray?"

"You know him?"

"Yes, I hired him."

"Oh..."

"Well, you can have your reunion another day. The food will be ready in fifteen minutes."

The phone clicked, and she sat listening to the dial tone. Ashley gathered her wits about her. She picked up the phone and dialed Charles' villa.

"Yes, hallo," he answered rather coldly.

"Charles, this is David's first night in the Kingdom. I'm just not going to do him that way."

Charles let out a disgruntled noise. "Oh, very well. I've made plenty of food. I'll ring him up and invite him as well."

Ashley showered, changed clothes, and walked toward Charles' villa.

As usual, he'd left the front door slightly open. She walked in. There were sounds of preparations coming from the kitchen.

"There you are!" Charles greeted. He was carrying a plate of steamed food to the dining room table. The Brit was dressed for the occasion. Instead of his usual starched white shirt and tie, he was sporting tight jeans and a black silk V-neck T-shirt.

"You're looking pretty buff, baby," Ashley complimented, then realized, "but...that's the point, isn't it?"

"When will David's wife be joining him?" Charles returned bluntly.

"He said in about two weeks."

Charles handed Ashley a wine glass. "Don't worry. It's just club soda—so, two weeks, you say?"

"Yes, sir."

"Hmm. Well then, that's his timetable."

"Excuse me?"

"His timetable. It's all very clear, you know. He's on a short schedule, and has to work fast before his wife gets here."

Ashley put down her pretend wine drink. "Charles!" she said, exasperated. "David's wife and I grew up together. I was in their wedding. We are all good friends!"

Charles seemed unabashed. "And I'm sure he'd be more if you let him."

"Aaaa—!" Ashley threw up her hands. "Just what is it about this country?" Her rantings were interrupted by the smell of a thick scent emanating from Charles' direction. "Think you have enough aftershave on?"

The Brit's reply was interrupted by a knock on the door.

"Go answer it. It's probably your American friend."

She opened the door. "Hey, Dave! A slight change in plans…"

"Hey. I, uh, brought a bottle of wine for Charles. One of the guys just came back with it from Bahrain."

Charles peered out of the kitchen. "Oh, hallo, David. Just a sec."

The Brit carried in dishes of food. He lit candles.

"Uh, I brought you some wine, Charles." David held up his offering.

Charles coolly inspected the label. "Yes, that's quite good. Ashley, darling, would you get the corkscrew, please?" He glanced at the forlorn American male for effect. "You know where it is."

Ashley rolled her eyes and muttered under her breath, "Stinker." David looked bewildered.

"Sit down, sit down," Charles magnanimously offered David a chair. "Ashley, darling, do come join us."

Charles gallantly pulled her chair out, then pushed her gently to the table. Ashley gave him a sideways glance of displeasure. She wondered if the Brit understood how naive most Americans were, and how he was messing with this poor guy's head. Dinner progressed pleasantly, with Charles playing the charming host.

"No, I've never been to England," David admitted during the course of the conversation.

Charles took a sip of wine and pushed his chair back. Ashley's eyes glanced toward Charles' obvious male endowments, framed less than subtly in the form-fitting jeans, then quickly looked away. Charles knew exactly what he was doing. He locked eyes with David.

"We're not some piss-ant little country, you know," he stated imperiously.

David was flustered. "Uh...of course, you're not."

"Yeah, yeah, yeah," Ashley interrupted, "Birthplace of the Empire, originator and purveyor of our common language...and..." she locked eyes with Charles, "home of quite a few renowned rogues."

Charles smiled, in spite of himself.

Ashley turned to the American and brightly asked, "More dessert, Dave?"

"Uh..." he answered sheepishly, "I think I'd better be going."

"Oh, sorry," Charles replied, "I'll just see you to the door."

The door closed. Ashley picked up dishes and carried them into the kitchen. "I'll help you clean up. Then I have to leave."

Charles grinned smugly. She smacked him with a dishtowel as he walked past. "Did you accomplish what you wanted?"

"Yes, I think I did."

Ashley made a mental note to call and apologize to David when she was safely back in her villa.

Katie's Overture

Ashley shook her head as she loaded the dishwasher. There was a soft knock at the door.

"Now I wonder who..." Charles went to answer the door. The compound manager's wife, Katie, stood at the door, unaware of the American woman's presence in the kitchen.

"Well, Katie, good evening!" Charles greeted Sam's wife loudly. Ashley stopped loading the dishwasher.

"To what do I owe the honor of this visit?"

"I made these for you, Charles. I know they're you favorite."

Katie looked nervously outside. "May I come in?"

"Why, yes, certainly. Have a seat. Would you care for a drink while I'm up?"

"Yes, some beer if you have it."

"Sorry, darling, all I have is tea."

"Tea would be fine, then." Katie sat down on the sofa and carefully adjusted her dress.

Charles walked into the kitchen, his fingers to his lips. Ashley was leaning against the counter, trying not to laugh. Charles quickly made the tea while Ashley set cups on the tray. He carried the tray back to the living room.

"There now...white or black?"

"White, please."

"Here you go, then. By the way, where's Sam tonight?"

"Oh, he had to go to a meeting at the American compound. He won't be back," she emphasized pointedly, "until very late."

Katie tossed her head in a way she considered to be suggestive. Ashley, watching from the corner, choked back a laugh. The disparity between the two was almost comical. Charles was trim, polished, and professional. Katie was at least ten years older, her wrinkled, drooping face framed by stringy, gray hair, and she had on a loose cotton housedress in an attempt to hide her excess rolls of poundage. Her teeth were stained and crooked. Ashley especially was fascinated by the hairy, unshaven legs.

Charles sat in a chair across from Katie and began to pour tea.

"Charles, dear, come and sit here," Katie patted the sofa area beside her.

Charles was unflappable. "Thank you, dear, but I'm quite comfortable." He continued to sip his tea, waiting for the next overture.

"Are those new pants? They're very becoming."

"Thanks."

Katie gulped the rest of her tea. "Are you sure," she asked in her thick brogue, "that you haven't something stronger to drink?"

Charles had his legs crossed and his hands under his chin. "Sorry," he answered crisply, "fresh out."

Silence. Katie fidgeted.

"I just made a fresh batch of beer...would you like for me to bring you over some?"

"Not in the mood for beer tonight."

Silence. Ashley covered her mouth in preparation for the next volley.

"Charles, I just think you're so wonderful. I've admired you so much these past few years..."

"Yes, you and *Sam* are very dear to me, too."

Katie chose to ignore the implication, and pulled herself off the sofa with some effort. She approached Charles, arms out. "Oh, Charles, I just want you to know how much I truly care—"

"Oh, I forgot. I have something in the oven. You just stay put, Katie."

Charles quickly crossed through the dining room into the kitchen. Ashley could tell by his expression that he was tiring of this game. He bent over and whispered, "Go out the kitchen door, circle around, and knock on the front door."

Ashley turned the doorknob gently and eased out onto the patio. Charles opened and slammed the oven door shut.

"All finished!" he announced cheerily to Katie. He crossed back into the living room. "Now," he said, settling back into his chair, "where were we?"

Before Katie could respond, there was a knock at the front door. "Now, I wonder who that could be?" Charles jumped up and opened the door.

"Well, Ashley. What a surprise..."

"Hi, Charles. I just got Thursday's airline schedule, and wanted to get you a copy right away." She handed him one of his own recipe cards from the kitchen. He looked at it and chuckled.

"Very good. I'll take care of it."

Ashley looked past Charles. "Oh, hi, Miss Katie! I didn't know you and Sam were here..." Ashley looked around and called out, "Hi, Sam! Sam?" She feigned confusion. "Oh, he's in the bathroom again?" The American woman batted her eyes innocently.

Katie looked at Ashley with seething anger. "I'd best be off. I was just delivering Charles' favorite pastries."

Katie pulled her substantial weight off the sofa with some effort. For effect, she wrapped her arms around Charles. "I always enjoy our visits, Charlie."

She gave Ashley a smug look, then brushed past the young woman.

The two watched as Katie waddled down the sidewalk. Ashley turned to Charles and broke out in laughter. "Charlie?"

The Welshman shook his head in disgust. "Imagine...that...that fat, frumpy cow!"

"Yes, it was fun, but now Katie hates me more than ever," Ashley realized.

Charles pulled Ashley back into the house and shut the door. He playfully brought her to him, and lightly planted a chaste kiss on her cheek.

"Be off with you, then. We don't want any of the good neighbors talking."

"Right. I'll just go make my apologies to David."

She walked out into the starlit sky. Jeddah at night. She inhaled the sweet scents of the night blossoms. Not bad for December.

Calling His Bluff

Ashley was looking forward to getting on the clinic bus the next morning. There were just so many personal complications in this compound.

During a break at work, Camille faced her sister and signed, 'Charles—what's up?'

Ashley looked around the room. She signed back, 'He's making me crazy. He's playing with the illusion of romance, when we both know there is no future between us. It's hurting me, and it's keeping him from getting on with his life.'

'So, what are you going to do about it?' her older sister signed back.

Ashley stopped for a moment. She strolled over to the snack area and made herself a cup of tea. As the spoon stirred round and round, the answer became clearer. She sat down and looked at her sister.

'I'm going to shock him into reality. I'm going to call his bluff.'

Camille sat back, folded her arms, and considered her sister's response. 'Have you considered all the ramifications?'

Ashley took a slow sip of tea. 'I've thought this out carefully. I just can't keep playing these cat and mouse games,' she signed back.

"Well, then, good luck..." Camille answered aloud.

After work that night, Ashley picked up the telephone. "Hello, Charles? You know, you've been making me all those wonderful meals... well, I want to reciprocate. How about if I whip us up some down-home cooking and bring it over tomorrow night? Six-thirty? Great."

Ashley and Camille were able to get the clinic bus to leave early the next day. Both sisters quickly put together a Creole meal they'd been taught by the inimitable Miss Kay-Dee. Camille helped Ashley walk the baskets of food to Charles' villa.

"You know, Sis, Charles might not be talking to us anymore after you're finished."

"I know, Cammy. But I just want to resolve this. Talking just doesn't seem to be working."

Camille sighed as they walked, "What a waste. He is decorative."

"Yeah," Ashley laughed, "he is great eye candy..."

Camille looked at her sister, shocked at her uncharacteristic commentary. "Ashley!?"

Charles opened the door.

"Hi, Charles!" Camille smiled. She handed him one of the baskets of food. "Bye, Charles!"

Ashley organized the food in his kitchen. "My God, Charles...you had to wear Drakkar Noire?"

"Don't you approve?"

"Approve? Do you want to get assaulted?"

"Ashley, don't talk that way!"

"You're quite the package, you know? You come in here looking all fine and smelling good. Then you act all stiff-assed, which just makes it all the more challenging."

"Ashley, stop it!" Charles sat down very properly at the dinner table. "I'm hungry...I didn't get any lunch."

"Well, my dear," Ashley snapped open a linen napkin with a flourish and draped it suggestively on Charles' lap, "I'm sure you will like this dish."

"Here now! Quit that playing!"

Dinner progressed quietly. After dinner, Charles made coffee for his guest. As he handed her the cup, Ashley looked at his finely chiseled, classic features. "My God, you're handsome."

A look of fear crossed Charles' face. "My dear, you have to leave now. It's late, and we can't have the busy bodies talking."

"They're just frustrated gossips," Ashley protested. "We haven't done anything."

"Yes, that's true. But we must keep up appearances," Charles stated quite primly.

For some reason, his words inflamed Ashley. She stood up angrily, possessed by the strength from years of carefully watching every word and action. "Yes, we must keep up appearances, at all costs!" She reached out and grabbed Charles by his shirt collar, pulling him roughly to her. Now, eye to eye, Ashley snarled, "I'll knock that starch right out of your stuffed British shirt!" Then she let go of him.

Charles reeled back, dazed, and sat down on his sofa. Ashley laughed softly, incredulous at her own uncharacteristic behavior.

Charles seemed upset by her laughter. "It's not funny, Ashley."

The sudden realization struck Ashley like a thunderbolt. "I have been keeping up appearances my whole life, no matter what the cost..." She cocked her head as the decision came to her. Her smile was one of a tremendous burden lifted from her. "And, I'm not going to do it anymore. It may sound trite, but it's true...From now on, I'm going to follow my heart."

She grabbed the confused Charles one more time, and with the ecstatic feelings of this life-changing decision, kissed him soundly on his lips. "Thanks, Charles!" she said, as she let go of him.

The always-controlled Charles was now fighting to define their new relationship. "Friends?" he asked tentatively.

Ashley turned back and smiled at him. "Always."

Ashley walked out the door. She didn't notice that Katie, the manager's wife, had been watching from her kitchen window.

Leave Her Alone!

Ashley felt better the next morning. As she jogged around the compound, she thought she was getting her life back in control. As she turned the corner, David was reaching for his morning paper.

"Hi, Dave!"

"Hey, Ashley. Just brewed some coffee...got time for a cup?"

Ashley looked at her watch. "A few minutes." She stretched out her leg muscles for a few moments then followed David into his villa.

"Let's see…you only like cream, don't you?"

"Thanks." Ashley took the cup. "How's work?"

"Alright. I'm a little lonely, but Abby will be here next week."

"Good. We'll have y'all over for dinner then." Ashley downed the last swig of coffee. "Bye."

As she turned to leave, David's phone rang. Ashley opened the door, then realized she didn't know what day David's wife would arrive so she could plan a menu. She turned around. David's face was white as he held out the phone.

Ashley gave a puzzled look as she walked toward the phone receiver David now held toward her. A loud, harsh metallic-sounding voice emanated menacingly, "LEAVE HER ALONE!"

David hung up the phone. He looked at the other American. "My God…"

Ashley shook her head, speechless. She put her hands in the air to indicate bewilderment, then walked back toward her villa.

Camille met her at the front door. "You'd better hurry up and get ready, girl."

Ashley pulled Camille away from the front door and explained what had just occurred.

"Who do you think it was?" her sister asked.

"I don't know. The voice was disguised. But I sure hope it wasn't—"

"Charles?" Camille finished. "No, it couldn't be…"

CHAPTER 8
Christmas In The Kingdom

Naomi was already at the clinic when Ashley and Camille arrived. She looked up to see the two women settling in, and called across the room, "Camille, may I see you a minute?"

Camille walked into Naomi's office, closed the door, and prepared herself. Naomi put her head down into her hands. "The architects and contractors are seriously behind schedule. The new clinic building isn't going to be ready for at least another five months."

"Oh, no!" Camille exclaimed in disappointment. "We were all ready to move in after Christmas!" At that moment, she realized her work here was almost at an end. "Naomi—the budget, supplies, operating manuals, computer software—they're all ready. What are we going to do for five months?" Camille glanced toward the door. "And...what am I going to do with Lilly?"

Naomi looked up. Camille could see the sadness in Naomi's large, luminous eyes. "She's your problem. I've got my own."

Camille turned to leave. "Naomi?"

"What?"

"Thanks for letting me know."

Ashley spent the day at her desk, drifting in and out of reverie between tasks. 'I'll never understand this country,' she signed to Camille.

'And…' she looked up at her big sister, tears welling up in her green eyes, 'I miss Remmy.'

'Call him!' Camille signed back.

Ashley nodded.

After work, Camille and Ashley stepped off the clinic bus.

"Wait!" Camille grabbed her sister's arm. "Let's talk out here for a minute."

"What's up?"

Camille looked around to make sure they were alone. "The clinic building is five months behind schedule."

Ashley's eyes opened wide. "Five months? Cammy, we're almost finished setting up. And, we can't hire any staff or see patients until we're in the new clinic building."

"I know," Camille nodded. "Ashley…I think…our work here is pretty much finished."

"You mean…" Ashley realized, "we could go home?"

"There's no longer any reason to stay. Next week is Christmas. We'll wait until after the holidays, then bring it up with Naomi. I'm sure she'd be relieved not having us use up the clinic budget when we'd just be sitting around, bothering her."

Ashley grinned. "I hear that." She waited as her sister opened the villa door.

"Hello, Mum," Samantha greeted. "Dinner fixed. Just like you said."

"Thanks, Samantha."

"I go now?"

"Yes, you may go now."

Beau, Ashley, and Camille were finishing dinner when the phone rang.

Beau jumped up. "Hello? Mr. Remmy? How's everything going there?" Beau looked at his aunt. "Sure, let me get her for you."

Ashley rose from the table and walked to the phone. "Hey, Remmy!" She stopped and looked at her sister and nephew, who were watching her attentively.

"Oh, alright," Camille acknowledged. "Son, we'll finish our dessert on the veran-dah!"

Ashley turned back to the phone.

"Well, do you want to talk to me now?" Remmy asked.

"Yes, Remmy, I do."

"Did you mean what you said in the last call?"

"You mean about doing something important?"

"No, not that..."

"Oh. That...I love you?"

"Yes, ma'am. That's the part."

"Yes, hon, I meant it. And you know what, Remmy?"

"What?"

Ashley hesitated. She knew the Arabs in the guardhouse were probably listening, but she didn't care. This was important. "It looks like...I'll be coming home real soon."

"You will? May I ask when?"

"I'll know after next week."

"Baby, that's the nicest Christmas present I've ever had. Oh, by the way, have you heard about Jimmy?"

"No. It's hard to get letters, and phone calls are so expensive."

"Well, he quit his little piddlin' private practice. He's got a job singing with the Legends show at the Imperial Palace in Biloxi."

"No way!" Ashley laughed. "Which star is he impersonating?"

"Elvis."

Ashley broke into waves of laughter. After she caught her breath, she finally understood about Jimmy. "Remmy, I was the one who pushed Jimmy into being a minister. Performing was what he really wanted to do all along, wasn't it?"

"Exactly." Remmy was relieved she'd figured this out on her own. Now they could get on with their lives. "Ashley? I love you, too. Just give me a date...alright?"

Ashley thought about his choice of words. "I will, hon."

"Bye."

Charles Takes a Trip

Charles had been frustrated all day. David, the new American engineer, was acting strangely toward him. And, he certainly couldn't figure out Ashley's sudden coolness. Americans. They'd take over the whole bloody Kingdom if you let them.

What he needed was a few weeks back in Wales, his own country.

He was glad he'd had the foresight to apply for holiday leave months earlier.

He'd made the usual "bread run" that afternoon for friends in the compound. All the fresh-baked loaves had been delivered, except for Camille and Ashley's. Well, they could just do without. He unlocked his door and put the bread in an old-fashioned bread box. Then, he walked over and switched on his stereo. The same Tina Turner song was playing again, 'What's love got to do with it, do with it? What's love, but a second-hand emotion...'

Charles laughed bitterly. Bloody hell. Yet another American. Well, he might as well deliver their bread and be done with it. He walked briskly toward the sisters' villa. As he knocked on the door, he heard the sound of a flute.

"Hey, Charles!" Ashley grinned. "Oh, good. You brought the bread. Beau was just asking for a sandwich. C'mon in."

"Who's playing the flute?"

"Oh, that's Camille. It's her stab at culture."

"Is that...Bach?"

"Well, that's her unique rendition of it."

"She's not butchering it too badly," he commented charitably.

"Would you like some iced tea?"

"Well..."

"Oh, c'mon." Ashley grabbed his arm and pulled him into the living room. "Cammy! Charles just brought the bread!"

Camille walked downstairs, flute in hand. "Charles! Hey, I just learned a Welsh folk song for you."

Camille played lightly through a Welsh tune Charles recognized from his childhood. A small grin appeared on his face, then was replaced with a more serious look.

"Well," he stood up, primly adjusting his tie. "I must be off. I have to pack."

"Pack?" Ashley asked. "Where y'all going?"

"You-all," he replied, trying to imitate them, "is going home for Christmas."

"You know," Ashley replied, "you have been looking a little tense."

"I'm glad you concur," he answered bitterly. "I'm so relieved you won't be devastated."

Camille looked at Ashley and smiled. "Let's sing Charles a song to send him off. Hmm...what would befit his current...state of mind?"

"I know," Ashley replied blithely, picking up her guitar. "The Rose."

"Excellent choice, Ashley. What key?"

"Key of C, a good country key."

"Really, I must get on with my packing," Charles protested.

"Sit down, Charles," Camille ordered, pushing the surprised Brit onto the sofa. "This will take...how do you say.. just a 'sec'?"

The two sisters nodded at each other, then started singing. As the song progressed both women pointedly looked at their seriously unhappy friend.

'It's the heart afraid of breaking that never learns to dance.
It's the dream afraid of waking that never takes the chance.
It's the one who won't be taken who cannot seem to give,
And the soul afraid of dying that never learns to live...'

Song finished, Ashley looked into Charles' troubled aquamarine eyes. "It's been two years now since your wife died, Charles. Don't you think it's time to get on with your life?" she asked softly.

The troubled Brit didn't respond. Confused about his emotions, he continued to sit.

"Yeah, get on with your life!" Camille laughed. "Now, get out of here before we start singing 'Desperado'."

Given his leave, Charles gratefully exited. Camille put her flute down and grinned mischievously at Ashley. "You know, we're going to have to find that man a new theme song."

Noel

Charles had given Sam his company tickets to the Jeddah Christmas concert. "Take Katie, she's been in a mood lately," he instructed his friend.

Katie, for some reason, didn't feel much in the Christmas spirit. "Why don't you take those awful American women and their upstart son?" she angrily suggested.

"Alright, I will," Sam answered, surprised at yet another behavior change. He needed some relief from her incessant whining lately.

Sam picked the three Americans up at their door. As they were seated in the concert, Camille whispered, "I didn't know they even allowed Christmas concerts."

"Not always. But, since we won the war...It depends on the political climate. Of course," he chuckled, "some of the songs have to be 'modified'."

The program was well planned, and the singers were surprisingly good. "Noel, Noel, Noel, Noel," the choir sang, "Born is the king of—" there was an uncomfortable, collective pause, "Beth-le-hem."

Beau grinned and looked at Sam. "They can't say the word 'Israel'?" he whispered.

"No, not in public."

After the concert, Sam returned them to their villa.

"Thanks, Sam. It sure was nice of you to take us," Ashley said.

"Yeah, and I bet Miss Katie is gonna make you pay for it," Beau added astutely.

"Beau!" Camille admonished her son. "Tell Mr. Sam you're sorry."

Beau hung his head. "Sorry, Mr. Sam."

Sam grinned and said a pleasant good night. As he walked toward his own villa, he said aloud to himself, "But the boy is right." He looked anxiously at the upstairs window and saw his wife sitting in her rocking chair, holding her cat. She'd been doing a lot of that lately.

Christmas Cards

The next day, Eddie, her maid's husband, drove Camille and Beau around Jeddah for Christmas shopping. One of the shopkeepers looked at the Americans, then warily glanced around the store. He motioned for Camille to come over to him. "Christmas cards?" he whispered, pointing under the counter.

Camille chuckled. "OK, let's see..."

He looked around again, then flashed her the front of a card. "How many?" he asked.

"Oh, give me six."

The shopkeeper quickly took her riyals. Instead of the regular shopping bag imprinted with the store name, he stuffed the cards into a plain brown bag.

"Sorry," he apologized, "no receipt for these."

Camille smiled and turned to leave.

"Oh, Miss?" he called softly. Camille turned back to him. He glanced furtively at the shoppers. "Merry Christmas," he grinned.

Camille walked the few steps back. "Merry Christmas to you, too," she said softly.

Her son bounced up to her. "Did you get Dad some shaving lotion?" she asked.

"Yeah," Beau pulled the bottle out of his shopping bag, "his usual stuff. Uh, Mom…can I get Charles some shaving lotion, too? He's been real good to me."

"Well, I suppose so. But, he won't be back until after New Year's."

"I know, Mom. Charles wears some great aftershave…"

"Yeah, I hear you. It's also very expensive."

"I already checked the price. Mom, he's helped us out a lot." Beau studied his mother for a moment. "And…you and Aunt Ashley aren't getting him anything for Christmas, are you?"

Camille smiled gently. "No. The intent might be misunderstood."

"Well, then, I'll do it."

Camille saw her son maturing into a thoughtful person. She gave him a little hug. An Arab man glared at her as he passed. Camille remembered, "Oh, that's right. Can't show your son affection in public. Hey, kid, do you want to look for a Christmas tree?"

"Sure."

Camille and Beau explored three large nurseries. All the potted pines had already been sold. One small, scrawny Norfolk pine was left, for the equivalent of $60. Camille sighed. "Beau, would you mind terribly if we didn't put up a Christmas tree this year?"

"No, Mom. I don't care that much, anyway. I thought you wanted it."

Many of the expatriates had left for the holidays, so the compound was unusually quiet. The clinic was also fairly quiet.

Two days before Christmas, Safiya cheerfully appeared at the clinic with a basket of small, wrapped gifts. "Merry Christmas!" she greeted everyone cheerfully. "I wanted to give you all a little remembrance."

"Oh, Safiya! Thanks, but we didn't expect it," Camille blurted out.

Safiya grinned and passed out the gifts. "I know you celebrate Christmas, so I'm letting you all go home now. You won't need to come back until the twenty-eighth. The bus driver will be here any minute."

Everyone seemed caught by surprise. The staff looked around at each other.

"Got to go! Happy holidays!" Safiya disappeared through the door.

Almost at the same time, the staff remembered. Today was payday. Naomi usually waited until the end of the day to hand out the paychecks. What would happen now? They waited anxiously. The bus driver stuck his head in the door.

"Ready to go!"

The staff looked at Naomi. She showed no reaction. Unhappily, the workers filed toward the bus. Camille couldn't imagine how or why Naomi would do this to the workers. There were no automatic teller machines, and the banks would be closed all weekend. Camille knew some of the staff was depending on the money for holiday expenses.

Hala was the last out the door. She tentatively walked within a few feet of Naomi. "Doctora Naomi?" she asked in a small, quivering voice.

Naomi looked up from her work. "Yes?" she asked coldly.

Hala hesitated for a moment. "Merry Christmas." Hala turned and walked out the door.

As Camille rode the bus home with the silent group, she thought about Naomi. Maybe, she speculated, Naomi wanted to show the Arabs that Christian holidays wouldn't get in the way of clinic work. Naomi, she reasoned, probably still didn't feel secure in her new position. Whatever her reasons, she had certainly put the damper on the Christmas spirit.

Camille got off the bus at her compound. As she unlocked the door, Beau came rushing out.

"Oh, hi, Mom. I left you a note."

"Where are you going?"

"Jason's dad is gonna drive us to the video store."

"Then you'll be at Jake's?"

"Yeah."

"OK...just check back later."

"See ya!"

Camille sat down. What was there to do? She didn't feel like working on her book. She looked at her watch.

Hans had gone to Wisconsin to visit his family for Christmas. It would be nine p.m., still early enough to catch him.

Hans' father, Gunther, answered the phone. "Cammy! How are you doing way over there?"

"Oh, fine, Gunther. A little lonely. How are you?"

"You know…this old body always has some aches and pains."

"Sorry to hear that. Is Hans home?"

"No, he's over at Uncle Otto's. Do you want him to call you?"

"No, that's OK. Just tell him I called."

Camille hung up the phone. She sat on the sofa, staring at the wall. Now what, she thought to herself. I know, I'll make some Christmas cookies.

She heard the key turn in the door. It was Samantha, her maid.

"Oh, Doctora! I didn't expect you home."

"Safiya gave us extra days off for Christmas. Samantha, I'm glad you're here. I want to make some Christmas cookies. Would Eddie mind taking you to the store?"

Samantha grinned. "Oh, shopping! Yes! Just write down what you need."

Camille wrote the list. "Let's see—flour, sugar, vanilla, eggs, oh—spices—some cinnamon, and nutmeg…"

Samantha frowned. "Sorry, no nutmeg."

"This is the land of fresh spices. Why wouldn't there be any nutmeg?"

"It is not allowed."

"Not allowed? Why not?"

Samantha blushed. "They consider it to cause…um…certain feelings between men and women…"

Camille looked up and laughed. "Nutmeg is considered to be an aphrodisiac?"

"Yes, Mum. But, I can get you other spices."

"Oh, OK, Samantha. I'll work around it."

"Very good, Mum." Samantha took the list and closed the door behind her.

The next few days passed quietly. Camille read and worked on her book. Ashley seemed to have found her voice again, and was working on musical arrangements.

New Year's Eve

Now it was New Year's Eve. Beau came bounding in with all his characteristic enthusiasm. "Mom, you know they're having a New Year's Eve party at the compound tonight."

"I know, sweetie." She put her reading glasses back on and jotted a revision for the last chapter of her book.

"Are ya going?"

"Huh? No, honey, I don't feel like it."

"But—I can still go, right?"

"Sure, hon. It's right here. Just come home around twelve-thirty or so."

"No problem."

By nine p.m., Beau was headed over to the party with his friends. Camille sat on her sofa with a cup of cocoa and one of the last books she'd brought from the States, a science fiction novel, *The Talons of Time*, by an author named Paul Twitchell. By ten-thirty, she was asleep in bed.

A hand touched her shoulder, waking her. "Mom, Mom!"

"Who...what? Beau? What time is it?"

"It's twelve-thirty, just like you asked. Mom, I just had to tell you about this—it was great! Ashley sang and played the guitar, and everybody clapped a lot. Then, we all held hands at midnight and sang Old Lang Syne. And people asked about you—"

Camille gave her son a hug. "Honey, I'm glad you had such a good time. It'll be a nice memory for you."

"Yeah, I guess. OK, I just wanted to tell you. Goodnight, Mom." Beau reached down and gave his mother a kiss on the cheek. "Happy New Year!"

Camille settled back in bed. What would the new year bring? she asked herself as she drifted back into sleep.

CHAPTER 9
Haram! Forbidden!

The holidays were over, and people were starting to filter back. Jack, the personnel director, arrived at Camille's front door early the next morning. "Tonight we're all going over to a place to smoke the hubbly-bubbly pipe. Would you care to join us?"

"That depends, Jack. What on earth is a hubbly-bubbly pipe?"

"Oh, you sit on high stools and everyone has a pipe leading from the big main pot."

"Uh, it sounds—interesting. I don't smoke, though."

"It will be a cultural experience for you. Come by my villa at six. There'll be at least two cars going."

"Alright…" The clinic bus honked. "Oh, gotta go."

As the clinic bus was pulling into the palace gates, Gerald was in the clinic pouring himself a cup of coffee. He walked over to the fax machine and sorted through the new messages. He pulled out a paper with a publisher's heading on it. Curious, he started reading.

"Dear Dr. Kohl: Enclosed are the editorial comments on the final two chapters. As you know, we're under a deadline. Please complete the revisions and fax them back as soon as possible. The editorial committee is meeting in three days. Thanks, Janette Simmons, Editor-in-Chief."

"Damn! What the hell is Camille doing having her personal things come to the clinic!" Gerald angrily crumpled the pages and tossed them into the garbage can.

Camille and the rest of the staff members walked in moments later. Camille stopped for a cup of coffee then passed the fax machine. "Gerald, were there any faxes for me?"

Gerald became intent on his computer screen. "No."

"Hmm..." Camille took a sip of coffee, still looking at the fax machine. "Oh, well." She sat down with the clinic therapists to review their work projects...not that there was much work left.

Lilly, the Egyptian-American therapist, looked at her work assignment. "Is that it? What am I going to do the rest of the day?"

"Lilly, I've given you everything that needs to be completed for the next week."

"For the next week? What am I supposed to do?"

"Lilly, the construction problems have put us five months behind. You don't want me to give you busywork, do you?"

"Well, no."

"Then read some of the new books on therapeutic techniques. Now's your chance."

"Oh, alright."

Camille spent the day reading, too. Yet, she felt there was something she should be doing...

Camille arrived at her villa that afternoon more tired than usual. Her throat had been hurting her, and now she had a fever. She downed a few aspirins and lay down on the sofa to sleep. She drifted off into a deep sleep.

Ashley and Beau walked in and saw Camille asleep on the sofa. Ashley put her finger to her lips. "She's really tired. We'll get some sandwiches, take them upstairs, and play Monopoly, alright?"

"Sure, Aunt Ashley."

Camille awoke to the smell of fresh coffee. She looked out the window, surprised to see the sun breaking over the horizon. She glanced at the clock—six-thirty a.m.

"Uh—" Her throat felt swollen. She could barely squeak out a word.

"Well, you're finally awake," her sister commented. She crossed over and felt her big sister's forehead. "You've got a fever. Why don't you call in sick for once? You deserve it."

Camille nodded her head in agreement.

"Besides," Ashley laughed, "I kinda like it that you can't talk back to me..."

"Mom, I'll fix you my special tea when I get home from school. Then you can talk again," Beau added.

Camille smiled at one and frowned at the other.

The two left. Camille wondered if the morning paper had arrived yet. She walked out to the front step, and bent down to pick up the green-colored newspaper.

Jack was locking his villa door, ready to leave for work. He glanced up to see Camille. Camille gave him a weak greeting wave. Jack looked at her through clenched jaws.

"Oh, hubbly-bubbly..." she squeaked out. "Sorry..."

"Yes, you will—" he hissed, "you will be sorry." He turned and walked toward the gate.

Camille felt a sense of foreboding, but was too exhausted to deal with it. She entered her villa and called the clinic. "Hello, Fatma? Camille. I'm sick. You'll tell Naomi?"

Camille walked upstairs and fell into bed, exhausted. Hours passed. The ringing phone woke her.

"Uhh...hello?"

"Cammy? Hi, this is Lou."

"Lou?"

"What's wrong with your voice?"

"I'm sick."

"It's getting to you, huh?"

"Yes."

"I called the clinic and they said you were out today. I was going to take you to lunch. Why don't I bring you some beef *schwarmas*? I'll bring some extra for Beau and Ashley."

"Sounds good," she grunted.

Within an hour, Lou arrived loaded with paper bags filled with food. The two had a pleasant meal, with Lou doing most of the talking.

"I heard Charles is gone on holiday."

Camille nodded. "Went back to Wales."

Lou looked philosophical for a moment. "You know, he may eventually marry again. But, being Welsh, he'll always remember his first wife, Christine."

Camille took in this information. "They're a pretty loyal people, huh?"

"Oh, yes," Lou assured her, "your friend for life. Now..." Lou leaned forward, "is it true that Ashley and Remmy are back together?"

"Yes," Camille smiled.

"Good," Lou replied as he opened a silver suitcase. As he talked, he walked around the villa taking readings. He stopped now and then and pointed to the location of a listening device. Camille nodded.

"Well, I'm so glad to hear about Ashley and Remmy. They'll work out fine. Maybe I can make it to the wedding..." Lou looked at his watch. "Gotta go. I'm picking up my girlfriend, Heidi, at the hospital."

Camille walked Lou to the door. "Thanks."

"Not a problem. Call me whenever you need something."

She watched her friend disappear out of the gate. The Arabs in the guardhouse also watched her distinguished friend leaving.

"I wonder what he had in that suitcase?" one of them asked.

Beau burst into the door after school. "Hi, Mom! Feeling any better?"

"Yes, Beau. Mr. Lou brought over beef *schwarmas* for us."

"Beef *schwarmas*...I like those." He wolfed one down, then went back into the kitchen. A few minutes later, he appeared with a cup of tea. "I remembered my promise...Uh, Mom? Me and Jason—"

"Jason and I," she corrected.

"Sorry. Jason and I rented some movies. May I go watch them?"

"Don't you have any homework?"

"No. I got it done in school."

Camille gave him a questioning look. She was too tired to pursue the subject right now. "Alright."

Beau grabbed another beef *schwarmas* then looked at his mother again. "Can Jason have one, too?"

Camille nodded.

"Thanks, Mom! I'll be home by nine-thirty." He skipped out the door.

Your Husband Can't Come

The next morning, Zayad stopped by the palace to talk with Safiya.

"I need some more time. I've taken steps to stop her husband's entrance visa."

Safiya sighed. "This will cause problems."

"I know." Zayad rose to leave. "Is she here?"

"She's downstairs."

Zayad walked down the steps and entered the work area. Camille had her long, natural light blonde hair pulled away from her face. As she bent over the table, a golden strand fell across her face.

"Oh!" she said, aggravated. "I'm tired of this. I'm going to get this mess cut."

"No!" Zayad said reflexively.

Camille spun around. Narrowing her eyes, jaw set, she marched over to the telephone book. "Beauty parlors—let's see—ah, a place named 'California Cuts'. That can't be too bad." She picked up the phone to dial the number.

Zayad watched her for a moment, then slipped out the pool entrance.

"Are you going to talk to Naomi?" Ashley reminded her sister.

"Yes, right now."

Camille walked across the room and tapped on Naomi's door. Naomi had just put the phone receiver down and was sitting, staring into space. Why did there have to be so many complications, she thought.

She looked up at Camille. "Yes?' she asked wearily.

"Naomi, we need to talk—"

"Your husband can't come," Naomi bluntly interrupted.

"What?"

"His visitor's entrance visa wasn't granted."

Camille let this sink in. "Why?" She remembered Zayad's morning visit. "Just let me guess..."

Naomi couldn't confirm her suspicions, or she'd get herself in trouble. "I don't have that information," she answered.

Camille thought quietly for a moment. "Who does?"

"The Saudi government."

"A name, Naomi. Who would he contact?"

Fear drifted across Naomi's eyes.

"Naomi, you don't know Hans. He's one hard-headed German. No matter what, I'll guarantee you he'll be here." Camille rose from her chair, then turned. "Oh, by the way, Naomi—Hans' two-week visit is specifically addressed in my contract." She started to leave, then heard Naomi let out a deep sigh.

"Wait." Naomi pulled out a leather appointment book and leafed to one of the last pages. She knew getting involved would cause problems for her, but handed Camille the information anyway. "Here's the name of the Saudi expediter that might help him."

"Thanks." Camille stopped and took a long look at Naomi. "This is harder on you, isn't it, Naomi? It would make your life easier if Ashley and I leave—especially if we're sitting around doing nothing for the next five months and eating up the clinic budget...Just think about it."

Naomi nodded with a far-away stare.

Camille took the paper and walked to the phone next to her desk. She called the Saudi expediter, and he took the information. Camille hadn't used the clinic phones for long distance calls. This was an exception. She dialed Biloxi.

"Hans, we've got to talk—no, we're OK. No, listen...Hans—there's some hang-up on your visa...Hans, calm down. I've just called the Saudi expediter. He's working on—what? You're calling our senator?"

Camille paused for a moment. This particular senator was chairman of the Overseas Base Allocation Committee. The Saudi people understood politics. "Hans? I think that's a fine idea. Call our senator. And stick around the phone. The expediter said he'd be calling you in a little while."

Camille hung up the phone. She knew Hans well enough. He was already dialing the senator's office.

That afternoon, Camille tried a new beauty salon. This one was run by a blonde California woman.

"Cut it. I want to try something...business-like."

"How short do you want it cut?"

Camille thought of Zayad. "Short," she answered.

As the two women chatted lazily, the beauty shop owner relayed the story of how she came to be in the Kingdom. "I married a wealthy Arab," she said. "At first, I thought I had everything I wanted." The California woman gestured around the expensive beauty shop with marble floors. "I do have money, but..." she hesitated, "no freedom."

"Can't you take a trip to California and see your family?" Camille asked.

The woman looked down at the floor for what seemed a long time. "I haven't seen my family," she said quietly, "in nine years."

A cold chill ran through Camille. She thought of Hans. Would he be able to come and get her out of the Kingdom?

When Camille arrived back at her villa later that afternoon, she saw an Arab standing in front of Jack's villa. He grinned at her. "You are Doctora Camille?"

"Uh, yes...are you visiting Mr. Daniels?"

"No, Jack is gone. He moved this morning."

"This morning?" asked the stunned woman. "And—you're already moved in?"

The Arab smiled. "The workers can be very efficient when properly... motivated. I am Amin. I am the comptroller for all the company businesses."

"It's...uh, nice to meet you, Mr. Amin. But why are you here in a Western compound? I thought the compounds were totally separated."

"Yes, almost always. It is a..." he paused and looked serious for a moment, "special arrangement."

Camille frowned. Amin ignored her reaction and waved his arms graciously toward his new villa. "And tonight, Doctora Camille, I have prepared a very special Egyptian feast for both you and your son. You come at six thirty!"

"Sounds more like an order than an invitation, Mr. Amin."

"You will be here, yes?"

Camille sighed. "I will be here, yes."

"And remember to bring your son!" he called after her.

Camille entered her villa.

"Hi, Mom."

"Beau, I'm so glad you're home."

"Yeah. I'm starting to get bored."

"The 'new' has worn off, huh?"

"Yeah, and I never thought I'd say this, but...I miss Dad."

"Honey, I miss him, too. But, tonight, we're going to have an Egyptian meal cooked by a real Egyptian."

"Where?"

"Right next door."

"Doesn't Mr. Jack live there?"

"He moved."

"Oh. Well, when's the meal? I'm pretty hungry."

Camille looked at her watch. "In just a few minutes. Go clean up, and it'll be time."

At six-thirty, Beau and Camille walked next door and knocked. Amin immediately opened the door, grinning with two glistening gold teeth flashing in the center of his mouth.

"Wow! Are those real gold teeth?" Beau asked with fascination.

"Beau! That's not polite!"

Amin laughed heartily. "Nice to meet you, Beau." The Egyptian shook her son's hand. "Come, come! I hope you are very hungry!"

"I am."

Amin was a gracious host. He brought out different, well-prepared dishes, all presented on silver trays.

"Eat more, Beau," Amin insisted, heaping a third portion of tasumi on the boy's plate.

"I can't eat anymore, Mr. Amin. Can I...I mean, may I be excused?"

"You sure you're still not hungry?"

"Oh, I've had plenty. Thank you, it was great." Beau turned to his mother. "I'm going over to Jeremy's for awhile, OK?"

"OK, but be home by—"

"Yeah, yeah, I know...nine-thirty." Beau left.

Camille suddenly felt uncomfortable. She rose from her chair. "Let me help you with the dishes."

"Oh, no, no. Sit, sit. My maid will be here early in the morning." Amin smiled and looked at Camille. "I have a special family heirloom to show you."

"OK."

"It's upstairs. In my bedroom."

"Well, Amin, bring it down. I'll wait."

"No...you don't understand. It's fastened to the wall..."

Camille cocked her head, studying Amin. "I don't think that's a good idea." She put her linen napkin on her plate and stood up. "Thanks for the meal. It was delicious, and I know you spent a lot of time preparing it." Camille walked to the door, opened it, and then turned around. "Goodnight, Mr. Amin."

She walked quickly back to her villa, entered, and sat on the sofa to think. Why had Jack left so suddenly? Why had an Arab moved into an all-Western compound? Why had he invited her to dinner? And, why had he asked her to his bedroom? She doubted he would have made any physical overtures. Just what was going on here?

You Can't Do That Here

The next morning, Camille opened the front door and started her usual morning jog. She loved early mornings in Jeddah...the smell of the winter flowers, the gentleness of the early morning sun. She finished thirty minutes then slowed to a walk. Her mind was pleasantly occupied when she was disrupted by a sharp clucking noise. She turned to see two Arab women sitting in front of Amin's villa.

"Good morning," she greeted them.

The women stared at Camille's jogging outfit with obvious disapproval. One of the women spoke angrily in Arabic, pointing to the American woman's bare legs.

Amin came out of the villa to investigate the noise. "Oh, Doctora, you're wearing shorts."

"Yes, Amin. I always wear shorts when it's eighty-five degrees and I'm jogging."

"The two women do not approve."

Camille turned from the main sidewalk and approached Amin. "When I signed my contract, it stated that I was going to live in a Western compound where I could continue my Western lifestyle. I'm not about to give up exercising because these women do not approve."

Camille looked at each woman for a moment, then started back to her villa. Just then Ashley rounded the corner, still dripping wet from her morning swim.

"Camille, what the hell is going on here? Some crazy Arab women were screaming at me to get out of the pool!"

Camille chuckled in spite of herself. She'd never heard her sister swear before. "I don't know, babes. Suddenly it's gotten just plain crazy around here."

Camille heard the phone ring, and sprinted to answer it.

"Hello?"

"It's all set," Hans greeted perfunctorily. "Pick me up at the Jeddah Airport Monday night at seven-fifteen. I'll be on Swiss Air Flight 7797."

"Hans, you mean it? You can really come?"

"Yes, I—"

Hans' conversation was interrupted by a click as the phone went dead. Camille didn't care. Her husband had managed, most likely with some political intervention, to get into the country.

Across town, another conversation was ensuing. "Yes," Safiya said, "I heard her husband got his visitor's visa."

"Well, he may come to visit the Kingdom if he must," Zayad acknowledged angrily. "But, I have assured that his entry will not be a pleasant one."

Charles in Wales

Charles had thoroughly enjoyed Christmas in Wales. He walked with old friends from house to house, singing Christmas carols. Back in his homeland, he felt centered.

After Christmas, he carefully picked out flowers and walked slowly to his wife's grave. It had been a year since he'd been able to visit. Charles bent down on his knees, and placed the flowers on the grave. The searing pain swept through him again, and tears ran down his cheeks.

"Christine," he said, surprised at the anger in his voice, "why did you leave me here? Why did you have to go?"

He let his pain pass through him. He realized after an hour had passed that there would be no answer. The winter breeze cut through his jacket, and he realized how cold he was. He stood up. His legs were sore from kneeling.

Suddenly he saw a figure kneeling over a grave in the distance. He watched for a few minutes, understanding the feeling of loneliness mixed with the sense of duty. The figure stood up and looked his way. It was a woman. She continued to stand, looking at him expectantly.

Charles moved his legs stiffly in her direction. As he grew closer, he also grew more intrigued. She was a young woman, with long, auburn curls that had a freeing effect on him as the cold wind lightly played through her hair. Then he stopped in his tracks. Long, dark lashes framed a pair of startling cornflower blue eyes. He stood transfixed, unable to say anything. Finally, he was able to mumble a question.

"Whom are you visiting?"

"My father. He's been gone seven years now. And who might you be here for?"

"My wife."

"How long has it been?"

"Two years."

The woman looked up at him. "That's no time at all now, is it?"

Charles felt a surge of warmth replacing the bitter English cold. She understood. But, of course she would. She was Welsh.

"What's your name?" he asked.

"Anna."

"Anna, my name is Charles. Would you care to have a pint with me at the pub?"

Anna smiled sweetly. "I'd be delighted."

Hans Arrives

It was Monday morning.

"Beau!" Camille yelled up the stairs. "C'mon down now. These eggs are getting cold."

"OK, OK!" Beau took the stairs in jumps. "Yah got any ketchup?"

"Yeah, yeah." His mother placed the bottle on the table.

Beau looked up from his breakfast. "Mom? What time is Dad coming tonight?"

"Seven-fifteen. Why? Do you want to go with me?"

Beau grinned. "No, not really. It's like, my last night of freedom, you know?"

Camille tried not to smile. "I know. Besides, you never know what kind of delays there'll be at the airport."

Later, when Camille arrived at the clinic, the air was thick with tension. Naomi glared at Camille.

"Naomi! Be happy for me. My husband's arriving tonight!" Camille quipped brightly.

Lilly sidled up to Camille. With her teeth clenched tightly in a forced smile, she commented quietly, "I don't think they're so happy."

"You got that right," Camille answered.

After work that night, Samantha's husband, Eddie, arrived to drive her to the airport. Camille had learned to trust Eddie and his dependability. Camille gazed out the window, trying to hold her excitement in check. Hans...it was only a few more minutes now. Her driver parked the car, then met her inside the airport.

"Well, Eddie, the board says my husband's plane has just arrived. It shouldn't be too long now..." Camille watched the passengers through the glass window as they entered the Customs room. She waited. No Hans. The flow of passengers trickled down. The room was empty, except for a few officials.

"Oh, oh," Eddie commented. "You probably should have brought a Saudi expediter." Eddie approached an Arab official. In Arabic, he asked him if Hans was one of the passengers on the plane.

"American...Kohl...*iwa*."

Eddie asked why he had been detained. The Arab frowned and disappeared. He reappeared within minutes and answered Eddie in Arabic. "He has to wait."

"Why?"

"He has to wait," the guard repeated.

"How long does he have to wait?" Eddie persisted, knowing he was close to crossing the line himself.

"Until we are finished with him," was the official's nebulous reply.

Eddie came back to Camille. "You heard that?"

"Yes, Eddie. This may take awhile. If you want to go home..."

"No, no," Eddie seemed almost offended. "I'll stay with you."

Camille looked at him gratefully. "Thanks."

Another hour crawled by. It was now nine-thirty. Camille thought she heard Hans' voice. She walked over to the door.

"*La! La!*" a guard angrily warned her.

"Look, I'm tired of waiting. Either send my husband out now, or I'm coming in!" One thing Camille had learned—the Arab men hated it when a woman made a scene. Two guards came from the inner room to see what the commotion was about.

Camille stood firmly planted with her arms crossed. She wasn't budging from the spot, unless carried off. And she planned to make that effort a challenge.

The first guard looked disgruntled. He disappeared to the inner room. She heard Hans' voice again. Then she heard noises of suitcases being closed and shuffled around.

Hans appeared sullenly in the doorway. "They made me stand on a damned white line for two hours," he greeted her. He looked angrily at one guard. "Just to prove they could do it!"

"Well, hello to you, too, Hans," Camille greeted him back.

"Look, I'm sorry. It's just that I've been on a long flight, and then this...Hon, I'm glad to see you."

Hans stopped and looked at his wife. "You cut your hair." He studied the cut for a moment. "Cammy, that makes you look sharp. You should always wear your hair that way."

"Thanks, I like it."

Camille turned to her chauffeur. "Eddie, why don't you go get the car?"

"Yes, Mum."

Eddie quickly returned the couple to the compound. Camille paid the Filipino in dollars.

"Thank you, Mum. Have a good night."

"Thanks for sticking with me, Eddie. Good night."

The next morning, Camille let Hans sleep in. She made Beau's breakfast and sent him off to school. The clinic was as usual. Camille was not surprised when Naomi didn't ask about Hans' trip. Camille called her villa that afternoon.

"Hey, this is great," Hans happily reported. "The personnel director had them drop off a new Volvo for me to drive."

"I suppose Mr. Daniels didn't mention we'd be renting it from the clinic," Camille tried to hide her sarcasm.

"No...well, he said something about settling it from your account..."

"I'm sure he will."

"Well, anyway, I found this supermarket. They had this great beer, so I stocked up."

"Beer? Hans, what are you talking about?"

"It's nonalcoholic, of course, but it tastes good."

"Oh, yeah...that. They brewed it to keep the German workers happy."

"Oh, by the way...this American guy, Henry..."

"Yes? What about Henry?" Camille asked warily.

"Well, he stopped by this morning and introduced himself. He said he was your sponsor."

"Oh, he did, did he?"

"Yeah. And he's gonna treat us to dinner at a seafood restaurant tonight. He said Beau could stay with his son, who's the same age."

"Uh, Hans, Henry's just—"

Hans excitedly cut her off. "Henry says they have a lot of terrific seafood fresh from the Red Sea."

Camille could tell Hans was set on this, and she would get no peace if they didn't go. "OK. Henry wins—this time."

Hans was cheerful when Camille arrived home that afternoon. "Hurry up and get ready, Cammy. Henry will be here any minute!"

Camille groaned as she walked up the stairs. She was changing her clothes when the doorbell rang.

"Well, Hans!" she heard the obnoxiously loud, harsh nasal twang of Henry. "Is Camille ready?"

"Cammy?" Hans called up the stairs. "Are you ready?"

Camille quickly zipped up her long skirt. "Yes, I'll be right down," she said through clenched teeth.

Henry watched intently as Camille descended the stairs. She could sense he was planning his strategy. "Hans, you follow me in your car. Janice and I have to make another stop on the way home that's out of the way." Henry's eyes had a hard glint as he delivered these words.

Hans was excited as they got into their car. "Cammy, look!" he laughed, pointing to one of the many whimsical statues of this beautiful port city.

"Hans, I want you to enjoy your first night out. But I also must warn you that Henry has an agenda, and it isn't benevolent."

"Oh, he's fine," Hans assured her. The thought of a gourmet meal in an exotic location had made Hans oblivious to any potential problems.

The two American couples pulled up at the white-pillared restaurant overlooking the Red Sea.

"Just look at this menu, Cammy!" Hans commented excitedly.

Henry dominated the conversation, while Hans was content to eat.

"Males and females are so restricted from being together here," Henry continued his lecture. "Some men actually have their limo drivers take them down to certain shopping districts. They pay for shopkeepers to get in their limos with them, and, while their chauffeurs drive them around, the shopkeepers perform...favors."

Hans put down his shrimp. Camille knew what was coming. Hans had never liked to talk about sex, and especially perversions, in public. "Henry, I'm not interested in hearing about that."

Henry was not discouraged. "Well, Hans, actually..." he turned menacingly toward Camille, "it's a lot less grief than messing with the wrong women."

Camille stared coldly at Henry. "Hans, there's very little in the way of activities for Westerners here in Jeddah," she explained. "Some of them focus on their neighbor's lives, and gossip about them for sport. Some..." she looked at Henry pointedly, "are pretty malicious."

Hans was more interested in the dessert tray that the waiter had just rolled up to the table. "Bananas Foster? You have that here? Well, I'll just have to have it! Cammy, you want some, too, don't you?"

"No thanks."

"None for us either," Henry stated. "We'll just have coffee. Someone accused us of being fat."

Camille laughed. "I'm not the one who brought up the comparison, Henry."

Henry sipped his coffee slowly, waiting as Hans contentedly polished off the last of his dessert. He looked ready to pounce.

"You know, Hans, we are all pretty close in the compound. There's one Brit that Camille and Ashley are especially fond of..." He put his napkin down and centered his full attention on Hans. "They've spent quite a lot of time with him." Henry waited intently for Hans' reaction.

Hans wiped his mouth with the linen napkin. "So? Cammy has male friends."

"Yes, but I believe Charles is...special."

Hans looked at his wife. "Cammy, who's this Charles?"

"Charles lost his wife two years ago. He's done nothing but help Beau and me, and he's been a good friend for Ashley."

Henry's neck was starting to turn a motley red and white mixture, which was moving up into his face.

Hans looked at Camille. He knew her to be imminently practical. And, Hans was ever the pragmatic German-American.

"So?" he asked Henry.

Henry seemed angry at the direction of this conversation. His eyes narrowed and a look of hatred overcame his face. Hans watched the transformation with interest.

"So?!" Henry responded, almost hissing. "They are very close. Do you know what I am saying here, Hans?"

Hans sat back and folded his arms. He looked at the man, and immediately sized up the situation. "You invited us out to eat so you could accuse my wife?" Hans sat for a moment, then looked at the angry stranger in front of him. Hans leaned across the table.

"You're one sick puppy, aren't you, Henry? So, you're trying to cause trouble in my marriage." Hans lowered his voice and moved closer to Henry's face. "Once we leave here, Henry, you had better hope I never lay eyes on you again. Do you understand me?"

Henry's eyes widened when he realized the meaning of Hans' words. A look of fear slowly registered in his face.

"With neighbors like you," Camille realized aloud, "no wonder poor Charles has been so uptight."

The waiter walked up to Henry and handed him the bill.

"Uh...I'll get this. I promised—" Henry fished nervously for his wallet.

"We'll pay for our own meal," Hans told the waiter. He tossed $70 on the waiter's tray. "Does that cover it?"

"Oh, yes, sir. Very good, sir."

Hans pulled Camille's chair out for her. "Let's get out of here," he said.

Hans waited as the valet brought their car. "That scheming son of a bitch," he said angrily, "where the hell does he get off—" He handed the valet a tip.

"Hans, do you know how to get to the compound from here?"

"What? Oh, sure. I was watching the roads."

Hans drove through Jeddah and parked on the side of the compound.

Camille unlocked the villa door. She went to the phone and rang Henry's number. "Send Beau home. Now." She hung up.

"What the hell is wrong with these people?"

"Oh, by the way, Hans...be careful what you say in the house."

"Why?"

"The villa is bugged."

"Bugged?" he asked incredulously.

"Yep. Bugged."

"No. They wouldn't..." Hans' face turned angry. "You mean, they're listening to everything we say and do?"

"Everything."

"Even upstairs?"

"Even upstairs."

"I...I've gotta go for a walk."

"Have fun. You've got a whole block."

Hans stormed out the door.

Charles had returned from Wales with new purpose. Assessing his life, he realized how many options he had. For years, he'd scrimped and saved, carefully investing most of his substantial earnings. He could actually retire if he wished. And, now he'd finally found a woman who understood him.

Charles had heard that Camille's husband had arrived. Not the smallest scrap of news escaped the compound. He was unsure how this man would react to the time spent with his family. He'd made the usual "bread run," and it was time to deliver to their villa. The Brit sighed and picked up the bread. It was time to face him, he decided.

He knocked tentatively on the villa door. As the door opened,

Charles found himself looking up at a solid figure that blocked out most of the door area.

"My God, you're a mountain," the words slipped out.

"I'm Hans, and who might you be?"

"Oh, excuse me. I'm Charles."

Hans grinned. "THE Charles? The infamous Charles?"

Charles relaxed. "Exactly."

"Well, c'mon in. Thanks for helping my family."

"I brought...the bread."

"Mr. Charles, you met my dad?" Beau skipped down the stairs.

"Yes, he's quite...sizeable."

"Oh, he used to play football in Wisconsin. But I bet Brett Favre could beat him in golf."

Charles was confused. "Who's Brett Favre? A golfer?"

"Oh, Mr. Charles, that's funny," Beau laughed, and ran back upstairs to his videogames.

Camille entered the room. "Charles, you're back! And you brought the bread. We were just getting ready to leave. Hans wanted to look at some pictures from local artists to bring back to the States."

"Oh, are you an art collector, Hans?"

"Well...something like that," Hans sheepishly responded.

"What artists do you collect?"

"Hans," Camille interrupted, "has one of the finest neon beer sign collections in the South."

Charles regarded this man with new appreciation. "Oustanding!"

"And," Ashley entered the room, "be sure and check out his website. Perhaps you've heard of it?"

"Sorry? Can't say that I have."

Hans proudly handed Charles a card. "Beertasterscertified.com. It's my hobby."

Charles took the card and laughed. Ashley studied Charles for a moment. He looked, well...different.

"Hans, Charles just got back from vacation. He really needed a rest after what he's been going through these past few years. In fact, we were telling him he needed to get on with his life..."

Camille turned her attention on Charles. "You look well rested, Charles. Relaxed, even. And look at those rosy cheeks..."

Hans grinned and inspected the Brit. He recognized the look. "I would say," Hans summed up astutely, "that Charles has gotten on with his life."

"And," Charles expanded, "I intend to do a lot more getting on— with life, I mean."

Ashley and Camille looked at each other. "Charles gets his new theme song!" Ashley picked up her guitar, and the two conferred for a moment, then broke out singing, "I'm so excited, I just can't hide it, I'm about to lose control and I think I like it..."

The group laughed together. Hans was feeling much more relaxed. "You know," he planned, "Maybe we should all just take a little time off tomorrow and see some of the country...you know, take a little road trip to some of the different cities."

Three people simultaneously shook their heads at him.

"No, you can't."

"Whadda ya mean—no, I can't?"

"You will need a visa to visit each different city," Charles explained.

"What?" Hans sat down, flabbergasted. This was just too much for his brain.

"Just another little restriction. But..." there was a definite twinkle in the Brit's aquamarine blue eyes, "I've got a phone call to make. Bye." Charles waved as he walked out the door. "See y'all."

CHAPTER 10
Don't Touch Him!

Ashley was bubbling over with excitement as they rode the clinic bus to the palace. "Will you ask Naomi today? Please? I want to start making some...plans."

"Alright, Ashley. First thing."

There was tension in the air as the women walked in. Camille was grateful when Safiya cheerfully entered the room.

"Camille, I have a favor to ask."

"Certainly, Safiya."

"One of my friends has a son who's had difficulty with his speech. Therapy hasn't helped. They're upstairs. I'd like you to take a look at him."

"Not at all," Camille said gratefully. "Our first patient! Alright, therapists," she called to the others, "let's go to work!"

They walked upstairs to a room where a young teenage boy stood, lanky and unsure of himself, as boys anywhere were at his age. His mother stood behind him in the room.

"Good afternoon," Camille greeted. She looked toward the boy. "What's your name?"

He looked at his mother for reassurance. She nodded.

"Muhamm..."

"Mohammed, right? Mohammed, how old are you?"

"Er-een."

"Hmm, thirteen..." Camille crossed the room and pulled a list out of the file drawer. "Mohammed, I want you to read the words on this list."

The boy took the list, and started.

"Lilly," Camille addressed the Egyptian therapist, "do you notice a sound pattern developing?"

"He has difficulty with dental sounds," Lilly answered with assurance.

"He may be tongue tied," Hala meekly added.

Camille looked at the group. Mohammed was their first clinic case, and they most probably could easily solve this problem. "So, what do we do next?"

"Easy. Clip the lingual frenulum," Lilly answered, hands on her hips.

"Right. Of course, one has to be careful that there's not any blood vessels or nerves in the way. Mohammed, hop up here on the table."

Camille picked up an examination light and a tongue depressor.

"Open wide." She held Mohammed's jaw to steady it, then began to raise his tongue with the tongue depressor.

Three Feet Away

"What are you doing?!"

The group turned to see Naomi storming toward the therapists. Frightened, the boy clamped down on the tongue depressor.

"I'm doing a standard exam, Naomi. Nothing different than we've done a hundred times before."

"No! Not here! You can't touch him."

"What?"

"You have to be at least three feet away from him at all times."

"Naomi, I can't see his tongue real good from three feet away."

"I told you once already," Naomi was openly hostile, "that you can only touch other females."

"Naomi, we have no male therapists. What are we going to do with male patients?"

"You can work with them. You just have to be across the table."

Camille slowly and with finality put her exam light down on the table. She looked at the other therapists, who appeared confused and afraid. A realization slowly filled her. She couldn't perform her job. Given these restrictions, there was no way.

"Naomi, I think we'd better talk..."

"Yes, I think that's a good idea."

The two women walked into Naomi's office. Naomi closed the door.

"Naomi," Camille started softly, "I was brought over here with the understanding that I would work with neuromuscular retraining; you know—the laying on of hands? Can't do that if I can't touch 'em. I think it's best if you started looking for someone to replace me. Someone who's comfortable with this particular cultural—restraint."

Camille waited. No response. "Alright, then..." Camille rose to leave.

"Camille?"

"Yes, Naomi?"

"You're right. I'll make the calls."

Safiya seemed to feel badly about the confrontation. At least the boy's problem had been diagnosed. Two days later, the surgery was performed. Within a week, the boy's speech was improving.

"Why don't you bring Beau to work with you Saturday morning? He can watch movies with my children," Safiya offered.

"Thanks, Safiya. I think Beau would enjoy that."

The next morning, Beau arrived with his mother at the palace. He seemed to enjoy the company of Safiya's children, as they all ran laughing upstairs to watch a movie.

It was quiet in the clinic that morning. Safiya had given the other therapists the morning off.

After a few hours, Naomi emerged from her office. "Camille, do you have anything more to do here?"

"Not a thing."

"Well, then, you may call the clinic bus to take you home."

"Good. I'll just call upstairs for Beau first." Camille picked up the phone.

"By the way..." Naomi turned back.

"Yes?"

"I...made those calls. It looks like the problem will be resolved shortly. Maybe, even, within the next few weeks."

Camille sighed in relief. "Excellent."

Beau was quiet on the bus ride back to the villa. Finally he spoke. "Uh, Mom? You know that they have a TV satellite dish at the palace..."

"Yes, hon, I know."

"Well, the kids started watching this movie, you know? It was from France. Mom, you'd tan my butt if you caught me watching something like that. I can't believe the servants just let them..."

Camille scrutinized her son's bewildered look then quietly thought about the whole scenario. "The servants were probably afraid to say anything," she concluded.

As the bus drove on, for the first time Camille became aware of the many TV satellite dishes topping the rooftops of the more affluent dwellings. What an irony. Because of censorship, technology was slow in coming to this country. Yet, technology had opened the worldwide airwaves to the wealthy Arabs.

Back at the compound, Ashley found out that Amin and his wife would be in Cairo for three days, so she decided to take advantage of their absence to go swimming.

"I'll take Beau in the pool for a swim," she volunteered, "then you and Hans can try out that Moroccan restaurant he's been talking about."

"Thanks, hon. That'll give us a chance to talk," Camille looked around the villa, "away from here."

Hans was good with maps. He seemed to easily find his way through the tortuous, haphazard road system of Jeddah.

"We're on what's called the 'Shaky Bridge' now," Camille explained.

"It is shaking. Why?"

"Something to do with construction problems..."

Hans shook his head. "Gheeze, then let's get off this quick."

He drove further and was happy to see the Moroccan restaurant ahead. Once inside, Camille was impressed. The floors were polished marble, tropical plants abounded, and a large fountain dominating the center of the room lazily sprayed water.

"Cammy, have some almond milk," Hans encouraged. "I think you'll like it."

Meal ordered, Hans turned to his wife. "Alright, I'm rested and calm now. What's going on at the clinic?"

"We just saw our first patient today."

"Oh, that's good."

"No, it was a disaster. It was a young male, so I couldn't touch him to examine his mouth."

Hans put down his napkin. "What? I've never heard of such a thing!"

"Apparently, the cultural restrictions also apply in a health-care setting. Women therapists are not allowed to touch male patients. They must work with a table separating them by at least three feet."

Hans wiped his mouth and looked out into the distance. "How..." he wondered, "no, that just won't work," he concluded.

"Exactly. Besides, we are all set up, but the new clinic building won't be ready for five more months."

"Five months?"

"Oh...and Ashley wants to get home so she and Remmy can get married."

Hans gave a startled expression. "I should have seen that one coming," he laughed.

"Hans, Naomi and I talked. She's finding replacements for Ashley and me. We may be able to go home with you, if..." Camille gave him a mischievous grin, "if that's OK with you."

Hans leaned toward his wife. "Hon, you don't know how happy that would make me."

Back at the pool, Ashley and Beau were in high spirits. They took turns doing cannonballs off the edge of the pool, seeing who could create the biggest splash.

Charles had been on the phone with Anna, his new love. He heard Ashley and Beau's laughter outside. I have to tell Ashley, he decided. She'd be so pleased with Anna... He quickly changed into a T-shirt and shorts, uncharacteristically relaxed clothes for him.

Beau saw him first. "Hey, Mr. Charles, catch!"

Charles laughed, caught the beach ball, and sat at the edge of the pool.

Ashley paddled over. "So..." she coaxed, "tell me, darlin', who's got you so happy?"

Katie's Revenge

Sam hadn't had the heart to tell Katie that Charles had finally found a new love. Her name was Anna. He sensed that it would drive her fragile emotional state to the breaking point.

Up on the balcony, Katie watched her precious Charles sitting beside the pool. So, she thought, he looked so happy. He was probably going to become part of this American family. He'd probably move to the States with them, and she'd never see her handsome Charles again.

Katie sat in her rocking chair stroking her Siamese cat and inwardly seething. Her grasp of reality had been quietly slipping away. Almost no one paid much attention to her, or they would have seen the signs. Her husband, Sam, had noticed she was acting more peculiar lately, but hoped she'd somehow get better if he just humored her.

Katie's thoughts became more circular, then more angry, then more circular. How could Charles do this to her? Due to a childhood illness, Katie had been left barren. Couldn't Charles understand that it wasn't her fault? She sat, rocked, and continued to seethe.

Beau's playful screams from the pool caught her off guard. Charles had picked up Beau, ready to chuck him into the water. Katie's smoldering hatred ignited as she watched. She suddenly gripped her cat hard. Her Siamese gave a startled cry and sprang away from his mistress. What little reason Katie had was washed away in a torrent of hatred.

Katie had been patient, but this was too much. She had to get rid of these Americans, who were turning her beloved Charles against her.

"Katie, I'm going to market. Want to come along?" Sam, her husband, asked pleasantly.

"No."

"Well, alright then, love. Won't be gone long."

Katie waited until she saw her husband's car back away. Madame Safiya's phone number must be around somewhere. Since Sam was manager for all the Western compounds, she knew he had it in his workbook. Katie shuffled through Sam's desk drawers.

"Ah! Here t'is!"

She leafed through the pages and stopped at one entry.

"Yes..."

The look of hatred gave Katie's plain face an eerie, chilling appearance as she dialed the phone. There was no force on earth that would stop her now, for she was about to get rid of her perceived competition once and for all. Charles would be hers. It was just one phone call away.

Abayas Up!

Meanwhile, Beau was tiring of the pool. "Aunt Ashley, could we get some ice cream?"

"Doesn't your mom have any in the refrigerator?"

"No, she forgot to tell Samantha to buy some."

"But, Beau, we'd have to rent a limo, and prayer call is coming up shortly..."

"Oh, I'll drive you," Charles volunteered. He was in a magnanimous mood. "But—you're going to have to hurry. We've got about twenty minutes."

Ashley rushed in and threw a T-shirt and shorts over her wet bathing suit. She tied her jogging shoes and threw her *abaya* over the haphazard outfit.

Charles honked the horn outside their villa. The three of them climbed into his car. "We may just have time—we'll go down the street to the local grocers."

Charles parked the car and all three jumped out. Ashley had never been in this local neighborhood store before. The American had been told to shop the larger, nationalized grocery chains and avoid the more militant faction in this neighborhood.

As Ashley raced to the counter, she crossed over the metal grids that blew an updraft of chilled air to block the outside heat. Caught by surprise, her *abaya* billowed over her head for a moment, showing her bare legs and arms covered only by a wet T-shirt and shorts. A great sound of disapproving noises arose as eyes fixated on her.

"Well, now you've gone and done it!" Charles chided, trying to be serious. The Brit took on an air of mock sternness. "Just wait until I get you home!" His critical tone and promise of retribution appeared to appease the male Arabs.

Beau shrugged his shoulders. He couldn't see what all the fuss was about. At one of the check-out stands, two guards from the Western compound were waiting in line. One of the guards from their compound smiled deviously as he looked at the other guard.

CHAPTER 11
It Has Come To My Attention

The tide had turned in the Kingdom. A respectable amount of time had elapsed since the Gulf War, and the Saudis felt safe once again. Also, the Christmas holidays had been tolerated.

The English and Arabic writing on all the road signs was changed. Now, there were only Arabic road signs. Since there were more expatriates than Arabs in the Kingdom, and not all Arabs could read the written Arabic, this caused more confusion and increased traffic accidents.

The president and members of the Jeddah Sailing Club were arrested at the docks as their yacht returned from an approved outing.

Hoda Beach, where Westerners had been able to scuba dive and swim with a relaxed dress code, was now heavily patrolled for anyone who might not be following strict dress codes.

And Eddie, the husband of Camille's maid, Samantha, was taken into custody for interrogation.

At the beginning of the next work day, Ashley was even more insistent. "Cammy, would you please get some more information from Naomi about when we can leave? Just think, after all these years, Remmy and I are officially engaged. I don't want to delay the wedding much longer."

"Yes, Ashley, yes."

As Camille entered the clinic room, however, she could sense something was very wrong. Fatma, the Lebanese secretary, looked fearfully toward Ashley.

"Miss Ashley, Madame Safiya wants to see you right away."

"Oh, alright."

Ashley climbed the stairs, walked into the office, and seated herself in front of Safiya's desk. Safiya took a moment to study the young woman in front of her.

"It has come to my attention," she began seriously, "that you have not been following our laws."

"I haven't?"

Safiya stood up and paced behind her desk. "My life is an open book. I have no secrets," Safiya continued. "But you, Ashley, have not learned how to properly deal with…relationships."

Ashley realized she must be talking about Charles. Both women looked at each other for a long moment.

"It has even been reported…that you have even gone to—dinner parties!"

Safiya's last statement sounded so incongruous and anticlimactic that Ashley had to stifle a laugh. "Well, yes I have, Safiya."

Safiya frowned. "I am having our personal business manager write up a statement for you to sign. It will say that you acknowledge that you have broken our laws and that you will never break these laws again. Then we will be finished with this unpleasant business. I will expect a signed copy on my desk by tomorrow afternoon. That is all."

Ashley rose from the chair, opened the office door, and walked downstairs. She poured herself a cup of coffee, sat at her desk, and stared at the wall.

Comforted to see the young American back and in no apparent distress, the staff seemed to relax. Ashley listened to the far-away, melodic prayer call with sadness. She was surprised to find she would actually miss this "come to God, come to God." What human being anywhere wasn't trying to come home to God?

Ashley watched thoughtfully as Hala emerged from the bathroom after performing her ablutions and quietly rolled out her prayer rug for midmorning prayer call.

Camille, ever watchful of her younger sister, walked over to her desk. "What was that all about?" she asked in a low voice.

Ashley looked around the room. "I can't tell you right now."

After lunch, a Saudi businessman opened the clinic door and walked in with the characteristic flourish. He sat abruptly next to Ashley, without asking for the usual permission. The young American woman looked disapprovingly at him. She placed him in his sixties, a person of some moderate importance who obviously wanted to impress his extremely wealthy mistress.

"Yes, what is it?" she asked coldly.

"I have worked very hard to get good words for this document," he stated proudly in a thick Arab accent. "I have exactly the words that you need to sign."

He presented his document. Ashley took the paper and read through it slowly. "This is to state that Miss Ashley Ladnier, being an employee of Madame Safiya Malinara, has without conscience violated the sacred laws of Saudi Arabia and the religious tenets of Islam. Further, she willingly agrees that she will never violate these laws again, and apologizes for her disorder of judgment."

If the situation hadn't been so serious, Ashley would have laughed and made copies for her friends back home.

The Arab man pulled out a gold pen from one of the crevices of his white robe. "You will sign it now."

Ashley put the document down on the table. "No. This is something which requires careful thought."

"You don't sign it now?"

"No. I will have to think about it."

Obviously at a loss, the man left the room with much less flourish.

Sign the Bloody Thing

Camille watched her sister as they rode the bus back to the villa. Ashley was in an introspective mood. There was a part of her that would always love this fascinating land and the people she had met here.

Hans was busy on the phone when they walked in. He cupped his hand over the receiver for a moment and looked at his sister-in-law. "Your neighbor Charles called. He wants you to come over to his place and talk about something to do with work." He went back to his conversation.

"Oh…OK." Ashley dropped her briefcase and walked the short distance. She knocked on Charles' door.

"It's open."

Ashley entered Charles' living room. His curtains were drawn and only a small table lamp was lit. Charles sat in a chair in the corner.

"Sit down," he ordered.

Ashley pulled an ottoman next to Charles and sat facing him.

"Katie took it upon herself to call your boss, Safiya. She told Safiya that we were having a torrid affair."

"But we're not!" Ashley protested.

"She asked me again just last week if I'd have an affair with her." His words suddenly became bitter. "I told her I was not having an affair with anybody, and certainly would not with her." Charles turned his head in the direction of Sam and Katie's apartment. "How could she even delude herself into the notion that I would actually want to have sex with her—that, that—rumpled sack of potatoes!"

Ashley giggled at his description in spite of herself. Charles glared at her. She covered her mouth and became serious again. "Does Sam know what she did?"

"Yes. The word got back to him immediately. He doesn't know about her other unwanted advances toward me, of course. I would never tell him. But, he's sending his faithful wife back to Britain for a 'rest', he calls it."

Ashley sighed. "I like Sam."

"I do, too," Charles replied softly. "He's always been a good friend to me."

"Charles, Safiya called me into her office today. They want me to sign a statement."

"What kind of statement?"

"Oh, just that I've broken the laws, and I will never do it again." Ashley handed him the file folder. "Here, take a look at it yourself."

Charles took the document and read it. He looked up at her. "Sign the bloody thing."

"No, Charles."

"Ashley, sign the bloody thing, and be done with it. Then you can get back to your work. It's important, you know."

"Charles," she worried, "your career won't be hurt because of this, will it?"

Charles laughed sarcastically. "What career? You call this a career? I've made my decision. I'm going back to Wales."

"Well, I'm glad for you, Charles. But will you get in trouble for what Katie said?"

Again Charles laughed sarcastically. "Of course not, Ashley. They always blame the woman."

Now it was Ashley's turn to be sarcastic. "Oh, yes. How silly of me. I forgot for a moment where I was."

She stood up and gave Charles a light kiss on his forehead, then tousled his hair. "Gotta go." Then she stopped. "Charles, if I don't see you again, remember...we are always friends."

Charles smiled. He hesitated for a moment, then reached up and unclasped a solid gold chain that was under his T-shirt. "Here," he said, fastening the chain around Ashley's neck. "Keep this until the next time I see you. Then I want it back."

A tear escaped from the corner of Ashley's eye. "It's been great knowing you, Charles."

Ashley walked back to her villa.

"What did Charles want?" Hans asked.

"Oh, we're having some problems with the same people," she explained. "Hans, Safiya wants me to sign a document saying I've broken the laws of Islam." She handed the paper to her brother-in-law.

Hans quickly read the paper, snorted in disgust, and threw it on the table.

"Don't sign anything! You're coming home with us!"

Beau entered the room at that moment with one of his British friends.

His friend turned to Beau. "Tell them," he ordered.

"Tell us what?" Camille asked.

"You tell them, Beau, or I will."

Beau still hesitated. "But, Colin, then they won't let me go to the mall anymore."

Colin faced Camille and Hans. "We were just walking back from the mall with some of the guys from the Swedish soccer team. We figured we'd be safe that way, because there were six of us. Three Arabs pulled up and started trying to stuff us into a van."

Beau put his head down. "So, we pulled their red picnic napkins over their heads, kicked a couple of 'em in the butt, and ran away."

"Some Arabs," Colin explained, "especially like to kidnap blonde boys. They take them out of the country."

"Beau!" Camille cried out.

"It's already happened two other times," Beau admitted.

"And you didn't tell us?"

"Mom, you would never have let me out of the compound."

"I think you should call the American embassy," Colin concluded. "My parents are calling the British embassy tomorrow."

"That's it!" Hans slammed down the steak plates.

"Thanks, Colin," Camille said.

"No problem." Colin looked at his watch. "I've got dinner waiting, too."

Beau was left standing by himself.

"Beau, don't you ever keep anything this serious from us again!" his mother angrily ordered.

"Now go wash up," Hans added.

Beau ran upstairs to his bedroom. Camille and Hans looked at each other. "We're outta here," Hans decided. "No matter what, I'm taking you all back home with me."

Hans walked upstairs and opened Beau's bedroom door. "Beau, we're not taking any more chances. If you want to go somewhere, you can go with me."

"But, Dad—"

"No, son. This is just too dangerous."

I Hope You've Learned Your Lesson

No matter what clucking she had to endure from the Arab women now entrenched in her western compound, Camille needed to go jogging the next morning. She knew it was going to be a pivotal day at the clinic, and she had to clear her head. After twenty minutes around the compound, Camille stopped suddenly as she rounded the sidewalk by Charles' villa.

Charles had already gone to work. There were ladders leading to his roof. Workers were busily pulling out wires. Camille froze. Charles' villa, she realized, had also been bugged. She knew now what was going to happen this morning. The decision had been made for the Americans to leave, and the listening devices in Charles' home would not be needed anymore. As she walked back to her villa, she prepared herself for what was coming.

Ashley expected a summons as soon as she reached the clinic. However, it wasn't until midmorning that the call came. Fatma put the phone down. "Madame Safiya wants to see both of you upstairs."

The sisters looked at each other, then slowly walked up the stairs and knocked on Safiya's office door.

"Yes?" Safiya answered sharply.

They opened the door and walked in.

Safiya looked aggravated. "Well, Ashley, you've caused quite a bit of trouble around here." She waited for a reply, but the American woman remained silent.

"Are you going to sign the confession?" she continued.

Ashley locked eyes with the Arab woman. "No, Safiya, I am not."

"Well, then, I have no choice but to ask for your resignation."

"No problem, Safiya. However, I do expect six weeks' severance pay."

Safiya looked startled, then angry. She shook her head, as if in unhappy resignation. "Oh, very well. You may have it." Safiya leaned over her desk. "What bothers me most is how I explain your sudden resignation. I don't want to hurt the reputation of the clinic."

"I understand, Safiya. Just tell them the truth. I just became officially engaged to a gentleman from my hometown."

Safiya appeared confused. If the woman was engaged, then maybe the accusations about the Brit...no, she didn't even want to think about it. She turned to Camille. "I suppose you want to leave, too."

"Yes, I do. And I want the same severance pay."

Safiya looked perplexed, then threw her hands up in exasperation. "Oh, very well. But, what do we tell the staff about you?"

"Easy...the truth. My husband is here, and I've decided to go back with him."

Safiya cocked her head thoughtfully. "Yes. Yes, that will work. After we finish, you may go downstairs and tell this to the staff. Then you will go home and pack."

Camille nodded in agreement.

Having satisfied herself with all the arrangements, Safiya leaned close to Ashley. The Arab woman looked around the room, as if someone could be watching. In a low, confidential tone, Safiya asked, "Just what is it about you?"

Ashley looked confused. "What do you mean?"

Safiya pulled herself back. "What is it that makes you get along so with men? I can't see it, myself."

Ashley and Camille looked at each other with sudden realization. It was so simple.

Ashley let out a chuckle. "Oh, Safiya," she said lightly, "Soul equals—"

Camille suddenly put her hand to Ashley's lips, cutting off the rest of her statement. For some reason, she realized that Safiya was not ready to hear this explanation.

Ashley looked questioningly at her sister for a moment, then came quickly to the same understanding. A concept that was obvious to the two sisters would somehow cause trouble for Safiya in her world.

Safiya had been leaning forward, ready to be enlightened. Now, she had been deprived of some special knowledge. The woman broke into an uncharacteristic fit of frightening rage.

Camille knew this woman had the power to make them disappear and never be seen again. Yet, Safiya was a highly-principled woman, and the American knew Safiya wouldn't harm them. She watched as the Arab woman's anger boiled over.

"You!" she pointed to Ashley then stuck her finger up in the air for emphasis, her voice evolving into a high-pitched shriek. "Are the most immoral, corrupt woman I have ever met! The sooner you leave this country, the better!"

Ashley looked hurt and confused. No one had ever called her immoral before.

Now it was Camille's turn to be angry. "Now you just hold the fort one cotton-pickin' minute, Safiya!"

In spite of the grave situation, Ashley found herself amused by Camille's mixed metaphors. But her sister was on a roll.

Camille stood up and gestured toward her sister. "You don't know this girl's story. We're talking minister's wife here, for God's sake! Even if she is my sister, I've never seen a more moral person in my life!"

Ashley looked in awe at Camille's pronouncement. She'd never heard her sister defend her so adamantly before.

"Oh," Ashley remembered, "speaking of ministers...we'll be needing our travel expenses paid, too."

"Huh!" Camille exclaimed, astounded. "You go, girl!" she cheered.

Safiya was tired of being double teamed. "No!" she stomped her foot. "Nothing more!"

Camille stood up and put her hands on her hips. "You're actually going to make us pay to get out of this country? Well, fine, if that's what it takes."

Safiya took one last look at this vexing pair. "You may leave now, and I hope you have learned your lesson."

The two women rose and left the office. As they stood at the top of the stairs, Ashley looked at her older sister. "I wonder what lesson that is?"

"I don't know," Camille shrugged.

Ashley composed herself. Camille followed her younger sister down the stairs, realizing she had a newfound respect for her.

As the women were readying themselves to face the clinic staff, Zayad slipped into Safiya's office. Safiya's husband, Sami, had also just come home and had gone to see his wife.

"Did Camille's sister sign the statement?" Zayad ask eagerly.

"No. I'm sending them both home."

"What? I am not finished with Camille."

Sami looked over at the man. Safiya's husband had graduated from UCLA in California and had difficulty understanding about all the fuss. "Zayad, just leave them alone."

Zayad's eyes flashed. "No, I will not. Camille will pay through her family. Her sister will face the Council. Her son—" he broke off, not ready to reveal all of his plans. "And, I want to look into the eyes of Camille's husband!"

Both Sami and Safiya groaned at the same time. Zayad straightened his *thobe* and *gutra* then walked purposefully out of the room on his mission.

Ashley paused briefly at the clinic door, slowly placed a smile on her face, and then drifted into the room. "Listen, everybody!" she announced. "I have an exciting announcement to make..."

The room quieted.

"Last week, I became engaged to the most wonderful man from my hometown. His name is Remmy. We've decided to get married next month. Doctora Camille," Ashley continued, placing her arm on her sister's shoulder, "also has an announcement."

"My family realized we needed to be together, so I'm leaving with my husband and son."

The staff sat in stunned silence. Camille walked over and shook Hamad's hand. "Good luck, Hamad. You'll make an excellent business manager for the clinic." She laughed and patted the colorful Lebanese secretary on the back. "Fatma, I'll miss your sense of humor."

Lilly stood at the table with tears in her large brown eyes. "Don't go and leave me here alone," she said quietly, her voice quivering.

"I must." Camille hugged the Egyptian. "You understand that better than anyone."

Ashley turned and looked at the sweet, delicate Saudi therapist, Hala.

Hala looked up at them, tears trickling down her face. "What will we do without you two?"

Ashley smiled gently. Hala had taught the Americans by example, rather than words, the true spirit of Islam. With compassion and quiet devotion to her faith, Hala embodied the best.

Ashley took the young woman's hand. "You'll do fine, Hala. I'll be thinking of you…and your first baby."

Hala lowered her head and wiped away the tears.

The now-former clinic director looked toward Naomi's office. "By the way, where are Naomi and Gerald?"

"Oh, they went to the American embassy," Fatma volunteered.

Camille and Ashley exchanged curious glances. Why?

She's Not Going Anywhere

The two sisters rode the clinic bus for the last time. Hans was waiting at the door for Camille. "I got the call. They said our movers would be here to pack in an hour. Is that right?"

"Yep. Ashley wouldn't sign."

"Good for her. So, when are we going home?"

"Friday morning. But, Hans, Safiya is making us pay our own moving expenses to get out of here."

Hans dropped the box he was holding. "What the hell—"

His thoughts were interrupted by a sharp rap at the door.

"Now what is it?" an angry Hans opened the door.

Two tall Arabs in *thobes* and *gutras* stood on the doorstep. One of them was Zayad, Safiya's cousin. His smile bore a vindictive quality that concerned Camille.

"Zayad," she acknowledged, "why am I not surprised to see you here?"

Zayad turned and studied Camille's short hair. "Your hair," he began, "I told you—"

"You told my wife what?" Hans demanded, his anger building. Both men stood eye to eye, openly assessing each other.

Zayad finally broke off his stare. "Your sister-in-law would not sign a document, which would have been the most prudent decision. Since she was uncooperative about this matter, she must come with us to be personally interviewed by the Council."

Hans leaned forward. "She's not going anywhere," he growled protectively.

"She must, or her exit visa will not be issued."

Ashley stood up and threw her silver *abaya* around her. "Thanks, Hans, but I can handle this."

Hans walked over and blocked the door with his massive body.

"Please, Hans," Ashley implored, "I can get through this. I want to go home with you."

Camille looked at Zayad. "I'm sure she'll be back in an hour or two, and intact, won't she, Zayad?"

"Perhaps so," he said noncommittally.

The two Saudis escorted Ashley to a black limo. They drove to the main company headquarters. Quickly escorted through the lobby, the woman was hurriedly ushered into a room with twelve Arab men at a long table.

The twelve Saudi men fired questions at her.

"Do you believe in Islam?"

"All religions are valid," she answered.

"But do you believe in the tenets of Islam?" the elder man insisted.

"The tenets of Islam are needed for those experiencing a certain state of consciousness."

The men looked at each other. They couldn't argue with these nebulous statements.

The older man, apparently the leader, cleared his throat. "Have you violated our laws?"

"I have not violated the spirit of your prophet, Mohammed's teachings. He taught compassion and love for all, didn't he?"

Ashley waited. "I have my own question," she said when it became apparent that no one was going to answer her. "It takes twelve men to question one woman? Why?" She looked around the table. "I have no quarrel with you," she said, "and you have no quarrel with me."

The men sat quietly for a moment. The elder at the head of the table nodded, and another put typed papers in front of the young woman. With relief, she realized they were her exit visa documents.

Zayad and another Arab escorted Ashley to the limo. Zayad sat across from her. Ashley looked into his golden eyes, and found them troubled.

"I'm sorry," he apologized. "It was not you I intended to hurt."

The two men drove the American woman back in silence.

Camille had been waiting, and rushed to the limo. "They didn't hurt you, did they?"

"No," Ashley held up an envelope. "And I got my exit visa."

"Well, alright!" Hans appeared relieved. His relief lasted for only a few moments as he turned to the two Arabs packing boxes.

"No! Don't put the crystal glasses underneath the pans!" Frustrated, he turned to his wife. "I have to stay on top of these guys every minute!"

Beau ran in with his friend Colin.

"Beau, are your games packed?" Hans' question followed his son up the stairs.

"Just about, Dad."

"I'll see," Camille said and followed her son. She entered Beau's bedroom. "Look!" she went over to his closet and picked up a lone shoebox from the top shelf. "You were going to leave your shoes?" She opened the box and frowned. Inside was a bottle with some kind of liquid.

Beau's eyes grew wide as Camille unscrewed the cap. "What is this?" she sniffed. She touched the liquid to her finger and tasted. "Beau! You were trying to make wine? Who taught you this?"

"I did," Colin volunteered. "Do you like it?"

"Oh!!" Camille answered, exasperated. "Colin, go home! Beau, you pour this stuff out and get back to packing!"

"I'll just be off now," Colin grinned and walked down the steps and out the door.

Camille stood in the middle of Beau's boxes.

"Sorry, Mom."

"Cammy!" Hans called. "There's a man here with some money for you and Ashley."

Camille walked down the stairs. An Arab held an envelope with Saudi riyals and a letter.

"You sign for money," he instructed.

"What's the money for?" Hans inquired.

"Oh, we told Safiya we wanted six weeks' severance pay."

"Good."

"You sign—you sign," the Arab insisted.

"Just a minute, I'm reading." Camille frowned. "I'm being charged for a doorbell they put in? Two hundred riyals? And the extra phone upstairs? Four hundred riyals?" She looked angrily at the poor Arab messenger in front of her.

"I no do, I no do," he protested.

Hans hotly let out his breath. "Well, sign the damned thing and get it over with!"

"Yes, yes." The little Arab man held out the paper and Camille scribbled her name. The man gratefully scurried out the door.

The phone rang. "I'll get it." Hans crossed the room. "Yes? Yes, this is Doctora Camille's husband. The movers will be here when?" He glanced at his wife. "Just a minute; let me write this down. Tomorrow morning at nine? OK, we'll be here. And...what about the car? OK, yes, I need to bring the car back to the dealer tomorrow afternoon...Yes, I'm writing down the address..."

"Wait!" Camille interrupted. "How will you get back to the villa?"

Hans rolled his eyes and covered the phone receiver. "They hadn't thought about that. They went to ask someone." Hans waited for another minute. "Oh, you're back? Yes? You're going to send who?" He looked toward Camille. "The clinic bus driver?"

Camille groaned.

"He'll be here at our villa at twelve-thirty? Alright." Hans finished.

"They gave us the slowest-witted one of the bunch," Camille complained.

"Well, at least they gave us someone," Hans countered. "Hey! It's our last night in Jeddah, and we have to take the car back tomorrow.

Cammy, we're going to the Hilton for the big seafood buffet!" He walked toward the stairs. "Kid, what're you doing up there?"

Beau's blonde head appeared at the top of the landing.

"C'mon, boy, we're going to a big restaurant to get some of those shrimp you like so much!"

Beau grinned. "Alright, Dad!" The boy rushed down the stairs and the three headed for the compound gate. Now that he was driving in the afternoon sunshine, Hans' spirits seemed to lift. He downshifted the Volvo as they came to another roundabout.

"Whee!" Hans called as he deftly turned the corner. Beau laughed delightedly from the back seat. "Want me to do it again?" Hans asked.

"Sure, Dad!"

Up ahead was another roundabout. "Hold on, kid!" A large silver Mercedes approached from a side street. Although Hans had the right-of-way, the Arab swerved to cut in front of him. Hans' jaw clenched. The two cars were at an impasse, and both stopped.

The Arab glanced at the family in the car with obvious disdain. The look was not wasted on Hans. His anger had been building all day, and this man's lack of respect was the trigger. Hans and the Arab shot each other angry glances.

The big American unlocked the door and stepped out. "C'mon, you son of a bitch!" Hans stomped toward him. "Let's go for it!"

Beau jumped excitedly up and down in the back seat. "Alright, Dad! Get him!"

The Arab looked at the six-and-a-half feet of angry American headed with purpose toward his Mercedes, and his face changed from disdain to fright. He quickly backed up and sped off in the other direction.

Hans stood for a moment in the roundabout and shook his hand at the disappearing Mercedes. "Anytime, asshole!" he bellowed in challenge. He got back into the car.

Beau patted his father's shoulder appreciatively. "You could've beat him up easy, Dad!"

Hans looked at the oncoming traffic, then started back down the road.

"Feel better now?" Camille asked.

Hans grinned. "Yeah. You know...I do."

Lost Again

The next morning passed quickly. The movers showed up almost on time, and the seven large boxes were loaded. The mover from the day before warily approached Hans.

"We're all finished."

"*Sukran*," Camille thanked him. The mover grinned and left quickly.

"What time is it?" Hans wondered.

Camille looked at her watch. "Oh, God. It's twelve-fifteen already. Let me fix you a quick sandwich before the bus driver gets here."

Hans and Beau wolfed down their sandwiches.

"Can I go with you, Dad?"

"I suppose."

Camille frowned. She felt uneasy, knowing the clinic bus driver's problems with new routes. "Hans...maybe not."

"Sure he can."

The clinic bus driver buzzed from the outer gate.

"You've got the directions with you, right?" Camille asked her husband.

"Yeah...right here."

The clinic driver flashed a jagged, toothy grin when he saw Camille and Beau. "Mr. Beau! Ride up front!"

Hans walked up to the bus driver. "Now, you know how to get to the car dealership, right?"

The little Arab had started nodding before Hans had finished his sentence. "*Iwa, iwa*," he assured him. He reached out and snatched the directions from Hans' hand.

"Then I'll follow you," Hans decided.

Camille looked unconvinced. "Uh, guys, I'll stay by the phone, just in case."

The bus driver, with her son, sped away. Camille could see Hans' look of determination as he sped after him. She shook her head and walked back inside the villa, feeling uneasy about the whole unfolding scenario.

The phone rang ten minutes later.

"Yes, Hans?"

"How did you—? Oh, never mind. I'm at a pay phone. The driver took off like a bat out of hell, and I couldn't keep up with him. Give me the phone number for the car dealership. I'll call them for directions."

Camille picked up the invoice and read off the phone number.

"Got ya…stay by the phone."

The outside buzzer sounded. Camille opened the gate. There stood the clinic bus driver.

"Mofi," Camille addressed him sternly. "Where is my husband?" Then she looked inside the bus. Beau was gone. "And…where is my son?"

Mofi sobbed. "Oh, Doctora, I stupid, I stupid. I lose Mr. Hans, and Mr. Beau got out…"

"Beau got out?! Where?!!" Camille felt panicked. Beau was alone somewhere?

"Oh, I so stupid!" The little Arab started banging his head against the bus in contrition.

"Yeah, yeah, that's what you need…more brain damage…Wait! I hear the phone—" Camille ran back into the villa and picked up the phone.

"Hans?"

"Yeah!"

"Where are you?"

"I'm at the car dealership."

"Hans, is Beau with you?"

"No. Why should he be? He was with the driver."

"The driver is back here, and he said Beau got out of the bus."

"What?!" Hans screeched.

"Doctora! Doctora!" Mofi's head appeared at her door. "Mr. Beau—he back!"

A sweaty, out-of-breath Beau appeared. "Mom!" he gasped.

"Hans—never mind. Beau is here!"

The driver was ecstatic. "I go get Mr. Hans now. I make it right!"

"Mom, the car place isn't even a ten-minute walk from here," her son explained.

"Hans, give the bus driver ten minutes. He's already left to get you."

"Jheesh—" Hans exclaimed and hung up the phone.

Camille looked at her son. "Beau—why did you get out of the bus?"

"Mom, when I realized the driver lost Dad, and I saw how close the car place was, I got out and started walking back. I thought Dad would be coming down the road, and I could show him how to get there."

Camille sat at the table, head in her hands. "Kid, I know you were trying to help Dad, but it's not safe for you to walk around here... especially alone. Remember?"

Her son looked sufficiently penitent. "Yes, Mom."

Twenty minutes later, the buzzer sounded. Mofi, the driver, stood by the gate, flashing his jagged-tooth grin. "I make it right!" he said proudly as Hans walked through the gate.

Camille laughed. "*Sukran,* Mofi! You made it right!" She looked gratefully at her reunited family.

"Hey, got any of that nonalcoholic beer left?" Hans opened the refrigerator door.

"Mom," Beau wondered, "are we gonna take these riyals back home with us or what?"

No Dollars

Camille groaned. "Money! We have to get the money out of our bank accounts!" She looked at their plane schedule. "We're leaving tomorrow morning before the banks open,"

"Well, now you tell me. I just took the car back." Hans sounded stressed again by yet another complication.

"Eddie!" She picked up the phone and dialed the Filipino's extension. "Oh, Eddie, I'm so glad you're home. Listen, I have a big favor to ask you. We need to get our money out of the bank tonight before it closes. Could you drive us?"

Eddie hesitated. The Americans didn't know he had been interrogated for hours about them, and then let off with a warning.

"Eddie, please!" Camille begged.

Eddie took a deep breath. "OK, Mum, I'll be right over."

Camille and Ashley threw on their *abayas*. There was a light knock at the door. Eddie was standing there.

"We have one hour before the banks close," he stated.

The women got in the back of his car. Eddie skillfully negotiated the late afternoon traffic of Jeddah. He pulled into a parking space in front of the bank.

Camille and Ashley entered the bank and stood in line. The two men in front of them finished their business and the women stepped up to the counter. The Arab man looked at them, puzzled they were alone.

"Good afternoon. We're going back to the States in the morning," Camille explained. "We came to close our accounts and get our money for the trip. Here's our account numbers and identification."

The Arab man looked at her and sighed. He walked to the back of the office and in Arabic discussed the situation with another man. The man came back.

"Only riyals available. No dollars."

"Why is that?"

The Arab looked uncomfortable. "Bank president gone for the day. Only he has keys for dollars."

The two women were getting more anxious by the moment.

"We put dollars in this bank," Ashley joined in, "we want dollars OUT—OF—THIS—BANK!" She stomped her Nike running shoes up and down. Her *abaya* fell open to reveal blue jeans and a New Orleans Saints T-shirt.

The bank teller shook his head and went to the back room again. The line of customers was backing up behind the two women. Now another teller was making a phone call and gesturing wildly. They heard the back door unlock, and a third man scurried in. He pulled a metal suitcase from under the counter and unlocked it with a key. He looked at the women, then counted out the money.

The teller quickly reappeared at the counter. "Yes...dollars." He skillfully dealt the dollars in front of them.

"That's only $8,000. We have $8,456 in our accounts."

Eddie, the driver, entered the bank. "Doctora!" he called out. He looked frightened. "We must go!"

"Just a minute, Eddie." She turned back to the teller.

"This is all the dollars we have. We send your dollars to your home in the States."

"Doctora!" Eddie's voice was becoming more insistent. Camille looked at the anxious Filipino. Then she turned back to the counter.

The older manager stepped forward. "We are an honorable bank. We send you the money."

"Sure you will. You didn't even ask for a forwarding address. Here's my husband's business card. Send the rest of the money to that address."

The teller took the card and nodded. Eddie was motioning to Camille. She stuffed the wad of bills into her purse and wrapped the *abaya* around her. "Eddie, what's the matter?"

"This area…it's getting dark. This is a dangerous area for a Filipino after dark."

"Oh, Eddie, I didn't know. I'm sorry."

"Please hurry."

Eddie led them to the car. Just then, the frantic sound of squealing tires jolted the air. Eddie, Ashley, and Camille heard a loud thud. Their heads went up in unison as a Saudi man in his white *thobe* and *gutra* was hurled into the air. He fell limply onto the street.

The terrified driver who had hit the Saudi, anxious to flee the scene, tried to back up. There wasn't enough room. They heard the sickening crunch of bones as the car drove over the Saudi's left shoulder to escape.

"Oh!!" all three cried in unison. Ashley clutched her stomach for a moment.

"Doctora! Miss Ashley! Get in the car!!"

The women jumped in the car and slammed the door. The loudspeakers began to broadcast the evening prayer call.

"God help him," Eddie intoned quietly. "Now it is prayer call. I hope the ambulance will come."

The group drove back to the compound in a saddened, yet thoughtful state about the tenuousness of life.

"Here, Eddie," Camille extended her hand with dollars.

"Doctora Camille, that's too much," Eddie protested.

"No, it's not. I put you in a dangerous position. Please, Eddie, take it. You and your wife, Samantha, have made our lives so much better here."

Eddie smiled and took the money. "You treated us good."

Camille sighed and looked up at the full moon. She would never forget the compelling magnetism of the moon in Jeddah.

As soon as Ashley hit the door, she bounded upstairs. "Now I really have to pack."

Hans had his suitcase on the dining room table. He stuffed his neatly-rolled socks into his suitcase then looked at her. "What took you so long?"

Camille threw her *abaya* onto a chair and kicked off her shoes. "The bank didn't want to give us dollars," she explained.

"Well, I hope you got them anyway."

"Most of it." She stopped and looked out the window. "Somehow Hans, under all the restrictions and fear, this country has a seductive beauty..."

Hans looked at his wife in disbelief. "Oh, yeah...right," he grunted sarcastically. "Now you'd better finish packing. Our limo will be here at seven a.m."

That night, Hans' breathing was peaceful. Camille looked down at this big, gentle, good-hearted man. There was a rhythm to her life. Hans was an underlying part of this rhythm. Their marriage, she chuckled to herself at the analogy, was like a musical chord. Through the years, the flats and sharps of discord had been worn away, and now what was left was a basic harmony. She laughed softly at the irony. She had to come all the way to Saudi Arabia to learn this.

Camille felt Hans' large hand reach out to her in the dark.

"Are you alright?" he asked.

"Yes, Hans...you know what?"

"What?"

"I love you."

"*Mein schatzi*," Hans chuckled and pulled her into bed. He held her gently until they both fell back to sleep.

CHAPTER 12
Home Again

Mom!" Beau bounced on the bed. "Time for our trip!"

"Son," his mother groaned, "how come you're never up this early for school?"

Hans rolled over.

"Hans!" she smacked him on the rear. "Get up! The limo will be here soon."

"Mom, can I go out and torture some cats one more time?"

"Beau, you didn't really do that, did you?"

Her son grinned mischievously for a moment. "No, not really," he admitted.

"You can go hang by the pool...just don't go any further."

"OK." Beau headed out the door.

The rest of the family scurried around with purpose.

"Hans! You've got the passports and visas?"

"Cammy, calm down. They're all in my briefcase."

The buzzer sounded.

"Beau, come in and get your bags. The limo's here," his father called out to him.

Your Son Can't Go

The limo driver efficiently loaded the suitcases in the car. The morning sun already glistened against the fountains and tall, modern buildings. The sign ahead announced their destination: *'tariig al-mataar'* (Airport Road). The family was quiet for a moment as they viewed the white pillared canopies that looked like dozens of pristine tents from a distance.

The limo driver pulled to the curve. Hans handed him the rest of his riyals. "Thanks. We can handle it from here."

The family made their way inside. They lifted suitcases onto the conveyor belt and handed their papers to the agent. The agent punched some information into the computer, looked at Hans, then nodded.

Next, he punched in Camille's information and scrutinized the feedback. He repeated the same process for Ashley, and they all breathed a sigh of relief.

Then, the agent punched Beau's information into the computer. He frowned, then punched the keys again. He shook his head. The agent called for a supervisor. In Arabic, they conferred. Camille heard something about a "police record."

The supervisor turned to Hans and addressed him. "Your son, he must stay in the country."

"What? Why?" asked an astonished Hans.

"Because...we had some—complaints. He hurt some men."

"Dad, I told you about that," his frightened son explained. "These men tried to kidnap the Swedish soccer team and me. We beat them off."

Beau turned pleadingly toward his mother. "Mom, we were just defending ourselves!"

The Arabs led Beau into a side room and closed the door. Hans and Camille stood speechless.

Hans recovered first. "Cammy, no matter what, we are all staying together."

Camille nodded numbly. The supervisor motioned impatiently for the three of them to continue to the concourse. They were holding up his line. His obvious disregard for her son's plight angered Camille. She looked at the supervisor. "NO WAY!!"

A voice came from behind her. "Doctora?"

Camille spun around. "What?"

In front of her was a distinguished-looking Arab man. "I am Ghasan. I came to help." Ghasan turned to the supervisor, and they disappeared into the room where Beau was being held.

Fifteen minutes of anguished waiting passed. Ghasan finally emerged, his arm around the frightened twelve-year-old boy. "You may all leave now," he informed them.

"Ghasan—how did you ever accomplish this?" Beau's grateful mother asked.

Ghasan grinned. "Trade secrets."

Camille laughed appreciatively.

Ghasan stepped closer to the couple and lowered his voice. "I have a brother who's a doctor in New Orleans." He looked around, then surreptitiously handed Hans a card. "Here's my business card. His name is on the back. Do me a favor. Look him up and say 'hello' for me, OK?"

Camille smiled and then bowed to the Saudi. "Thank you, Ghasan, for keeping our family together. *Allaah yisallimak* (May God make you safe)."

Ghasan beamed, then waved his hand. "No problem." He walked out the door.

Hans glanced down at Ghasan's card, and then let out a gasp. "Cammy, look at this!"

The card gave Ghasan's full name with his title—American Consulate General, American Embassy.

Hans and Camille looked at each other, and wondered aloud. "Who?" Who were the ones who had come to their rescue?

An Arab shouted at them. "The shuttle—get on the shuttle! The plane is boarding!"

The family climbed on the shuttle with the rest of the passengers. The shuttle drove the short distance, and they gratefully climbed the ramp to the jumbo Swiss airplane.

Once inside, Camille and Ashley joined the other women in the ceremonious finality of peeling off their *abayas*. Hans put his head next to his wife and whispered, "Don't get too comfortable. We're not off the ground yet..."

The flight attendants proceeded through the standard preflight instructions. The plane taxied down the runway and lifted into the bright sunlight.

The movie screens silently glided down. On the screen in front of them, the passengers saw a map of the Middle East and the Red Sea. A line was drawn through the Red Sea, indicating the boundary for Saudi Arabia. The picture of the small plane moved across the map. Most of the passengers sat transfixed, looking as the plane moved closer and closer to the line. As the plane crossed the borderline, an announcement came over the intercom.

"This is your captain speaking. We have just crossed over into Egyptian airspace. Food and beverages are now served."

An almost collective, audible sigh of relief emanated from the passengers. As if on cue, the flight attendants rolled well-stocked food carts down the aisles.

For the first time in weeks, the tension was gone from Hans' face.

"What would you like to drink?" the attendant asked Hans.

"Ein Bier bitte."

"Was trinken Sie?"

"Beck's."

"And you, ma'am?" the flight attendant asked Camille.

"You know, I think I'll have a glass of white zinfandel."

"Yes, ma'am." The flight attendant looked at Ashley. "And you, miss?"

Ashley's face showed the faintest trace of rebellion. "Well, I think the most immoral woman on the planet deserves a glass of champagne." She put her chin up and chuckled, "Somehow," she philosophized, "it's quite a feeling of freedom."

Hans and Camille looked at Ashley, shook their heads at her unexpected pronouncement, and laughed. They all held up their glasses.

"Here's to our outrageously immoral Ashley!"

"Here, here!"

They clinked their glasses together.

Beau looked questioningly at them. "Are you gonna drink those? It's still morning."

"Not in Biloxi, it isn't," Hans replied happily, downing his beer. He held out his glass for one more toast. "And...to Beau's escape from Saudi!" They clincked Beau's soda glass.

"Well, boy," Camille put her arm around her son's shoulder, "was that enough adventure for you?"

Beau grinned. "Yeah. This will hold me for awhile."

Camille turned to her sister. "And you, Ashley? Was this enough serious adventure for you?"

Ashley laughed. "The only serious business I have now is Remmy."

Remmy's Proposal

A song played on the radio as Remmy drove his car to the airport to pick up Ashley. He had to smile at the words.

"I don't care what you say or do...cause you don't love me and I don't love you..." Remmy listened and laughed at the change in meaning at the end of the song..."cause you do love me, and I do love you." He felt it was fitting for the beginning of his new life with Ashley.

As Remmy saw Ashley walk through the revolving doors, he held up a dozen red roses.

"Oh, Remmy!" Ashley cried when she saw him. Ashley raced to him and gave him an uncharacteristically passionate kiss.

Beau made a face and turned to his mother. "Oh, yuk!"

Remmy seemed pleasantly startled. "Damn, baby...can I have a lifetime of that?" He pulled out a small jewelry box and handed it to Ashley, and then slipped the ring on Ashley's left hand.

Ashley held up her hand and watched the light sparkle on her finger. Several passengers clapped and cheered. Camille's attention was riveted on the diamond. It was well over two carats, she guessed with a jeweler's precision.

"Oh, no!" Camille realized. "Her ring's bigger than mine!"

"Now you've gone and done it," Hans whispered to his future brother-in-law.

All eyes looked toward Camille.

"Can you accept it?" Ashley asked anxiously.

Camille stood in the airport lobby as she thought about this turn of events. Then she remembered Ashley facing the council of twelve men.

"Yes," Camille decided. "Girl, you have earned it."

The group gave a collective sigh of relief.

"Now," Camille planned aloud, "we'll hold the engagement party at Vrazel's, and the wedding party at the Beau Rivage—"

"How about the Blow Fly Inn?" Beau chimed in, wanting to add someplace a little more interesting for his friends.

"Yeah, the Blow Fly Inn..." Hans considered.

"Absolutely not!" Camille answered.

"Hey!" Ashley took command. "This is my wedding. We'll hold the engagement party at the High Cotton Grille and the wedding party at Mary Mahoney's." She looked up at Remmy. "Is that alright, honey?"

"Fine by me, baby. I'm just glad you're home."

Ashley and Remmy said their goodbyes to Camille, Hans, and Beau.

As Camille was getting into their car, Hans grinned. "Oh, by the way...did you hear about Jimmy?"

"You mean Ashley's former husband, the defrocked minister? No, what?"

"Well, he had plastic surgery to look like Elvis, got a job performing in Vegas, left his wife Susie, and is now living with a Bellagio showgirl."

Camille sighed with satisfaction. All was right with the world. "Good for him," she commented, as they headed for home.

Coastmusician.com

Later, Ashley and Remmy came to Camille and Hans' house for dinner.

"Well," Camille reported to her sister, "I may have lost the planning rights your wedding, but I'm going to help with your singing career. I've already got your website started."

"Oh, yeah?" Ashley asked with some fear. "What's the name?"

"Coastmusician.com," Camille answered proudly. "Oh, and that reminds me, Ashley...Georgene emailed me and said she put you on the planning committee for the 'Blessing of the Fleet'."

Ashley sighed. "Same old song...doesn't anything ever change around here?"

"Speaking of songs, Ashley," Camille continued, unperturbed, "I got inspired and wrote you a song. I think I'll play it on my flute for your wedding."

Hans rolled his eyes and looked at his busybody wife. "Here we go again..."

"Now, you have to rest up some, Ashley," Remmy instructed his bride to be. "You've got some Mardi Gras balls to attend. And tomorrow is the Pass Parade."

Pass Parade

Early the next morning, Remmy and Ashley pulled up in Remmy's large pick-up truck.

"Hey, Beau!" Remmy called, "get out here! We have to get to the Pass early for a good spot."

Beau scrambled out of the house. His eyes widened in amazement. "Dad!" he called back inside. "Come and see what Mr. Remmy put on his truck!"

Hans walked to the front port and laughed appreciatively.

"What's up?" Camille joined him. "Oh, my God..."

Fastened securely on the back of the double-axle truck was a six-foot port-a-potty.

"Hey, Remmy, good thinking!" Hans approved.

Mardi Gras

The next day, Hans' brothers and sister took the Amtrak train from Milwaukee to New Orleans for Mardi Gras in the French Quarter. Since there were mostly Wisconsin travelers, the train had to make an historic, unscheduled beer stop in Carbondale, Illinois, at two a.m.

Claudia, Hans' delicate blonde sister, was wearing her Green Bay Packers jersey as she waved for more beads on Bourbon Street at the Mardi Gras parade.

"Show us your boobs!" one of the men on a parade float shouted toward Claudia, as he held up a massive set of beads to tempt her.

Claudia looked tentatively toward Ashley. "Should I?" she asked, uncertain.

"Certainly not!" Ashley replied.

Camille looked around to make sure Hans was nowhere in sight. "Claudia, if you want the experience, fine. But, not in a Packers jersey. That's close to...sacrilegious."

Wedding Day

Camille had followed through on her threat to write a flute solo for Ashley's wedding day.

"I call it 'Ashley's Song'," Camille explained proudly as her younger sister cringed.

It was a multi-hued sunset of blazing oranges and soft amethyst colors on the beach overlooking the coast. As the sun readied to set, the wedding began. Four members from the Coast Symphony Orchestra provided the wedding music. The ceremony went smoothly, and only one song was left to play.

Camille stepped forward with her flute. Ashley squeezed Remmy's hand for reassurance that they'd get through this, too. As Camille played, everyone relaxed. It was a simple yet melodic tune, and Camille was playing it rather well. Except on the last bar, when she hit a loud flat note.

"Sorry," she grinned sheepishly, and finished the last chord.

Everyone laughed.

Ashley and Remmy turned and waved to the wedding party, then walked off down the beach by themselves.

Red Neck Mother

Ashley's singing career was blossoming. She was selective, however, with her singing engagements. After all, Remmy had been very patient.

One Saturday night, Remmy, Ashley, Camille, and Hans went to Mack Taylor's place, The Fiasco. Mack had his own version of "Red Neck Mother."

Ashley was in good spirits, and with Remmy's support, had become more relaxed and outgoing.

"Ashley, come on up here. Help me with this song," Mack encouraged. That night, the deaf education teachers were holding a convention, and many of them were in the audience.

"Yes, Ashley! Go on up and sing with Mack. We'll help!" they laughed.

Mack started. "So—it's—up against the wall, Red Neck Mother. Mother who has raised a son so well, SO WELL, SO WELL..."

Remmy, Hans, and Camille looked up at Ashley on the stage. She was leading all the deaf education teachers while they signed and sang along. Ashley continued, as the place exploded in an uproar of laughter. "She's thirty-four and drinkin' in a honkey-tonk café, kicking hippies' ass and raising hell..."

Where's Uncle Otto?

The next morning, Hans got a phone call. "Really? You're kidding, right? He really is? Crap. Well then, it's one more call to the American embassy."

"Hans, what is it?" Camille came yawning out to the kitchen.

Hans sighed. "It's Uncle Otto again. He's over in Czechoslovakia and got arrested."

"Got arrested?" Camille said, waking up. "What for?"

"Well, there was a protest march because the government wanted to raise the price of beer. And, Uncle Otto must have thought it was a good cause, because he took up a sign, joined the demonstration, and that's when they..."

We're Not Finished with You Yet

That night, a contented Camille settled down to sleep. "Goodnight, Hans," she lightly kissed her husband. She sat in bed for a moment, in a contemplative mood. "You know, honey, I'm glad our life is back to normal."

"Me, too," Hans said, wanting sleep more than a thoughtful exchange at this hour.

"And," Camille said, ignoring his back, "I'm very glad I'm finished with Saudi Arabia."

Hans shifted in bed and raised his head. "Amen to that!" Then Camille heard his breathing become regular as he drifted off to sleep.

In her dreams, she saw a tall Saudi woman in a black *abaya* approaching her. It was Safiya. As she grew closer, Camille could see a determined look on the Arab woman's face.

"We're not finished with you yet!" she announced.

A group of Arab men led by Zayad appeared. They grabbed Camille and strapped her into a roller coast seat, where Safiya was waiting in the adjoining seat.

The roller coaster slowly climbed a monstrous hill, reached the top, and then began a downward lurch. Camille's stomach shot up in her throat from the dizzying momentum and fear for her life.

Shocked by the intensity, Camille bolted upright in bed, sweat dripping from her. She sat in the dark, knees pulled into her body, with her arms wrapped around them for protection.

She thought she was finished with Saudi Arabia...Or was she?

www.ingramcontent.com/pod-product-compliance
Lightning Source LLC
Chambersburg PA
CBHW060449290526
45791CB00001B/42